CALLAWAY COUNTY, MISSOURI

MARRIAGE RECORDS

1821 TO 1871

COMPILED BY

Sherida K. Eddlemon

HERITAGE BOOKS
2015

HERITAGE BOOKS

AN IMPRINT OF HERITAGE BOOKS, INC.

Books, CDs, and more—Worldwide

For our listing of thousands of titles see our website
at
www.HeritageBooks.com

Published 2015 by
HERITAGE BOOKS, INC.
Publishing Division
5810 Ruatan Street
Berwyn Heights, Md. 20740

International Standard Book Numbers
Paperbound: 978-1-55613-494-4
Clothbound: 978-0-7884-6231-3

DEDICATION

This volume is dedicated to the CHATHAM families who settled in or journeyed through Missouri in the 1800's, and especially to the family of Mary Chatham, born 1777, in Virginia, who died in Callaway County, Missouri in September of 1849, and to the Josiah Chatham family who moved from Illinois to LaClede County, Missouri.

ACKNOWLEDGEMENTS

Special thanks to the staffs of the Missouri State Archives and Ellis Library.

TABLE OF CONTENTS

P R E F A C E

Callaway County was founded on November 25, 1820 from Howard and Montgomery counties. The county was named in honor of James Callaway, a Missouri Ranger killed by Indians during the War of 1812. Although many of the settlers to this area came from Virginia, Maryland, Kentucky, Tennessee and the Carolinas, the earliest settlement was made by the French at Cote Des Dessein. Daniel Boone came to the Callaway County area in 1808. Prehaps, it was his tales of the area that helped to lure those settlers from Kentucky and Tennessee.

It was not mandatory for a marriage to be recorded at the courthouse. Many of the marriages were performed by circuit riders and were recorded in a haphazard manner. Some marriages were never recorded or recorded in another county. The marriages from the first two registers of Boone County with stated Callaway County connections have been included in this volume as well as some that appeared in area newspapers. These marriages were included to help make a more complete compilation.

The following abbreviations were used to indicate the title of the officiants performing the marriage rites or the dates involved. A surname index is included in this volume.

MG - Minister of the Gospel or Preacher
JP - Justice of the Peace
MD - Marriage Date
PM - Place of Marriage
ED - Church Elder
UK - Title Unknown

I wish you luck in finding your ancestors within these pages.

John Abbot and Ann Plummer, (MG) Theodrick Boulware,
(MD) April 4, 1828.
James S. Day and Mary Bechel, (UK) Joseph T. Bryan,
(MD) December 13, 1847.
Elias J. Emmons and Mildred Newman, (JP) T. G. Jones,
(MD) December 7, 1830.
John B. Goodrich and Eleanor Jackson, (MD) May 20, 1869.
John Griffith and Eliza M. Williams, (UK) David Kirkpatrick,
(MD) November 25, 1830.
James M. Harrison and Jane E. Sayers, (MD) August 28, 1855.
Thomas Hornbuckle and Providence Baker, (JP) Robert Davis,
(MD) May 28, 1826.
Edwin Hubbard and Ann Eliza Philips, (MD) April 4, 1860.
Simpson Hyton and Eliza Boyd, (UK) Absalom Rice,
(MD) March 24, 1842.
William Kemp and Lizean Gardener, (MG) William Duncan,
(MD) October 16, 1834.
Clarence F. Kouns and Hester A. Hard, (MD)November 15, 1859.
Elisha Abbot and Frances Philips, (MD) March 7, 1851,
Groom is from Jasper County, Missouri.
George L. Baker and Mrs. Elizabeth E. Bridges, (MD)
April 26, 1859.
Angus Berry and Mary W. Suggett, (MD) February 26, 1857.
Jacob Ellington and Sally Matheny, (MG) Jabez Ham,
(MD) December 16, 1838.
John L. Farmer and Sarah E. Dickson, (MD) September 4, 1866.
William A. Foster and Matilda D. Harris, (JP) R. B. Jackson,
(MD) August 31, 1837.
Charles Hafenreffer and Mina Shirmack, (MD)November 4, 1855.
Peter Harris and Betsey Acles, (MG) William Coats,
(MD) May 5, 1833.
--- Abraham and Rachel Sheets, (MG) James Barnes, (MD) Oct-
ober 12, 1837, Groom is from Boone County, Missouri.
Presley Thomas and Frances Collier, (MD) March 27, 1851.
Griffin Todd and Jany C. Ham, (MG) G. K. Ham, Groom is from
Howard County, Missouri.
David Adair and Margaret Young, (MD) March 29, 1855, Groom
is from Iowa.
George Campbell and Sopronia Howard, (MD) July 12, 1867.
Franklin Dillard and Ann Elizabeth Bernard, (UK) S. Bernart,
(MD) July 29, 1844.
Given D. English and Jane M. Kemp, (MD) March 14, 1870.
John Finley and Nancy Woodland, (UK) Andrew Alexander,
(MD) January 7, 1838.
Thomas B. Jose and Susan Wilson, (MD) May 17, 1863.
John Lambert and Permelia Wade, (MD) December 18, 1870.
John W. Martin and Martha Everhart, (MD) December 6, 1858.
Elijah Adams and Elizabeth Leeper, (MG) David Kirkpatrick,
(MD) April 5, 1832.

1

Willis B. Alexander and Jane Hopper, (JP) Thomas H. Baker, (MD) March 8, 1826.

James P. Bailey and Ann R. McCrackin, (MD) August 16, 1853.

Elijah F. Cooper and Mary Jane McQentin, (UK) Thomas P. Stephens, Groom is from Saline County, Missouri.

Isaiah Craghead and Bethena Remp, (MG) John Young, (MD) December 31, 1840.

Dr. Franklin Dillard and Emily S. Bernard, (MD) May 3, 1860.

Thomas Edwards and Mrs. Harrier Davis, (MD)January 10, 1864.

Andrew Knapp and Elizabeth Wallace, (MD) December 10, 1867.

John W. Adams and Amanda Baysinger, (JP) Thomas J. Ferguson, (MD) February 2, 1854.

William B. Baker and Rebecca Meloany, (JP) Jos. T. L. Bryan, (MD) April 5, 1849.

Thornton Blankenship and Elizabeth R. Barry, (MD) June 25, 1854.

Hiram Calvin and Emma Neff, (MD) September 25, 1866.

George Adams and Mary Williams, (MD) February 17, 1870.

Thomas Musgrove and Cornelia Culbertson, (MD) December 29, 1850.

Richard B. Owens and Elizabeth M. Tolbert, (MD) August 2, 1868.

Edwin Revis and Mary E. Davison, (MD) March 10, 1869.

Hiram Adair and Mary Ella Sheets, (MD) December 3, 1856.

Jacob Houf and Elisa Stults, (UK) W. W. Kemp, (MD) March 30, 1848.

William H. Rose and Margaret A. Rogers, (MD) April 27, 1865.

John Scanland and Elizabeth Newton, (MD) May 16, 1868.

Abram L. Adcock and Amanda M. Cheatham, (MD) January 28, 1857.

Thomas H. Caldwell and Kitty Ann Elley, (UK) W.W. Robertson, (MD) October 8, 1845.

James G. Horn and Mary Z. Thatcher, (MD) May 7, 1856.

James T. Huffmaster and Elizabeth T. Huffmaster, (MD January 13, 1869.

Robert Jackson and Mary A. Gill, (MD) April 4, 1857.

John Riley Johnson and Mary Elizabeth Thompson, (UK) Zachariah Jones, (MD) April 1, 1869.

Granville N. Jones and Lucy E. Barker, (MD) March 13, 1856.

William G. Kemp and Sarah L. Kemp, (MD) November 12, 1851, Groom is from Pettis County, Missouri.

L. B. Murray and Elizabeth George, (MD) May 25, 1854.

James Reynolds and Margaret Crank, (MD) June 18, 1853.

Henderson Wright and Agnes McClintock, (UK)Robt. A. Younger, (MD) November 3, 1842, Groom is from Boone County, Mo.

Charles H. Yeater and Judith Jameson, (MG) Theo. Boulware, (MD) September 2, 1830.

David Allen and Martha F. Allen, (MD) November 20, 1862.

James M. Humphreys and Louisa A. Smith, (MD) April 21, 1869.

William Maddox and Mildred B. Jones, (MD) March 1, 1870.
William Richardson and Jane S. Holt, (UK) John E. Nevins,
(MD) November 9, 1843.
William P. Selby and Amanda P. Anderson, (UK) Irvine O.
Hockaday, (MD) March 12, 1836.
Hiram Adair and Alice M. Sheets, (MD) August 26, 1868.
Andrew J. Brown and Elizabeth Thompson, (MD) December 23,
1864.
George B. Hopkins and Ann Gray, (MD) July 27, 1857.
Washington Lynes and Susan Suggett, (MG) James Barnes,
(MD) July 28, 1836.
James M. Nichols and Pricilla B. Griffith, (MD) November 3,
1863.
Douglas A. Robertson and Susana E. Perrier, (MD) August 29,
1858.
John E. Adkins and Jane Lawson, (MD) February 12, 1860.
William H. Myers and Susan E. Custard, (MD) September 12,
1867.
William H. Rose and Hester Ann Patterson, (MD) February 14,
1867.
James A. Wood and George Ann Gibony, (MD) June 23, 1859.
John B. Adams and Mrs. Sarah E. Allen, (UK) James H. Tuttle,
(MD) May 25, 1862.
James Bellama and Martha Jane Harris, (MD) March 17, 1853.
Peter Day and Charity Ann Stark, (MG) J. Green, (MD) April
8, 1852.
Sanford Elliot and Martha A. Crosswait, (MG) T. G. Jones,
(MD) May 30, 1841.
John H. Adcock and Mary J. Sleby, (MG) Jacob Conns,
(MD) October 4, 1849.
Jesse Farmer and Sarah H. Winscott, (MD) December 26, 1869.
D. D. Ford and Martha P. Tate, (MD) May 4, 1848.
William A. Gregory and Elizabeth Mathis, (MD) February 11,
1857.
Christopher Hall and Martha C. Martin, (MD) February 3,
1848.
Hugh Maddin and Amanda E. Fisher, (MD) August 13, 1857.
Bailey Miller and Susan Jones, (JP) John A. Burt, (MD) Oct-
ober 20, 1831.
Edward Nance and Matilda Bradley, (MD) January 12, 1868.
William Robinson and Nancy C. Boswell, (MD) December 23,
1869.
John Adair and Eliza Sinclair, (MD) March 25, 1858.
William G. Dixon and Hattie Thornhill, (MD) September 20,
1866.
John English and Sarah Jane Medows, (MD) July 1, 1858.
John Ferguson and Agnes Jane Browes, (MD) January 23, 1845.
Edward Greer and Sarah Hamilton, (MD) December 27, 1853.
Samuel E. Hansard and Talitha Crews, (MD) February 13, 1866.

Daniel Buckner and Margaret Newton, (MD) July 11, 1867.
Joseph Adair and Sarah M. Adcock, (MG) Jacob Conns, (MD)
   August 14, 1845.
Silas Hornbuckle and Jane A. Wainscott, (MD) December 22,
   1864.
Joseph Isaacs and Cecelia Rolle, (MD) April 6, 1848.
Damascus G. James and Mrs. Virginia Robinett, (MD) October
   2, 1860.
Francis M. Johnson and Susan E. Finley, (MD)August 16, 1857.
Thomas Jones and Sarah Young, (UK) Jno. Pace, (MD) October
   20, 1836.
Robert B. Adkinson and Elizabeth A. Oliver, (MD) January 24,
   1861.
John Bassinger and Martha T. Morree, (MD) February 19, 1857.
Enoch C. Daley and Minerva Wilkinson, (MG) W. H. Burnham,
   (MD) October 24, 1866.
John Egan and Roxalina D. Day, (JP) A. L. Brashear, (MD)Feb-
   ruary 10, 1866.
Andrew Howard and Mary Burn, (UK) George B. Hopkins, (MD)
   March 27, 1846.
D. Johnson and M. A. Petty, (MG) Theo. Boulware, (MD) August
   8, 1833.
John L. Major and Eliza Blackwell, (UK) Peter Sternberger,
   (MD) April 5, 1848.
Joseph Adcock and Eliza Barger, (UK) Absalom Rice, (MD) June
   15, 1848.
Thomas W. Ferguson and Elizabeth J. Wayne, (MD)June 22,1870.
Andy Zumwalt and Isabella Cooner, (MD) January 2, 1849.
Seaton C. Owen and Cordelia Sheets, (MD) November 24, 1867.
George Criswell and Elizabeth Fitzhugh, (UK) John N. Nevins,
   (MD) February 2, 1843.
Michael Freeman and Louisa Wilson, (UK) Greenup Jackson,
   (MD) November 17, 1836.
Alfred Grise and Mary Ann Cobleritz, (MD) March 30, 1857.
John S. Martin and Sarah H. Martin, (MD) January 19, 1864.
Richard May and R. Crump, (MG) Theo. Boulware, (MD) December
   17, 1829.
T. B. Scholl and D. A. Boone, (MD) April 9, 1863.
William G. Williams and Sallie Babb, (MD) November 4, 1869.
John M. Allen and Mary F. Woods, (JP) William H. Neal, (MD)
   September 9, 1839.
Henry Herriford and Esther Vinson, (UK) Thomas Stephens,
   (MD) September 1, 1825.
William G. Oldham and Rebecca E. Ewing, (MG) J. L. Yantis,
   (MD) February 25, 1841.
Ignatius Renso and Elizabeth M. Carney, (MD) November 24,
   1853.
John T.LaFon and Evaline I. McKamey, (MD) February 4, 1866.
John Hurley and Rebecca Baker, (MD) April 1, 1858.

John Frey and Sophronia Hall, (JP) Adam Hope, (MD) November 7, 1822.

William B. Moad and Eliza J. Thornton, (MD)October 12, 1864.

Robert Orme and Matilda May, (UK) Andrew Alexander, (MD) April 5, 1838.

Henley C. Rusill and Arrana Overfelt, (MG) Theo. Boulware, (MD) December 6, 1837.

George W. Thomas and Sarah R. Reed, (MD) February 17, 1853.

Henry Utt and Mary Jane Edge, (MD) September 19, 1861.

Ralph Arthur and Margaret McClure, (MG) Joseph Coons, (MD) January 22, 1843.

William T. Brandenburg and Mary Jane Howard, (MD) August 28, 1870.

Thomas W. Herring and Mary Jane Young, (MD) February 11, 1864.

James Steward and Margaret Harman, (MD) March 19, 1865.

John B. Peters and Catharine Driskell, (MD)January 26, 1854.

William Arnold and Louise Scholl, (MG) James Love, (MD) February 27, 1840.

Admiral R. Dunham and Julian M. Beaven, (MD) June 8, 1857.

Isaac Kelsoe and Mary Sitton, (MG) Noah Flood, (MD) May 13, 1843.

John Magee and Elizabeth Bowen, (MD) December 15, 1847.

John W. Booth and Ann E. Hickerson, (MD) January 12, 1865.

Joseph M. Bright and Mary F. Anderson, (MG) N. L. Fish, (MD) January 21, 1869.

Isreal B. Grant and Mary Warren, (MG) Theo. Boulware, (MD) February 14, 1831.

Robert N. Henderson and Mary M. Turner, (MG) J. W. Wallace, (MD) November 26, 1863.

M. E. Jett and A. R. Galbreath, (MD) December 21, 1854.

James Woodland and Susan Everheart, (MD) February 22, 1865.

John W. Nichols and Elmore Bedsworth, (MD) March 12, 1861.

Armstead B. Fant and Susan H. Snell, (UK) Absalom Rice, (MD) September 26, 1843.

Francis Chick and Elenor Hays, (JP) Jno. A. Burt, (MD) December 16, 1835.

Thomas Hill and Janey J. Chafford, (MD) May 13, 1858.

Bartlett Rossen and Sarah A. Musgrove, (MD) March 29, 1855.

Enis C. Smart and Mary Foy, (UK) George B. Hopkins, (MD) March 7, 1869.

Philip W. Adams and Nancy C. Ming, (MD) March 11, 1855.

Caleb W. Babb and Annie Jennings, (MD) November 19, 1870.

Jonathan Estill and Clarissa C. Baker, (MD) July 5, 1860.

George Yates and Rebecca E. Kidwell, (MD) February 1, 1855.

James Turner and E. M. Hoalman, (MD) April 20, 1841, (MG) Theo. Boulware.

Benjamin F. Miller and Nancy E. Adkins, (MD)December 5,1855.

Darice C. Hays and Rachel E. Bunch, (MD) December 24, 1861.

Julius A. Fay and Sarah L. Bland, (MD) September 15, 1870.
William H. Nevins and Susan Maupin, (MD) June 7, 1866, (JP)
   W. B. Tucker.
Edward H. Van Hay and Margaret Adams, (MD) September 10,
   1847.
James A. Adams and Anne Mosely, (MD) November 22, 1855.
Walton S. Fisher and M. A. Terry, (MD) April 17, 1864.
Zachariah Petty and Mary Jane Bryant, (MD) August 7, 1833,
   (MG) Theo. Boulware.
John Sharp and Nancy B. McCordia, (MD) November 18, 1852.
Rufus Williamson and Manerva Langley, (MD) August 24, 1843.
Dr. Edward Duncan and Martha C. McMahan, (MD) May 10, 1866.
Stephen N. King and Elizabeth Bruner, (MD)September 6, 1846,
   (MG) M. P. Wills.
Thomas Musgrove and Cornelia Culbertson, (MD) December 29,
   1850.
James Thomas Davidson and Anna Elizabeth Davidson, (MD) May
   20, 1869.
James Clanton and Keziah Tharp, (MD) May 30, 1830, (JP) Wm.
   Crain.
William W. Moore and Sophia C. Basinger, (MD) December 13,
   1868.
Benjamin Foust and Sarah Jane Brackbill, (MD) March 6, 1861.
Abraham Zumalt and Juliet Hope, (MD) September 30, 1825,
   (UK) Christopher Zumwalt.
Thomas Herring and Mary Harding, (MD) April 9, 1868.
Henry Debo and Lucy Ann Sitton, (MD) January 24, 1855.
James W. Gibson and Annie E. Boswell, (MD) December 5, 1866.
Thomas C. Hudson and Rosanna M. Syms, (MD) January 3, 1855,
   Groom is from Boone County, Missouri.
James H. Jameson and Amelia Worthington, (UK) John Thatcher,
   (MD) January 30, 1840.
Louis Judt and Mary E. Harrow, (MD) April 26, 1855.
Andrew Louis Kemp and Mrs. Martha Foster, (MG)John A. Young,
   (MD) November 4, 1840.
James Land and Sarah A. Gordner, (MG) George K. Ham, (MD)
   September 17, 1848.
John Marrow and Nancy Agee, (MD) October 15, 1835, (JP) Jas.
   Stewart.
John F. Baker and Mollie C. Miller, (MD) March 24, 1863.
Thomas H. Howiser and Elvira Ann Moon, (MD)January 27, 1848.
Alexander M. McIntire and Griselda Boyd, (UK)W.W. Robertson,
   (MD) September 25, 1845.
Robert N. Patton and Margaret J. McClanahan, (MD) March 30,
   1848.
Henry B. Renoe and Eliza Jane Holt, (MD) October 27, 1853.
Louis Archer and Mary A. Cosby, (MD) January 27, 1870.
Larkin Fleshman and Jane Williams, (MD) December 12, 1843,
   (UK) John E. Nevins.

6

William Lambert and Susannah Burnett, (MD) April 13, 1828,
   (UK) Jas. Henderson.
John Allen and Martha F. Hampton, (MD) October 4, 1869.
William T. Mosley and Fanny Fitzhugh, (MD)November 29, 1848.
Bazel Z. Offutt and Mary C. Henderson, (MD) April 3, 1845,
   (MG) Theo. Boulware.
James P. Crews and Nancy Bright, (MD) March 8, 1866.
David Eastwood and Ann T. Moore, (MD) May 10, 1864.
Benjamin M. Linn and Sallie A. Atkins, (MD) March 6, 1868.
McAnius Marsh and Susan Williams, (MD) September 25, 1846,
   (UK) Z. N. Roberts.
Nathaniel B. Branham and Elizabeth Hobson, (MG) R. C. Hill,
   (MD) September 10, 1842.
William T. English and Frances Jones, (MD) March 5, 1858.
John H. Galwith and Narcissus McCowan, (MD) July 22, 1867.
William Baskin Hamilton and Margaret H. Allen, (UK) R. L.
   McAfee, (MD) September 7, 1837.
Wesley H. Knight and America H. Carisle, (MD) July 6, 1843,
   (MG) Noah Flood.
William Adams and Delia Cartmell, (MD) November 16, 1845,
   (JP) William J. Gilman.
William J. Callaway and Mary L. Kemp, (MD) August 19, 1852.
John C. Dyer and Mrs. Frances May Brashear, (MD) May 31,
   1870.
Morgan McIntire and Mary A. Atkins, (MD) May 20, 1854.
Hardin Nash and Sarah Adair, (MD) February 26, 1836, (MG)
   William Duncan.
John Yates and Elizabeth Dawson, (MD) April 26, 1833.
Charles Alford and Elizabeth Ginn, (MD) June 4, 1857.
Thomas Cunningham and Martha E. Jackson, (MD) July 31, 1861.
Thomas Jackman and Dicey Potter, (MD) September 6, 1832,
   (JP) John A. Barry.
William R. Martin and Mary Jane Davis, (MD) April 5, 1847,
   (MG) Noah Flood.
H. W. Neill and Nancy Ann Wisley, (MD) November 15, 1848,
   (JP) Isaac Langley.
Bethel Philips and Darly Estes, (MD) January 2, 1828, (MG)
   William Coats.
John Ramsey and Sarah C. Oliver, (MD) September 2, 1858.
Thomas Sanders and Letitia Breckenridge, (MD) May 25, 1837,
   (UK) Thomas M. Allen, Groom is from Tennessee.
John Bennett, jr. and Elvira J. Harrison, (MD) November 25,
   1852.
John Hopper and Mary S. Covington, (MD) May 23, 1869.
John W. Pulliam and Mrs. Nancy Robinson, (MD) July 24, 1854.
Thomas Wright and Sally Ann Howe, (MD) November 28, 1850.
Samuel Clark and Arabella J. Cleveland, (MD) November 15,
   1860.
John Grant and Sarah Harrison, (MD) January 20, 1859.

James M. Irvin and Julia F. Ming, (MD) December 15, 1859.
Thomas Morrison and Mary Jane Pugh, (MD) November 4, 1855.
Henry Adley and Nancy Schigley, (MD) May 17, 1853, (JP)
    Zadock Hook.
William S. Craig and Julia A. Riley, (MD) November 4, 1852.
Samuel Edwards and Levicy Williams, (MD) March 29, 1869,
    (MG) James McGuire.
John W. Foxworthy and Mary S. Burt, (MD) June 7, 1850.
Nathaniel Jones and Janetta Loy, (MD) July 16, 1866.
Peter Joseph Neidacker and Francisca Veerkamp, (UK) Joseph
    T. Bryan, (MD) March 25, 1842.
John H. Ravenscraft and Martha W. Meredith, (MD) December
    24, 1850.
William Rhodes and Rosannah Dougherty, (MD)December 3, 1821,
    (JP) James Nevins.
Andrew J. Wallace and Catharine Hudson, (MD) March 17, 1853.
Rueben Bullard aand Martha Selby, (MD) January 11, 1870.
Matthew Davis and Elizabeth Wilfley, (MD) July 7, 1835,
    (MG) Theo. Boulware.
Philemon K. W. Estill and Cassandra Collins, (JP) R. L.
    Miller, (MD) November 17, 1852.
Thomas B. Garrett and Mary Jane Taylor, (MD) December 24,
    1862.
Thomas C. Haskins and Mary G. Anderson, (MD) February 18,
    1835, (MG) Theo. Boulware.
Joseph H. Adkins and Mary Jane Dillion, (MD) January 15,
    1863, (JP) John K. Boyd.
Ela Black and Miss A. M. Mills, (MD) October 4, 1855, Bride
    is from Vermont.
John Mourning and Elizabeth Coons, (MD) November 10, 1853,
    (UK) Jacob Coons.
Thomas Ridgway and Marinda Lawhon, (MD) November 28, 1844,
    (UK) Thomas P. Stephens, Bride is from Boone County.
Samuel Walker and Kitty Townsend, (MD) December 31, 1835,
    (MG) William Duncan.
Glover Anderson and Martha Williamson, (MD) August 13, 1845.
John Holland and Susannah Dougherty, (MD) January 15, 1857.
Benjamin D. Yates and Agnes J. Grant, (MD) March 14, 1865,
    (MG) John F. Cowan.
William Stephens and Marianna Renfro, (MD) January 5, 1843,
    (MG) J. P. Barnes.
William Rutherford and Jane Jahs, (MD) May 4, 1822, (JP)
    George King.
Robert Purdy and Martha J. Culbertson, (MD) September 23,
    1852.
James Oliver and Nancy Bratton, (MD) December 13, 1832, (JP)
    Enoch Fruit.
Leroy Moore and Martha Basinger, (MD) January 19, 1865.
Silas Jones and Catharine Love, (MD) January 6, 1858.

Joseph S. Adkins and Martha C. Brown, (MD) October 22, 1863, (JP) John K. Boyd.

Waller B. Farmer and Mary C. Gillings, (MD) March 21, 1869.

Samuel Hall and Rachel Gray, (MD) October 29, 1835, (MG) A. Norfleet.

John T. Harris and Sally A. Bullard, (MD)September 13, 1859.

Elisha Roberts and Mary Ann McMahan, (MD) November 25, 1853.

Monroe Scott and Sarah Jane Irvin, (MD) February 23, 1843, (UK) R. S. Reynolds.

John W. Tate and Hannah Boone, (MD) December 30, 1869.

William Vaughn and Mrs. Elizabeth Batt, (MD) November 11, 1855.

Jeremiah Muir and Lucy J. Bagby, (MD) January 7, 1854.

John Miller and E. A. Stuerd, (MD) October 18, 1859.

William C. Leeper and Isabella Henderson, (MD) November 26, 1848, (UK) W. W. Robertson.

Erastus King and Mary Glasgow, (MD) February 10, 1846, (MG) Noah Flood.

Thomas Foster and Mary E. Early, (MD) March 23, 1855, (UK) Henry H. Dodd.

Benjamin F. Covington and Bertha A. Arnot, (MD) November 20, 1851.

Milton J. Hall and Frances Gilbert, (MD) November 13, 1862, (UK) John D. Gregory.

John McLaughlan and Ann E. Glover, (MD) February 11, 1858.

Christopher Meacham and Bearsheba Neille, (MD) October 22, 1835, (UK) George B. Hopkins.

William Quin and Mary Scaggs, (MD) December 20, 1860.

Isham Davis and Elizabeth Scott, (MD) December 28, 1848, (MG) Noah Flood.

William S. Evans and Maria W. Sanders, (MD) December 11, 1856.

John J. Ficklin and Mary F. Day, (MD) October 25, 1855.

William Harrison and Harriet J. Jameson, (MD) December 29, 1851, (MG) Noah Flood.

John C. Kidwell and Elira Hobson, (MD) October 10, 1866.

Mason Thatcher and Catherine McConnell, (MD) December 20, 1829, (UK) D. M. Kirkpatrick.

Berry Allen Watson and Clara E. Ward, (MD) May 4, 1865.

Isaac Atterberry and Polly Jane Gash, (MD) January 19, 1843, (MD) James Love.

William Berry and Are Ann Thompson, (MD) March 4, 1857.

O. C. Bowlan and Betty F. Dunavant, (MD) December 10, 1858.

Joseph O. Fletcher and Lucy W. Parker, (MD) May 18, 1837, (MG) Thomas B. Sutton.

James S. Henderson and Emily Boone, (MD) June 6, 1831, (UK) David Kirkpatrick.

George W. Johnson and Eliza Little, (MD) August 23, 1866.

Vincent Arthur and Nancy Ann Selby, (MD) April 20, 1862.

Anson G. Bennet and Mollie Ann Moore, (MD) April 14, 1825,
(MG) William Coats.
John E. Callaway and Edna Pratt, (MD) June 16, 1852, (JP)
William J. Gilman.
Achilles Dawson and Mary E. Wright, (MD) January 20, 1847,
(MG) Noah Flood.
Horatio Asa Jones and Frances Ann Rockard, (MD) March 13,
1843, (UK) David Coulter.
William Hans Lauther and Virginia Dyer, (MD) October 25,
1841, (MG) William Homman.
David Marshall and Mary Ann Ridgway, (MD) February 14, 1865.
Joel McConnell and Ann Thatcher, (MD) December 17, 1829,
(MG) Theo. Boulware.
John Adam Rayburn and Catherine Elizabeth Martin, (MD)
January 10, 1867, Groom is from Boone County.
James Thornhill and Agnes Robinson, (MD) November 4, 1847,
(UK) W. W. Kemp.
Robert B. Williams and Rebecca Kemp, (MD) November 6, 1850,
(JP) Isaac Langley.
Benjamin N. C. Adkins and Phebe Ann Brown, (MD) July 11,
1860, Both Bride and Groom are from Boone County.
Thomas Carlisle and Polly Ann Langley, (MD) August 9, 1849,
(JP) J. K. Allen.
Ira D. C. Green and Nancy E. Bishop, (MD) November 16, 1864.
Thomas Hamilton and Amanda G. Lail, (MD) march 28, 1855,
(MG) J. B. Carrico.
George T. Jolly and Louisa W. Smith, (MD) November 21, 1844,
(MG) Noah Flood.
William R. Maxwell and Mary E. Smith, (MD) May 24, 1853.
Alpheus MacCubbin and Mrs. Lucy H. Garrett, (MD) July 21,
1853, (MG) James E. Hughes.
Napoleon B. Neal and Louisa Jane Douglass, (MD) January 25,
1860.
James R. Thompson and Hennie A. Watkins, (MD) June 4, 1862,
Groom is from Morgan County.
John Winterbower and Elizabeth Zumwalt, (MD) April 11, 1839,
(UK) Abrams Norfleet.
William H. Adams and Mrs. Harriet Larue, (MD) November 28,
1867.
Thomas J. Trimble and Nancy Clark, (MD) June 29, 1845, (MG)
Noah Flood.
William G. Baynham and Tabitha Irvin, (MD) October 10, 1832,
(UK) William Duncan.
-- Hansberry and Susannah Boulware, (MD) June 9, 1835, (MG)
Jas. Suggett.
Joseph Marris and Martha E. Hall, (MD) April 1, 1863, Groom
is from Boone County.
Daniel Pasley and Jane Bradley, (MD) October 29, 1846, (JP)
W. J. Gilman.

William Agee and Hannah M. Thornton, (MD) August 15, 1837,
(MG) James Suggett.
William Matteer and Sally Hunter, (MD) August 27, 1829,
(UK) Thomas Durfee, Groom is from Ralls County.
Eugene B. Todd and Nancy Stephens, (MD) March 19, 1861.
John Wilson and Isabella Clatterbuck, (MD) July 26, 1865.
John R. Blount and Rebecca E. Cread, (MD) April 23, 1856.
William H. Dawson and M. A. Brandon, (MD) February 26, 1869.
Noah Martin and Virginia Closby, (MD) February 11, 1835,
(MG) William Duncan.
James F. Rootes and Edacia Wisely, (MD) November 4, 1866,
(UK) Thomas J. Ferguson.
D. W. Barnes and Susan C. Glasgow, (MD) June 28, 1865.
John W. Davis and Elizabeth Newton, (MD) January 16, 1866.
George A. Moore and Katharine Brite, (MD) October 28, 1860.
James Short and Rebecca Walker, (MD) August 10, 1851, (JP)
William Gilman.
William Weatherford and Evaline Harper, (JP) Robert Davis,
(MD) December 23, 1829.
Thomas I. Baker and Kate West, (MD) March 30, 1859.
George N. Kemp and Kae Gill, (MD) February 16, 1860.
James Bartley and Permelia Fitzhugh, (MD) January 24, 1849,
(MG) J. Criswell.
Henry C. Hawkins and Lavena Alexander, (MD) March 5, 1857.
Joseph N. Moss and Casandria James, (MD) July 27, 1848.
Elisha Vincent and Nancy Huddleston, (MD) April 9, 1829,
(MG) N. Ridgeway.
James W. Young and Eliza Jane Humphries, (MD) October 3,
1860.
William J. Bell and Lucy Jane Bell, (MD) September 22, 1859.
Wesley Criswell and Eliza Ann Holt, (MD) May 23, 1858.
Alford O. Hall and Elizabeth Coil, (MD) July 14, 1846, (UK)
Ninian Ridgway, Groom is from Kentucky.
Daniel Miller and Polly Moman, (MD) June 5, 1827, (JP) Wm.
Martin.
Elvis J. Nichols and Mary Irwin, (MD) April 19, 1866.
J. E. Rice and M. E. Coats, (MD) March 28, 1864.
James W. Hart and Susan C. Sayers, (MD) March 12, 1856.
John Green and Mary Fowler, (MD) January 31, 1847, (MG)
Stpehen Ham.
Samuel C. Patton and Eliza Jackson, (MD) March 7, 1866.
James M. Robinson and Nancy C. Cave, (MD) February 20, 1849,
(MG) D. Coulter.
William P. Smith and Mary E. Emerson, (MD) March 19, 1856.
Lewis Blackburn and Mary A. Garrite, (MD) April 19, 1855.
Francis M. Day and Debara A. Hornbuckle, (MD) December 5,
1860.
John P. Ferrier and Jane Goodrich, (MD) September 2, 1855.
Perry S. Holt and Elizabeth Emmons, (MD) March 14, 1867.

11

Ennis C. Smart and Eliza Herring, (MD) February 18, 1864,
(UK) Jas. A. Drennan.
David R. Bailey and Eliza Jane Zumwalt, (MD) March 1, 1862.
Jonathan Crowson and Sallie F. Smart, (MD)December 12, 1866,
(UK) W. W. Robertson.
William Sims and Mrs. Frances Gilbert, (MD) May 2, 1850,
(UK) J. S. Canterberry.
Daniel M. Tucker and Elizabeth E. Moss, (MG) Noah Flood,
(MD) January 21, 1846.
Elijah Potter and Rhoda Ham, (MD) June 24, 1837, (JP) John
A. Burt.
John W. McGhee and Georgia Miller, (MD) December 10, 1841,
(UK) Moses U. Payne.
Peter McCullough and Nancy A. Thatcher, (MD) December 1,
1859.
George W. Lynes and Jennette M. Finley, (MD) September 23,
1868.
Marcus D. L. King and Elizabeth C. Montjoy, (MD) December 1,
1870.
John J. Jones and Rebecca Reynolds, (MD) May 13, 1827, (JP)
Edward Ellis.
Jeremiah Hunt and Martha A. Craig, (MD) August 4, 1865.
Daniel W. Green and Endosia T. Finley, (MD) March 17, 1856.
Wilson Garrett and Mary McMahan, (MD) October 10, 1855.
John Estes and Cyntha Ann Martin, (MD) January 30, 1853,
(JP) William J. Gilman.
Charles A. Davis and Sarah Jane Overton, (MD) March 15,
1857.
William M. Crump and Mary Jane Shull, (MD) January 9, 1834,
(MG) James Suggett.
Thomas P. Butler and Sally M. Buckner, (MD) February 26,
1856.
Thompson Fry and Mary A. Brown, (MD) November 8, 1865.
John S. Gilbert and Maggie Newsom, (MD) January 28, 1868.
John G. Hansard and Emeline P. Pierce, (MD) January 6, 1858.
John Jacobs and Laura Houston, (MD) March 11, 1862, Groom is
from Boone County.
Archibald Langley and Lucinda Freeman, (MD) March 24, 1839,
(JP) H. S. Turner.
Marcellus Nichols and Sallie Irvin, (MD) January 30, 1866.
Fielding M. Oliver and Louisa Broughton, (MD) January 15,
1845, (MG) James Love.
George Randell and Isabella Turk, (MD) August 10, 1854.
Newton Ross and Elizabeth Coats, (MD) January 21, 1857.
Frederick Sanders and Martha Gray, (MD) December 22, 1840,
(UK) Milton Cleveland.
William C. Bailey and Helen Wipporen, (MD)November 28, 1859,
(UK) A. Campbell.
George Bartley and Margaret Jane Moore,(MD) August 29, 1847.

Bezel Benson and America L. Turner, (MD) January 10, 1867,
(MD) G. Tatum.
George S. Dehaven and Ann Eliza Dudley, (MD) February 17,
1864.
William Drinkard and Sarah J. Basinger, (MD) March 2, 1865.
John H. Early and A. Jones, (MD) January 20, 1862.
John Gregory and Elizabeth Scholl, (MD) July 17, 1842, (JP)
William B. Garrett.
James Langley and Elizabeth Smart, (MD) March 12, 1840, (UK)
Absalom Rice.
Aaron McMillin and Sarah Zumwalt, (MD) January 19, 1826,
(UK) James Henderson.
William A. Sanders and Ann Foster, (MD) January 10, 1840.
Caleb Williams and Sarah Updike, (MD) October 6, 1836, (JP)
James Harrison.
James M. Allen and Judith Wilson, (MD) March 18, 1852, (MG)
Theo. Boulware.
James Baskett and Elizabeth Reed, (MD) Ocotber 28, 1851,
(MG) M. P. Mills.
George Calvin and Mary Carter, (MD) August 16, 1866, Groom
is from Audrain County.
Henry C. King and M. J. Ficklin, (MD) December 22, 1867.
Robert H. Stewart and Nancy Jane Meadows, (MD) December 15,
1856.
Joseph Williams and Elizabeth Langley, (MD)February 6, 1825,
(UK) Felix Brown.
Jos. Richard Yates and Ellen Thrilkild, (MD) December 12,
1861.
James M. Armstrong and Nancy Hibberts, (MD) November 24,
1842, (JP) J. A. Burt, Groom is from Montgomery County.
Anderson J. Baker and Roberta G. Wayne, (MD)August 13, 1839,
(MG) Milton Cleveland.
William Bradley and Sarah Bowman, (MD) February 27, 1869,
(JP) George B. Moore.
William Calicot and Elizabeth Ann Callaway, (UK) Matthew
Davis, (MD) January 27, 1842.
Elijah Davis and Lucinda Haynes, (MD) January 15, 1828,
(UK) Thomas Stephens.
Joshua Myers and Margaret Myers, (MD) August 24, 1847, (MG)
John Green.
Henry W. Stokes and Elisa Bailey, (MD) November 28, 1839,
(MG) James Suggett.
Mathias Wagoner and Mrs. Mary Harkins, (MD)February 1, 1846,
(JP) Charles A. King.
Wiley Vinson and Elizabeth Whaley, (MD) October 10, 1869,
(MG) W. W. Jones.
John W. Scruggs and Sarah Ann Smith, (MD) April 24, 1855.
John K. Pemberton and Maggie Hord, (MD) April 20, 1870.
Caleb E. Berry and Ann M. Wells, (MD) November 21, 1854.

James W. Owen and Emily E. Foss, (MD) April 22, 1856.

Talton K. Patterson and Laura Elizabeth McAmay, (UK) R. L.
McAfee, (MD) January 30, 1868.

Albert Pratt and Lina Baker, (MD) March 6, 1865.

George Allen and Emily Dickerson, (MD) December 18, 1863,
Groom is from Boone County.

Robert H. Blackburn and Mary E. McCall, (MD) November 4,
1855.

Thomas J. Callaway and Mary E. Sanders, (MD) August 9, 1865.

Benjamin H. Cason and Malinda Beall, (MD) December 27, 1860.

Benjamin F. Clatterbuck and Lucy Ann Holt, (MD) January 11,
1866.

Henry Fletcher and Janes Estes, (MD) April 18, 1822.

William M. George and Ann Young, (MD) May 12, 1841, (MG) J.
L. Yantis.

Michael R. Hall and Amanda L. Callaway, (MD) December 15,
1870, (MG) Thompson Penn.

George W. Hamilton and Frances C. Hamilton, (MD) August 12,
1846, (MG) W. W. Robertson.

Samuel C. Heller and Victoria Morris, (MD)December 24, 1860,
Groom is from Boone County.

R. I. Hunt and Mary Ann Suggett, (MD) October 24, 1868,
Groom is from Chariton County.

Allen Kinkead and Mary Price, (MD) June 14, 1838, (MG) J. S.
Yantis, Groom is from Saline County.

Thomas H. Lane and Mrs. Mary Dunn, (MD) March 19, 1870.

Andrew J. Langley and Sarah E. Davis, (MD) February 4, 1870.

James F. Maddox and Margaret F. Jones, (MD) September 18,
1860.

Benjamin Overton and Ann Holt, (MD) July 15, 1830, (MG) J.
A. Suggett.

Henry F. Allen and Sallie E. Stephens, (MD) December 23,
1863.

John W. Brackenridge and Apalena Driskill, (MD) July 30,
1852, (JP) Joel Palmer.

Hiram Coats and Pamelia Walker, (MD) September 20, 1835,
(JP) James Stewart.

Callchill (sic) English and Susan M. Lynch, (MD) May 22,
1867.

William H. Freeman and Nancy Jane Davis, (MD) February 6,
1859.

John S. Gilbert and Elizabeth E. Miller, (MD) May 14, 1857.

Allen Goodman and Margaret Tate, (MD) January 11, 1863.

William Harrison and Mary T. Vinson, (MD) January 8, 1868.

John S. Herndon and Elizabeth Pratt, (MD) March 15, 1860,
(UK) Jeptha Harrison.

William James and Evaline Blackburn, (MD) May 24, 1838, (JP)
R. B. Jackson.

14

Samuel B. Jeffries and Mary Ann Conner, (MD) December 24, 1856.

George T. Kemp and Elizabeth M. Musgrove, (MD)April 3, 1851.

Charles C. Lawrence and Susan I. Wood, (MD)January 25, 1869.

Andrew Lisk and Mary D. Cobbs, (MD) March 8, 1855, Groom is Montgomery County.

Andrew Mahoney and Sally Ann Moxley, (MD) August 21, 1828, (JP) Enoch Fruit.

W. C. Bartley and Josephine Ramsey, (MD) July 29, 1863, (MG) E. G. Tenten.

James F. Custard and Sarah M. E. Dawson, (MD) December 23, 1858.

Thompson Crump and Louisa Hays, (MD) December 22, 1825, (MG) William Hays.

William A. Davis and Druzilla Smith, (MD) August 12, 1846, (MG) Theo. Boulware.

Joseph R. Derieux and Jane Dunham, (MD) March 1, 1843, (MG) Theo. Boulware.

William Divers and Martha A. Jones, (MD) December 25, 1863.

Enoch B. Dunlap and Amanda Jane Whyte, (MD) February 16, 1861.

James Ferguson and Catharine Price, (MD) October 20, 1834, (UK) George B. Hopkins.

William Fort and Margaret J. Wilburn, (MD) June 16, 1853, Groom is from Audrain County.

Francis R. Foy and Jane Langley, (MD) May 31, 1849, (JP) J. D. Mcgary.

James M. Glover and Martha A. Moon, (MD) November 16, 1856.

Henry A. Greenway and Sarah B. Keel, (MD) December 24, 1868.

William Nichols Hall and Matilda C. Howard, (MD) December 30, 1852, (UK) A. O. Hall.

William Ham and Martha McDaniel, (MD) June 22, 1843, (JP) A. Northpen.

Butler Harrison and Sarah Yeater, (MD) December 8, 1864.

John P. Jackson and Carrie Whaley, (MD) March 4, 1858.

Thomas Jameson and Margaret R. Martin, (MD) March 8, 1848, (MG) Noah Flood.

Hugh Allen and Mariah Board, (MD) February 25, 1847.

Reuben Murry and Catharine Wilson, (MD) May 17, 1844, (JP) A. Northphen, Groom is from Boone County.

Allen Nash and Evaline M. Oldham, (MD) April 18, 1844.

George Nichols and Hannah Brite, (MD) June 29, 1826, (MG) William Coats.

Samuel H. Owen and Amanda Ray, (MD) January 11, 1865.

John A. Pledge and Miriam Warren, (MD) February 14, 1831, (MG) Theo. Boulware.

William M. Potter and Jane Ann Boswell, (MD) August 12,1866.

Stephen Rice and Mary M. Ramsey, (MD) June 3, 1858.

John C. Stokes and Lucy P. Holt, (MD) March 21, 1862.

Henry M. Tate and Sarah J. Boone, (MD) December 11, 1865.
John Tennison and Ann McCormick, (MD) December 22, 1830,
(JP) Enoch Fruit.
Wickleff Thomas and Lydia Powell, (MD) March 12, 1861.
William R. Wilson and Ellen D. Grant, (MD) March 6, 1844,
(UK) William N. Robinson.
Thomas G. Williams and Mary F. Cook, (MD) August 17, 1845,
(UK) Absalom Rice.
Andrew J. Martin and Peggy Belcher, (MD) February 14, 1850,
(UK) W. J. Gilman.
Lafayette Linsey and Sarah Berry, (MD) January 2, 1849, (UK)
William J. Gilman.
Charles Lowe and Anna Derieux, (MD) March 24, 1870.
William B. Lenoir and Sarah D. Chappell, (MD) February 23,
1844, (MG) T. M. Allen.
James E. King and Sarah E. Marten, (MD) February 28, 1854.
William C. Kemp and Eliza J. Coons, (MD) December 23, 1850.
Andrew W. Jolly and Elizabeth G. Fisher, (MD) August 20,
1855.
William J. Jackson and Sarah E. Wren, (MD) October 31, 1839,
(MG) John Thatcher.
Robert Hunter and Martha Davis, (MD) October 23, 1864, (MG)
Stephen Ham.
William Hume and Emily Carter, (MD) October 10, 1844, (MG)
Noah Flood.
Joseph Howard and Mary Brannenburg, (MD) April 24, 1850,
(JP) Robert Jones.
Ambrose B. Hill and Elizabeth Williams, (MD) December 16,
1841, (JP) H. L. Turner.
James Craighead and Nannie Berry, (MD) January 18, 1866.
Edward Foster and Clarissa Jackson, (MD) September 19, 1858.
Moses F. Allen and Nancy Phillips, (MD) October 23, 1851.
Robert B. Farmer and Sarah J. Murphy, (MD) July 20, 1866.
William P. Myers and Mrs. Mary Wray, (MD) January 15, 1870,
(JP) John Vinson.
George W. Northcutt and Nannie Price, (MD) October 23, 1867,
Groom is from Boone County.
Robert H. Taylor and Mary E. Payne, (MD) March 2, 1870.
Dr. William E. Dillard and Elizabeth Hughs, (MD) June 17,
1841, (UK) William B. Douglass.
John Bowen and Eliza J. M. Newsom, (MD) November 11, 1868.
Allen Cobb and Palina Ann Hamiblin, (MD) November 28, 1844,
(JP) Joseph Scholl, Groom is from Montgomery County.
John M. Davis and Elizabeth Gibbs, (MD) March 19, 1843, (MG)
Noah Flood.
Moses P. Estes and Izabell Blankenship, (MD) October 17,
1858.
David D. Finley and Matilda Johnson, (MD) April 7, 1864.
James B. Gilman and Mattie J. Winson, (MD) March 26, 1870.

16

Harvey Hubberd and Martha King, (MD) December 17, 1850, (UK)
   W. W. Robertson.
Charles C. Lawrence and Rebecca F. Dudley, (MD) December 2,
   1866.
George Morris and Elizabeth McClelland, (MD) March 17, 1827,
   (MG) Alan McGuire.
Rober C. Baker and Susannah C. Devore, (MD) April 30, 1833,
   (ED) George Washington.
John Thomas and Elizabeth Craighead, (MD) June 8, 1854.
Benjamin Woods and Mary Tincher, (MD) September 19, 1867.
Oliver Craghead and Frances J. Payne, (MD) July 29, 1852,
   (MG) B. H. Spencer.
Reuben W. Farmer and Mary A. Saunders, (MD) December 24,
   1868.
Thomas M. Moss and Sarah Bowan, (MD) June 4, 1847, (UK) J.
   C. Renfroe.
John J. Griffin and Lucinda Shelley, (MD) April 17, 1856.
Thomas Bagby and Cintha Robinson, (MD) October 6, 1868.
William Hunter and Sarah Talbot, (MD) January 21, 1836,
   (MG) William Duncan.
Frederick W. Koch and Dara Hereford, (MD) June 7, 1862.
Cale C. Maupin and Isabel Dillon, (MD) October 9, 1865.
Frances McGown and Mary E. Lockridge, (MD) October 6, 1870.
Zacahriah Miller and Mary Ann Miller, (MD) July 31, 1851,
   (MG) Absalom Rice.
Irvine S. Nevins and Martha Dozier, (MD) March 12, 1856.
Nicholas Stephens and Sarah E. Gass, (MD) February 26, 1860.
Thomas J. Wright and Carrie T. Lovelace, (MD) September 20,
   1868.
David Zumwalt and Cordelia Merryman, (MD) February 20, 1863.
Luther Cheatham and Nancy Bowis, (MD) April 29, 1840, (MG)
   Absalom Rice.
Thompson B. James and Mary S. Crowson, (MD) June 21, 1855.
Nathan McBride and Elizabeth M. Carty, (MD) July 3, 1858.
Greenville Riggs and Mrs. Ann Bradly, (MD) January 29, 1858.
Wade H. Strickland and Bettie Brooks, (MD)February 27, 1855.
William Yancey and Martha Ferguson, (MD) March 14, 1839,
   (UK) J. F. Young.
Samuel Allen and Sarah Chappell, (MD) May 12, 1847.
William Kemper and Margaret Ann Murphy, (MD) March 21, 1856.
Moses McClintic and Sarah R. J. Price, (MD) December 10,
   1847, (MG) Theo. Boulware.
Alexander Read and Elizabeth Jones, (MD) February 9, 1848,
   (UK) William B. Douglas.
William Stanley and Nancy Jane Holt, (MD) April 28, 1836,
   (MG) Jas. Suggett.
Reuben B. Langley and Margaret Ann Hazelrigg, (MD) February
   1, 1860.
James T. Nelson and Mary E. Young, (MD) December 26, 1866.

17

Richard Smith and Eliza Waggener, (MD) March 15, 1835, (JP)
  Beverly Ramsey.
Samuel B. Rogers and Nancy E. Adkins, (MD) April 18, 1860.
Berry T. Owen and Elizabeth J. Spencer, (MD) February 4,
  1864.
Joseph Allen and and Ann Craig, (MD) March 10, 1841, (MG)
  John L. Yantis.
Elknah (sic) Brooks and Emeline Holt, (MD) June 1, 1848,
  (MG) Noah Flood.
John Coons and Sarah Arthur, (MD) March 13, 1850.
E. W. Blackwell and W. M. Beaven, (MD) June 22, 1854.
John Lane and Desiah Holland, (MD) November 15, 1858.
William A. Nash and Sophiah H. Adams, (MD) January 7, 1869.
Hiram Pace and Matilda Woods, (MD) February 29, 1824, (JP)
  James Nevins.
John Boyd and Emma Ferguson, (MD) December 14, 1843, (UK) R.
  L. Reynolds.
Smith A. Brandon and Eliza Ann Reynolds, (MD) February 19,
  1846, (MG) James Criswell.
Benjamin M. Gammon and Iretta C. Grissom, (MD) December 26,
  1867.
John Fullbright and Elizabeth Yount, (MD) October 2, 1828,
  (JP) George King.
Robert A. McCall and Elizabeth K. Kemp, (MD) February 15,
  1850, (UK) John Green.
Seaton H. Palmer and Mary E. Crum, (MD) August 26, 1863.
Richard Todd and Syntha M. Bane, (MD) April 3, 1870.
William C. Brown and Lucy Ann Bush, (MD) January 10, 1860.
John Gray and Mrs. Mary C. Warren, (MD) November 11, 1860.
David Painter and Frances A. Bernard, (MD) August 23, 1866.
Pemberton Gibbs and Polly Ann Rothwell, (MD) November 25,
  1847, (UK) Thos. P. Stephens.
Charles W. Baldwin and Jane Johndraw, (MD) March 12, 1857.
George W. Green and Mrs. Rebecca Humphries, (MD) June 22,
  1854, (UK) John R. Craighead.
William E. Hall and Mary E. Farmer, (MD) December 9, 1869.
Joseph T. Hughart and Ann Henderson, (MD) August 30, 1827,
  (UK) David Kirkpatrick.
Samuel Mateer and Louisa Miller, (MD) September 17, 1846,
  (UK) William B. Douglass.
Cash McDonald and Drusilla Davis, (MD) June 20, 1833, (JP)
  J. M. Doan.
John W. Pace and Sarah E. Pugh, (MD) August 15, 1866.
Jesse Selby and Elizabeth Hereford, (MD) November 5, 1828,
  (JP) William Martin.
Hugh Tincher and Susan Newsom, (MD) October 13, 1842, (MG)
  John F. Young.
John Arnold and Mary Susan Lale, (MD) June 28, 1860.
D. D. Johnson and Martha M. Buckner, (MD) November 27, 1856.

William Jones and Amanda Miller, (MD) February 20, 1834,
(MG) Jabez Ham.
John W. Martin and Amanda G. Balbertone, (MD) February 9,
1864.
Gabriel May and Elizabeth Craghead, (MD) December 4, 1823,
(JP) Thomas Fisher.
Thomas P. Petty and Narcisa W. Finley, (MD) February 14,
1861.
John Reed and Sally Moxley, (MD) October 31, 1835, (MG) Wm.
Coats.
Madison C. Allen and Julia Ann Wigington, (MD) July 1, 1858.
Thomas Austin and Jane Myers, (MD) April 2, 1840, (MG) Jabez
Ham.
William Beavans and Lucinda Ferguson, (MD) April 12, 1832,
(JP) Arthur Neill.
William R. Bernard and Margaret E. Buckner, (MD) July 28,
1850, (MG) W. W. Robertson.
James W. Bird and Zerilda Barger, (MD) April 9, 1851.
Thomas Jacobs and Lydia Dawson, (MD) November 9, 1834.
Louis Patterson and Ella Holland, (MD) January 27, 1870.
John Potts and Mattie Jane Henderson, (MD) March 24, 1864.
Thomas H. Baker and Marian Kirtley, (MD) April 13, 1845,
(JP) John R. Craghead.
Michael A. Burns and Mary McLaughlin, (MD) March 7, 1839,
(JP) H. S. Turner.
James Thomas Houseman and Nancy Jane Craighead, (MD) August
19, 1866.
William Jones and Elizabeth Jones, (MD) March 1, 1838, (PG)
Jabez Ham.
Thomas Langley and Sally Williams, (MD) May 16, 1838, (JP)
Arthur Neill.
James Sims and Patsy Beden, (MD) February 24, 1833, (MG) Wm.
Duncan.
John T. Smart and Virginia L. Smart, (MD) March 5, 1837,
(JP) Jas. Stewart.
John Williams and Eliza Graves, (MD) September 27, 1827,
(JP) William martin.
William B. Burt and Sophia E. Truitt, (MD) August 14, 1859.
Joseph Christy and Amanda Bowen, (MD) August 20, 1849, (JP)
Arthur Neill.
Michem D. Maddox and Mary Dudley, (MD) February 5, 1852,
(JP) Marshall Coats.
Allen D. Miller and Mary Ann Crowson, (MD) September 26,
1842, (MG) Noah Flood.
William B. Wright and Margaret A. Whaley, (MD) December 20,
1853.
A. Callison and Harriet A. Dickerson, (MD) November 1, 1859.
Ebenezer Finly and Mariah C. Moon, (MD) August 22, 1848.
D. Harkins and Sally Kenney, (MD) February 3, 1864.

Willis Hinley and Amanda Robinson, (MD) April 13, 1843, (UK)
Joseph Coons.
Jourdan Kemp and Mary Dunlap, (MD) May 19, 1831, (MG) Wm.
Coats.
Thomas Allen and Mrs. Eliza Langtree, (MD)December 20, 1864,
(JP) Stephen Scott.
Wildin Young and Susan Fruite, (MD) March 5, 1847, (UK) W.
W. Kemp.
James Murphy and Sofier (sic) Weaver, (MD) March 11, 1840,
(JP) Richard Swan.
George B. Moon and Francis Martin, (MD) August 30, 1841,
(JP) Hiram Yates.
Joseph Miller and Sarah Brown, (MD) October 21, 1847.
Levi McMurty and Fanny Chick, (MD) May 5, 1831, (JP) Enoch
Fruit.
Thomas M. Maughs and Ellen Everhart, (MD) October 4, 1859.
David Henderson and Mary Blattenburgh, (MD)December 1, 1834,
(MG) Theo. Boulware.
John Hamblin and Elizabeth Heasick, (MD) August 18, 1836,
(MG) Jabez Ham.
Thomas F. Guthrie and Mary Eliz. Clatterbuck, (MD) February
19, 1858.
Alexander Gilmore and Ann Hamilton, (MD) June 6, 1850.
Peter M. Gibony and Nancy Herring, (MD) December 6, 1860.
T. C. Foy and Mary F. Coonce, (MD) June 8, 1863.
Samuel Alkire and Mahala Ginson, (MD) October 13, 1831, (JP)
J. W. Johnston.
Nehemiah Kennett and Ann Eliz. Ficklin, (MD) March 2, 1854.
Jackson Lynes and Mary E. Harvey, (MD) February 6, 1845,
(MG) R. L. McAfee.
John McDaniel and Cynthia Alexander, (MD) August 5, 1824,
(UK) David Kirkpatrick.
James H. Miller and Sarah E. Harrison, (MD) October 16,
1866, (MG) R. S. Symington.
Jamey Pemberton and Martha Braley, (MD) January 7, 1840,
(ED) M. P. Wills.
Thomas Rupert and Rebecca Newsom, (MD) April 17, 1838, (UK)
John T. A. Henderson.
E. B. Sitton and Mariah Herring, (MD) July 6, 1843, (MG)
Theo. Boulware.
Wm. H. Wilson and Isabella J. Foxworthy, (MD) January 22,
1839, (MG) John S. Yantis.
Charles Hays and Dulcena L. Smart, (MD) February 22, 1844,
(MG) Absalom Rice.
James O. Harver and Betsey Philips, (MD) September 22, 1830,
(MG) William Coats.
Thomas J. Green and Sarah W. Bull, (MD) April 28, 1867.
Edward Gillow and Hariet Ely, (MD) August 29, 1851.
Gustave F. Carison and Ann Sheep, (MD) December 3, 1870.

Robert Carter and Martha Childers, (MD) January 7, 1841,
(MG) J. Coons.
William Jenkins and Hannah Walker, (MD) January 18, 1855,
(JP) J. K. Allen.
Richard K. McMahan and Elizabeth Black, (MD)January 5, 1846,
(MG) James Love.
James Muir and Rebecca Scholl, (MD) March 25, 1847, (MG)
James Love.
William H. Woolery and Mary E. Shoultz, (MD) March 19, 1863,
(JP) Green B. Todd.
Thomas N. Allen and Isabella Hamilton, (MD) April 4, 1839,
(MG) R. L. McAfee.
Benjamin Baker and Martha Rolle, (MD) May 28, 1840, (MG)
Thomas Allen.
Robert H. Branch and Sarah C. Barn, (MD) September 17, 1843,
(JP) Chas. A. Ming.
Stephen W. Gilbert and Mary Johnson Galloway, (UK) John F.
Cowan, (MD) October 11, 1864.
John D. Nevins and Mary Jane Fisher, (MD) September 5, 1838,
(UK) John T. A. Henderson.
James Sampson and Frances Selby, (MD) January 18, 1865.
Thomas Williamson and Nancy R. Colly, (MD) May 1, 1851.
Charles J. Bell and Mary Ann Custard, (MD)November 10, 1864.
J. W. Davis and America Dunlap, (MD) August 23, 1854.
James B. Fletcher and Mary Ann Blount, (MD) July 7, 1850,
(JP) Arthur Neill.
Martin Noland and Sarah Lampkins, (MD) March 2, 1826, (UK)
Anderson Woods.
James Porter and Mrs. Lucy Threlkell, (MD) October 17, 1852,
(MG) J. M. Wilson.
John Reed and Minerva E. Rothwell, (MD) August 27, 1861.
Aaron W. Rutherford and Mrs. Eliza Little, (MD) February 24,
1853.
Clay Sheets and Sarah S. Hardin, (MD) August 6, 1868.
Absalom Austin and Lydia Sitton, (MD) January 7, 1834, (MG)
Theo. Boulware.
Thomas Boyd and Mary F. Jefferies, (MD) July 17, 1855.
George Brown and Margaret Snell, (MD) March 15, 1848.
Austin Calhoun and Martha R. Craig, (MD) January 25, 1860.
Thompson Daniels and Jane McLaughlin, (MD) October 8, 1843,
(JP) B. Mathews.
William Ewing and Georgeanna Herring, (MD) April 19, 1840.
Julius W. Meyer and Emmelina Arens, (MD) November 26, 1868.
Norman Monroe and Martha F. Gregory, (MD) January 27, 1870.
James S. Samuel and Susannah A. Bartley, (MD) November 21,
1855.
John Unstead and Martha Jane Vaughn, (MD)September 28, 1860.
Stephen Plummer and Susan M. Davis, (MD) April 22, 1851.
David R. Baley and Mary Ann Zumwalt, (MD)September 18, 1856.

James M. Beaver and Salerda C. Holt, (MD) April 25, 1860.

T. J. Briant and Nancy Lowery, (MD) August 11, 1868.

Henry Elley and Sarah Fitzhugh, (MD) February 18, 1863.

Rowland Mumford and Mary S. Childs, (MD) June 10, 1868.

Thomas Scroghum and Susan Harryford, (MD) March 28, 1839, (UK) Joseph Coons.

Robert W. Turman and Mollie Cason, (MD) February 14, 1864, (MG) M. M. Fisher.

Willoughby P. Ferguson and Elizabeth Gee, (MD) January 18, 1838, (JP) Arthur Neill.

Dennis W. Bagby and Jane Payne, (MD) December 19, 1843, (MG) B. R. Johnson.

J. L. D. Basye and Mary Ann Larimore, (MD)December 30, 1851, Groom is from Jackson County.

Elisha H. Blackwell and Martha Ann Hutson, (MD) July 22, 1846, (MG) P. H. Steinberger.

J. G. Suggett and J. Curby, (MD) November 13, 1852.

Francis Tharp and Patsey Freeman, (MD) March 25, 1849.

Philip Blandenburg and Emily Atkinson, (MD)January 12, 1844, (MG) Jacob Coons.

Thomas Ficklin and America Ann Craig, (MD) October 30, 1845, (MG) Noah Flood.

John Jones and Polly Mateer, (MD) March 17, 1847, (UK) R. S. Symnington.

Augustus Murphy and Nancy Curry, (MD) November 28, 1833, (MG) Robert McAfee.

James A. Terrell and Hester A. R. Kelso, (MD) January 24, 1833, (UK) W. W. Redman.

Charles Bailey and Amelia Jameson, (MD) February 12, 1838, (MG) Theo. Boulware.

Wesley Criswell and Sarah L. Hawkins, (MD) October 24, 1866.

James Freeman and Elizabeth Gough, (MD) February 13, 1853.

John W. Mitchell and Eliza Snell, (MD) May 18, 1858.

Thomas W. Nichols and Sarah Kemper, (MD) September 8, 1864.

Robert Alexander and Mary Ann Sheley, (MD) October 8, 1843, (MG) Theo. Boulware.

John G. Cruso and Susan E. Carter, (MD) December 15, 1853, Groom is from Boone County.

Wm. H. H. Gentry and Nancy E. Early, (MD) March 13, 1860.

James McMurty and Sallie A. Berry, (MD) October 21, 1869.

Richard Netherton and Margaret I. Callison, (MD) September 4, 1856.

George W. Bellama and Sarah E. Thomas, (MD) September 12, 1864.

James M. Davenport and Rebecca Mosely, (MD) January 1, 1860.

John Ellis and Rebecca Derby, (MD) April 13, 1848.

John T. Gathright and Betty Jane Davis, (MD) April 29, 1858.

William W. McCall and Ettie Jackson, (MD) January 10, 1867.

Elijah B. Parker and Elizabeth Yates, (MD) December 15,1870.

James T. Harrison and Susan L. McKinney, (MD) January 15, 1867.
George McIntire and Frances Willing, (MD) March 1, 1863.
Jeremiah Moore and Sally A. Baynum, (MD) May 24, 1865.
Monroe Sampson and Pauline Shaw, (MD) October 20, 1853.
Tobias Byers and Amanda Ferguson, (MD) February 1, 1870.
Archibald G. Dawson and Louisa Harper, (MD) Septemer 17, 1855.
Richard C. Dunlap and Susan C. Berry, (MD) January 29, 1861.
Thomas Kemp and Mary M. Harris, (MD) November 6, 1868.
George W. Sanders and Nancy H. Ferguson, (MD) February 13, 1861.
George Thomas and Mary Ann Brown, (MD) October 21, 1857.
William H. Allen and Jane Ann Craig, (MD) November 11, 1852.
Joel M. Bolton and Eliza J. Scholl, (MD) October 14, 1868.
T. Farmer and A. Farmer, (MD) January 28, 1864.
Michael Gilbert and Elizabeth L. Kemp, (MD) April 14, 1856.
Frances M. McCown and Elizabeth Burdit, (MD)August 18, 1852.
James M. Obern and Mary M. Gibony, (MD) April 12, 1849, (UK) John R. Craghead.
E. Smith and Sarah Green, (MD) January 1, 1829, (MG) Theo. Boulware.
Samuel M. Dooley and Mary Wilkerson, (MD) December 13, 1855.
William Bryant and Adalade Bush, (MD) December 21, 1869.
John Hamilton and Agnes Hamilton, (MD) October 29, 1840, (MG) J. L. Yantis.
Frank F. Turley and Mary Weir, (MD) April 26, 1868.
Charles S. Yount and Mary Susan Conner, (MD) October 28, 1863.
James B. Curtis and Martha J. Adams, (MD) November 30, 1865.
O. Greensday and Mary Emmons, (MD) February 19, 1860.
James M. Jackson and Eliza A. How, (MD) September 11, 1855.
Richard F. Knox and Sarah Ann Dunn, (MD) February 3, 1867.
Harvey Level and Milly Boone, (MD) November 14, 1833, (MG) Jabez Ham.
John R. Newman and Mary A. Bartley, (MD) June 11, 1861.
David Wilson and Mary Dillard, (MD) September 8, 1870.
Stephen Terry and Kiziah E. Renny, (MD) January 9, 1867.
James Rogers and Virginia Madox, (MD) July 7, 1859.
James Freeman and Rozenna Green, (MD) April 3, 1870.
Columbus Dawson and Malvina Martin, (MD) April 4, 1850.
William Craig and Sidney Smith, (MD) December 12, 1838, (MG) Theo. Boulware.
Alexander Cleveland and Polly Ferguson, (MD) September 26, 1844, (JP) T. J. Ferguson.
W. A. Day and A. Winn, (MD) October 21, 1858.
Moses McClintic and Mary Black, (MD) January 26, 1854.
Abraham Vanhorn and M. Hall, (MD) March 10, 1869.
Benjamin Zumwalt and Fannie T. Green, (MD) January 15, 1868.

23

Benjamin H. Boon and Elvira H. Thornhill, (MD) February 6, 1866, (MG) Jas. H. Tuttle.

James S. Day and Elizabeth Farier, (MD) September 23, 1866, (MG) Stephen Hamm.

Sidney E. Fox and Fannie O. Scott, (MD) March 3, 1870, (MG) George W. Penn.

James Gathright and Hester Shackelford, (MD) July 25, 1844, (MG) Absalom Rice.

Thomas Harrison and Katharine Mattock, (MD) November 16, 1852, (MG) S. Scott.

David J. Judy and Nancy Ann Edster, (MD) April 7, 1860.

James A. Leeper and Florence McPheeters, (MD) October 28, 1825, (UK) W. W. Robertson.

Briton Matthews and Miss Zumwalt, (MD) April 28, 1831, (JP) Geo. Bartley.

William S. McCall and Martha W. Stucker, (MD) November 24, 1857.

Joseph J. Neal and Martha G. Garrett, (MD) September 13, 1855.

Benton Oliver and Mary E. Gray, (MD) November 9, 1870.

John U. Pemberton and Katharine Hunter, (MD) October 6, 1836, (ED) M. P. Wills.

Alexander Power and Patsy Ferrier, (MD) December 25, 1827, (MG) William Coats.

John W. Pullman and Elizabeth Heart, (MD) April 18, 1833, (UK) Robert McAfee.

Bazele Rose and Sarah Bryan, (MD) March 30, 1822, (JP) James Nevins.

William Sanders and Elmira Foster, (MD) June 14, 1855.

Thomas H. Berry and Mahala Davidson, (MD) February 17, 1836, (JP) James Stewart.

William H. Carthey and Catherine Hiller, (MD) December 25, 1856.

John Gaullee and Susan A. Wood, (MD) August 18, 1869.

Milton Perry and Zela O. Daniel, (MD) October 28, 1858.

Haydon King and Julinda D. P. Brun, (MD) December 19, 1850.

Henry Jones and Elizabeth Williams, (MD) June 3, 1842, (JP) A. K. Bell.

Dale Green and Martha Spry, (MD) March 23, 1853, Both Bride and Groom is from Boone County.

John Foster and Sarah Longley, (MD) April 24, 1828, (UK) David Kirkpatrick.

William Black and Mary Turner, (MD) April 4, 1860.

Thomas H. Beeding and Sarah E. Nichols, (MD) June 25, 1857.

William J. Dyer and Martha C. Keeling, (MD) July 30, 1861.

R. H. Fowler and Elizabeth Baily, (MD) February 18, 1858.

William Hutton and Martha Price, (MD) October 19, 1855.

Joseph Patton and Louisa M. West, (MD) February 1, 1859.

Abraham Vier and Mary McDonald, (MD) August 23, 1853.

Isaac Agee and Cordilly Thornton, (MD) November 25, 1831,
(MG) William Coats.

Joshua Anderson and Laurie Baker, (MD) November 13, 1825,
(MG) Wm. Coats.

James R. Baker and Margaret Blackenburg, (MG) October 27,
1842, (MG) Joseph Coons.

James W. Bagby and Lavina Brown, (MD) November 25, 1841,
(MG) George Smith.

Louis Barnes and Letitia Booth, (MD) March 11, 1863, (JP)
William Penn.

Joseph B. Callaway and Mary Ann Lawrence, (MD) November 25,
1852, (MG) M. F. Coats.

James Faris and Rebecca M. Annett, (MD) December 6, 1838,
(UK) J. T. A. Henderson.

James T. Gregory and Mary Eliz. McCall, (MD) February 28,
1865.

William Hall and Eliza Herron, (MD) April 6, 1859.

Thos. S. Hamilton and Mary Ann Kilbraith, (MD) September 18,
1845, (MG) R. S. Symmington.

Charles Hobbs and Mary Ann Ficklin, (MD) December 22, 1857.

Francis Sanreneo and Amelia H. Miller, (MD) December 31,
1857.

Luke Shiverdecker and Jane Vandeveron, (MD) September 6,
1855.

William Smith and Sarah Jane Ferguson, (MD)October 17, 1850.

W. H. Threlkild and L. M. Smith, (MD) June 11, 1841, (MG)
Theo. Boulware.

James P. Warfield and Catharine Spencer, (MD) September 30,
1869.

Napoleon B. Foy and Susan Boyer, (MD) February 17, 1868,
(UK) Thos. J. Ferguson.

James C. Galbreath and Henrietta P. Courtney, (MD) November
22, 1854, (UK) S. S. Laws.

Joseph House and Mary Malone, (MD) January 25, 1825, (UK)
Samuel Crockett.

Augusta Lambert and Joanna Rhodes, (MD) November 19, 1837,
(JP) Arthur Neill.

Henry Martin and Nancy Wright, (MD) August 12, 1869.

George S. McIntosh and Sarah Harper, (MD) December 16, 1841,
(MG) Noah Flood.

Moses L. Miller and Louisa Ferguson, (MD) June 15, 1836,
(MG) B. A. Ramsey.

Henry Neill and Deborah Lamsdun, (MD) January 9, 1844, (JP)
N. B. Ferguson.

William F. Powell and Lydia Jane Cheatham, (MD) January 23,
1840, (UK) Joseph Coons.

Edmund Randolph and Patsy McClelland, (MD) December 4, 1832,
(UK) William Duncan.

James Renoe and Eveline Boyd, (MD) September 22, 1852.

James Scott and Eliza Edge Booth, (MD) September 15, 1859.
William Buchannan and Martha Warren, (MD) February 14, 1831,
(MG) Theo. Boulware.
Dr. Thos. Collier and Casandra Ann West, (MD) May 26, 1853,
(MG) D. Coulter.
James McMahan and Amanda Crows, (MD) January 26, 1865.
Christian Stolle and Anna Marell, (MD) July 31, 1854.
Theo. Allen and Medora Scott, (MD) April 13, 1868.
Vinson Benson and Martha S. Allen, (MD) September 25, 1860.
Alexander Foxworthy and Emily Bryan, (MD) February 23, 1841,
(MG) Noah Flood.
John Kilgore and Margaret Willingham, (MD) January 28, 1831,
(JP) Isaac Black.
Daniel Miller and Eliza M. Atkins, (MD) August 31, 1859.
Archibald Campbell and Malicy G. Northway, (MD) October 28,
1869.
Strowther Fourt and Malinda U. Roy, (MD) September 12, 1868.
William N. Moore and Margaret Ewing, (MD) October 4, 1855.
Samuel Pratt and Matilda Hoalman, (MD) March 20, 1857.
Tyre Bishop and Rebecca W. Wilburn, (MD) June 7, 1838, (MG)
Jabez Ham.
James L. Gibbs and Harriet E. Crank, (MD) March 18, 1841,
(MG) George Smith.
William McLanghlin and Leny Callaway, (MD)February 19, 1829,
(MG) William Coats.
Benjamin Tenena and Lavina Jane Adcock, (MD) September 18,
1854.
Absalom Zumwalt and Mrs. Eliz. Zumwalt, (MD) October 10,
1860.
J. D. McFee and Mary S. Gaiter, (MD) September 26, 1870.
James D. Branch and Isabella Johnson, (MD) June 26, 1862.
John B. Fenley and Sarah Baker, (MD) September 14, 1847.
John L. Kale and Charlota A. Craigs, (MD) March 13, 1860.
Isham McDonald and Jane Boyd, (MD) October 17, 1835, (UK)
Robert A. Younger.
William Vaughn and Eliz. Jane Brandon, (MD) March 1, 1843,
(UK) John E. Nevins.
George W. Garrett and Susan S. Crump, (MD) April 30, 1867.
James S. Brown and Sarah Jane Hornbuckle, (MD) December 1,
1839.
Jeremiah Dyson and Catharine Hays, (MD) September 10, 1855.
George W. Gaw and Catharine J. Martin, (MD) March 8, 1849,
(UK) W. W. Robertson.
Samuel H. Lawrence and Margaret Dearing, (MD) January 29,
1862.
John Smith and Rachel Carpenter, (MD) February 5, 1857.
Lafayette Love and Sarah James, (MD) April 13, 1853.
Emanuel Neff and Amanda F. Benson, (MD) January 28, 1869.
James A. Purdy and Mary A. Hill, (MD) November 27, 1851.

William J. Gilman and Vicy Ann Callaway, (MD) October 18,
1838, (MG) Jabez Ham.
William P. Bryant and Sarah Herryman, (MD)February 19, 1857.
Thomas Hickenbottom and Mattie Arnold, (MD) April 30, 1868.
Richard E. Miles and Rose Anna Sheriff, (MD) January 24,
1856.
Robert N. Stewart and Caroline M. Smith, (MD) February 28,
1839, (UK) Joseph T. Bryan.
David Waggoner and Fanny Ronalls, (MD) September 18, 1834,
(JP) B. A. Ramsey.
John W. Duncan and Lucy D. Collins, (MD) March 6, 1867.
S. A. Burnett and Mrs. Martha C. Maden, (MD)October 5, 1869.
Obediah Dishman and Rebecca J. Hamilton, (MD) May 5, 1853.
Robert Glover and Martha Winn, (MD) September 22, 1848, (MG)
James Love.
John M. Hendrix and Bettie Wilkerson, (MD) April 27, 1868.
Richard Little and Adaline Suthern, (MD) January 20, 1841,
(MG) Samuel Day.
Julis Creesham and Ann Mariah Boyd, (MD) July 9, 1856.
James Brown and Hannah Ann Alderson, (MD) July 9, 1835, (MG)
William Duncan.
Thomas J. Atkinson and Mary J. Fisher, (MD)November 5, 1851,
(UK) B. H. Spencer.
Robert Brandon and Mrs. ELiza Dozier, (MD) April --, 1859.
John T. Buckner and Elen M. Burman, (MD) October 3, 1851,
(MG) W. Mayhew.
Robert R. Carrington and Julia A. Holt, (MD) January 16,
1866.
A. V. Dicus and Elizabeth Knight, (MD) April 16, 1860.
William B. Farr and Mildreth A. Wells, (MD) December 22,
1864.
Edward W. Hopkins and Cally W. Longley, (MD) April 1, 1854.
D. R. Knox and Alice Dyson, (MD) February 21, 1861.
Thomas G. Lewis and Artamesia Tharp, (MD) October 31, 1861.
Alexander J. Stansbury and Nancy Emmett, (MD) August 18,
1847, (UK) Jacob Coons.
Silas W. Wilson and Louisa George, (MD) January 6, 1858.
Harvey B. Allen and Mary M. Pledge, (MD) May 18, 1865, (MG)
C. Babcock.
A. P. Farmer and Fannie Dillion, (MD) October 14, 1868.
Morris A. Hardin and Elizabeth Galwaith, (MD) January 12,
1854.
James A. Henderson and Francis M. Holt, (MD) November 16,
1838, (UK) John T. A Henderson.
W. H. Moses and Laura M. Baugh, (MD) December 8, 1865.
James Steel and Thurza Langley, (MD) June 28, 1851.
William Wily and Mary Ann Scot, (MD) March 22, 1864.
Francis Forbes and Mary Ann McDonold, (MD) April 23, 1851.
Lewis Hord and Mollie B. Gant, (MD) November 10, 1858.

James McKinney and Martha Callaway, (MD) January 12, 1855.
I. M. Gilbert and Mary F. Oxley, (MD) January 25, 1869.
Hardin F. Hornbickle and Elizabeth Hinton, (MD)May 14, 1842,
     (UK) Absalom Rice.
Alfred Menifee and Mary Hunt Mason, (MD) November 25, 1830,
     (MG) Theo. Boulware, Groom is from Kentucky.
Bazel S. Tharp and Malinda Williamson, (MD) June 15, 1856.
John P. Ferree and Sarah Humphreys, (MD) November 15, 1868.
James Burnett and Miss E. M. Blount, (MD)September 25, 1867.
Joseph Wily Davis and Martha V. Meadows, (MD) January 18,
     1854.
Andrew W. Dickenson and Nancy Moore, (MD) October 27, 1858.
Jacob Potts and ELiza Jane Austin, (MD) March 9, 1858.
James Simpson and Charlotte Manners, (MD) October 5, 1859.
Andrew J. Douglass and Mary Collins, (MD) February 24, 1858.
Robert Gallaway and Jane McCrae, (MD) November 20, 1851,
     (UK) ---, Groom is from Boone County.
John Hughes and Mary E. Peyton, (MD) December 7, 1837, (JP)
     John A. Burt.
Jacob Madox and Louisa E. Morris, (MD) June 25, 1854.
John Moseley and Susanna Shortridge, (MD) July 30, 1845.
John Wadley and Nancy Ann May, (MD) August 21, 1856.
William Ellis and Sally Day, (MD) December 20, 1858.
James Clatterbuck and Catharine Miller, (MD) February 22,
     1845.
Leroy Griffin and Frances Gray, (MD) October 14, 1847, (MG)
     James Criswell.
John B. Moore and Elizabeth Nash, (MD) January 20, 1831,
     (UK) Geo. Bartley.
Elias Pickering and Caroline F. Holderman, (MD) January 2,
     1870.
William Henry Price and Eliza Dyer, (MD) October 31, 1854,
     (UK) D. C. Blackwell, Groom is from New York.
William Reynolds and Martha Ann Bennett, (MD)March 10, 1853.
Thomas Sheperd and Elizabeth Nickels, (MD) January 23, 1870.
William Yates and Mattie H. Tate, (MD) February 20, 1868,
     (MG) John F. Cowan.
William H. Rankins and Mary E. Spaunhurst, (MD) July 12,
     1860, (UK) --, Bride is from St. Louis.
Richard Sharp and Emma Dillard, (MD) February 22, 1865.
Frank F. Dean and Eliza Ann Zumwalt, (MD) December 24, 1867,
     (UK) Wm. E. Stephens.
Lemuel B. Coats and Elizabeth Maddox, (MD) July 6, 1849,
     (JP) W. J. Gilman.
Charles D. Harkins and Margeria Miller, (MD) September 22,
     1857.
Madison Pugh and Willimine Hardin, (MD) February 2, 1860.
Robert H. Woolfork and Bettie H. Slaughter, (MD) September
     --, 1861.

Ramson Agee and Siann Taylor, (MD) March 23, 1834, (MG) J.
B. Morrow.
James A. Baker and Martha King, (MD) December 13, 1842, (MG)
J. Coons.
Francis Bagby and Sarah Stokes, (MD) December 27, 1842, (MG)
R. S. Reynolds.
Milton Berry and Nancy H. Mosely, (MD) August 12, 1863.
Joseph Everheart and Lucinda Dycen, (MD) April 22, 1863,
(UK) Martin Bibb.
Kennel Gilbert and Francis Snell, (MD) November 8, 1842,
(MG) Theo. Boulware.
Richard T. Kavanaugh and Sarah Talbot, (MD) December 23,
1858.
William Quem and Mary Gregory, (MD) August 17, 1856.
Henry Bloom and Mrs. Clarissa Rainbow, (MD) June 19, 1869.
Lewis Walton and Julia Ann Ishmel, (MD) March 21, 1867.
Jesse Highfield and Malinda McKan, (MD) February 10, 1867.
Levan Ferguson and Jane Holloway, (MD) February 22, 1822,
(JP) George King.
Robert M. Craghead and Mary S. Findley, (MD) March 1, 1858.
Jesse Bano and Mary Malone, (MD) May 20, 1850.
Thomas J. Jackson and Orintha Tharp, (MD) January 15, 1857.
James G. L. Wells and Margaret Wyette, (MD) August 20, 1856.
Thomas Pledge and Florence C. Luper, (MD) February 22, 1838,
(MG) Theo. Boulware.
James H. Blythe and Martha E. Stokes, (MD) June 4, 1868.
William Jones and Josapheus Daugherty, (MD)January 27, 1864.
Fleming R. Pasley and Milly F. Kemp, (MD) March 13, 1869.
William Rogers and Mary Ann Saltsman, (MD)November 17, 1870.
John G. Wiseman and Sallie B. McClelland, (MD) December 19,
1860.
Thomas Barrett and Elizabeth Chasteen, (MD) September 23,
1869.
Robert Callison and Sarah A. Allison, (MD)September 3, 1856.
James Wilson and Judith Dawson, (MD) October 26, 1848, (MG)
Noah Flood.
Leroy Mullens and Elizabeth Woods, (MD) August 1, 1830, (UK)
Ninian Ridgway.
William Overtain Farmer and Martha Ann Sanders, (MD) April
2, 1862.
Matthew A. C. Davis and Mary E. Conner, (MD) May 18, 1856.
William Brocon and Margaret C. Curry, (MD) July 3, 1862.
John Armstrong and Virginia Garner, (MD) February 22, 1855.
George W. Bassinger and Charlotte C. Shaw, (MD) December 25,
1863, (JP) Thomas J. Ferguson.
Calvin M. Joiner and Martha Ann Davis,(MD) October 23, 1856.
I. Y. Miller and Martha J. Ramsey, (MD) October 14, 1868.
James W. Noland and Sarah Hord, (MD) March 9, 1870.
Louis Starke and Hellene R. Reimer, (MD) October 15, 1860.

Milton Allen and Mrs. Lucy J. Pemberton, (MD) January 5, 1871.

Isaac Baker and Ann Baker, (MD) January 18, 1826, (MG) Thos. J. Stephens.

Joshua T. Bagby and Lucy J. Allen, (MD) January 19, 1837, (MG) J. Green.

Robert C. Berry and Elizabeth M. Patton, (MD) August 10, 1854.

William Blackmore and Virginia A. Wilson, (MD) October 7, 1869.

John D. Gay and Mary J. Bratton, (MD) January 13, 1848, Groom is from Boone County, Missouri.

Thomas Harrison and Cyntha A. Estis, (MD) January 29, 1863.

William R. Haynes and Sarah Floos Blount, (MD) March 11, 1852, (JP) Arthur Neill.

James W. Waters and Susan F. Love, (MD) November 14, 1867.

Daniel A. Ferguson and Gilly A. Gilbert, (MD) December 23, 1858.

William L. Gatewood and Fannie A. White, (MD) May 3, 1860.

Samuel Lewis Griffin and Sarah Ramsey, (MD) May 7, 1856.

John R. Hasler and Mary Jane Bishop, (MD) February 21, 1856.

Campbell Hodge and Emily A. Given, (MD) May 17, 1860, (JP) B. A. Ramsey, Groom is from Kentucky.

David Hughes and Ann Eliza Pulliam, (MD) February 14, 1854.

Daniel Madden and Martha Coonce, (MD) April 9, 1862.

John L. Milone and Annie Gray, (MD) April 28, 1865.

Joseph D. Reagan and Eliz. E. Adams, (MD) July 27, 1835, (MG) D. Coulter.

F. S. Stephens and Sarah E. Bright, (MD) March 3, 1859.

John C. Games and Rhoda F. Duvall, (MD) February 20, 1853.

George H. Hess and Eliz. C. Malone, (MD) November 14, 1844, (MG) Absalom Rice.

James Jamison and Serena Bryant, (MD) May 13, 1850.

Dewit R. Lawrence and Margaret Lawrence, (MD)March 28, 1850.

David McGhee and Paulina Tharp, (MD) January 21, 1847, (UK) W. W. Robertson.

William H. Miller and Caroline B. Davis, (MD) January 30, 1846, (JP) Joseph Fisher.

Wm. Ripley Neal and Ellen Goodrich, (MD) November 7, ----, (UK) Marshall S. Coats.

George Nichols and Margaret S. Craighead, (MD) March 16, 1854.

Frederick Sheets and Margaret C. Houchins, (MD) November 11, 1869.

George P. Truitt and Sarah A. Trimble, (MD) March 10, 1845.

Carol Vincent and Hester B. Hobson, (MD) August 2, 1869.

Robert Humphres and Mary Yaits, (MD) July 29, 1860.

Berry Divers and Martha Ann Gilbert, (MD)September 25, 1856.

John Bull and Sinthy Davis, (MD) January 14, 1857.

Ezekiel Day and Sarah Branson, (MD) January 25, 1838, (UK)
Geo. B. Hopkins.
William Hook and Mealine M. Turner, (MD) September 26, 1847.
John Loid and Martha Gilmore, (MD) December 28, 1862.
George W. Neal and Mary A. Dudley, (MD) December 23, 1852,
(MG) John Green.
Jeffers R. Rogers and Mrs. Kizie Sheon (sic), (MD) November
24, 1843, (UK) Thomas Chandler.
Jeff Darby and Marietta Bruner, (MD) December 19, 1844, (ED)
M. P. Wills.
Howard James and Sarah Newsom, (MD) July 11, 1844, (UK) Jas.
Criswell.
James Pace and Zerilda Wayne, (MD) March 24, 1836, (MG) Jas.
Suggett.
Rufus K. Sander and Nancy I. Farmer, (MD) October 8, 1857.
Henry M. Thomas and Julian Zumwalt, (MD) January 15, 1857.
Thomas Allen and Nanny Jane Scott, (MD) September 9, 1845,
(MG) R. S. Symmington.
Thomas Blackburn and Ann Benson, (MD) December 15, 1846,
(MG) P. M. Richard.
Robert Gee and Mary Jane Wilkey, (MD) January 18, 1852, (MG)
James Love.
Jacob Paulsel and Mrs. Sarah Smith, (MD) August 27, 1835,
(UK) R. L. McAfee.
Arlis J. Vinson and Louisa James, (MD) May 3, 1847, (MG)
Noah Flood.
James Carrol and Margaret King, (MD) January 9, 1870.
James Peyton and Sarah Mateer, (MD) September 14, 1837, (UK)
R. L. McAfee.
Moses S. Ferguson and Mary Newman, (MD) October 2, 1850,
(JP) Geo. B. Hopkins.
William Kite and Tirisa Ann Hill, (MD) December 8, 1870.
P. B. Ross and Cynthiana Tharp, (MD) April 1, 1869.
James W. Shellnut and Lucinda T. Nichols, (MD) August 24,
1864.
Richard Epperson and Elizabeth Link, (MD) July 16, 1870.
John Debo and Ann Snell, (MD) September 23, 1835, (MG) Theo.
Boulware.
John L. Baker and Susan J. Duncan, (MD) January 7, 1867.
Walker Fields and Mary Ann Owen, (MD) November 17, 1859,
(UK) M. L. Bibb.
Dr. E. T. Scott and Louisa M. Offutt, (MD) october 21, 1858.
Robert H. Woolfork and Mariah E. Moore, (MD) January 12,
1859.
Charles Dile and Nancy Wadley, (MD) July 3, 1825, (JP) Geo.
King.
William W. Jones and Marcella M. Griggs, (MD) May 15, 1856.
Nathan C. Kouns and Anna O. Roots, (MD) October 30, 1867.
John Oscar Miller and Mary J. Willett, (MD) January 5, 1870.

J. S. Rogers and Cordelia Boulware, (MD) March 2, 1853.
Wesley Wright and Polly Potts, (MD) October 12, 1826, (UK)
  John B. Morrow.
William Hutchason and Eliza Harryman, (MD) March 27, 1856.
Levi O. Day and Malvina Winn, (MD) December 2, 1829, (UK)
  Absalom Rice.
C. J. Gibbs and Jane Frances Dulin, (MD) January 24, 1853.
Andrew Kayser and Martha Jane McGhee, (MD) October 11, 1855.
Isaac Langley and Sarah Neal, (MD) March 12, 1851.
Francis Parker and Letitia Will, (MD) August 26, 1863.
John Show and Mary S. Martin, (MD) August 19, 1861.
William T. Weldon and Ann E. Gills, (MD) December 12, 1865.
James Meredith and George Ann Hering, (MD)December 20, 1849,
  (MG) Noah Flood.
Marcellias Hoover and Sedonia Smart, (MD) November 18, 1844,
  (ED) M. P. Wills.
Garland Cruiso and Sarah R. Sheets, (MD) January 22, 1850.
John Bahr and Ann P. M. Vanstraten, (MD) June 3, 1861.
William T. Fullington and Mary E. Yates, (MD) December 5,
  1861.
Jasper N. Moon and Elizabeth Tharp, (MD) June 19, 1845, (UK)
  Wm. J. Gilman.
John A. Dallace and Susan M. Nowell, (MD) February 11, 1847,
  (JP) Chas. A. Ming.
Richard W. Knox and Top H. Dunn, (MD) September 6, 1855.
Lewis Myers and Nancy Ann Boggess, (MD) January 18, 1841.
William H. Allen and Rebecca Guardner, (MD) April 1, 1858.
William W. Davidson and Mrs. Levisa McBlashy, (MD) November
  14, 1844, (UK) W. W. Robertson.
Matillons (sic) Oliver and Miriam Jones, (MD) May 7, 1860,
  (MG) Jabez Ham.
John Sexton and Rebecca Green, (MD) October 19, 1869.
William S. Thatcher and Carlotte Westbrook, (MD)May 9, 1839,
  (MG) J. L. Yantis.
William Bloomfield, jr. and Helen Cole, (MD) March 29, 1852.
Ambrose Griggs, jr. and Martha Ann Miller, (MD) April 17,
  1870.
Milton Lockhart and Emily Sitton, (MD) March 17, 1859.
Elijah N. Thatcher and Nancy S. Griffin, (MD) August 11,
  1839, (MG) Robert C. Hill.
Samuel N. Gutherie and Ann S. Nichols, (MD) February 20,
  1856.
Edward Davis and Hamit (sic) McRoberts, (MD) October 25,
  1855.
Joseph C. King and Susan McKamey, (MD) April 22, 1858.
Hercules W. Neill and Sarah Gregory, (MD) April 1, 1841,
  (UK) Milton Cleveland.
Markus D. DeGrott and Ann H. Wolsh, (MD) March 4, 1860.
George Smith and Phoebe Crews, (MD) November 24, 1867.

T. Moon and Eliza Jane Tate, (MD) September 3, 1844, (UK)
W. W. Robertson.
Charles C. Hersman and Abby Machett, (MD) July 16, 1863,
(MG) J. B. Finley.
Robert Dawson and Mary Herring, (MD) November 3, 1842, (MG)
Noah Flood.
Thomas Crasenton and Narandy Ratekin, (MD)November 14, 1839,
(MG) Jas. Suggett.
Alexander Nichols and Mary A. F. Neal, (MD) November 26,
1863.
Moses Philips and Aney Agey, (MD) February 26, 1829, (MG)
Jabez Ham.
John Henderson and Mary E. Sbell, (MD) April 9, 1840, (MG)
J. L. Yantis.
Simon Davis and Ann Darby, (MD) June 9, 1842, (MG) Joseph
Coons.
Thomas Smith and Catherine Craig, (MD) January 29, 1828,
(MG) Theo. Boulware.
Samuel Woody and Sarah Day, (MD) November 23, 1846.
William Moore and Permelia Branch, (MD) December 17, 1860.
Henry F. Harland and Nancy McCall, (MD) December 13, 1860.
Thomas Smith and Mary Huddleston, (MD) August 16, 1829, (UK)
David Kirkpatrick.
Samuel Long and Mary Burnet, (MD) March 15, 1843, (JP) A.
Northphen.
George W. Hardin and Mrs. M. Willcoxen, (MD) November 23,
1857.
Samuel and Ann Swan, (MD) February 21, 1841.
Andrew Kayser and Mrs. Mary Sudlam, (MD) March 12, 1857.
James Song and Mrs. Susan Crews, (MD) August 11, 1857.
William J. Wayne and Elizabeth A. Bishop, (MD) November
3, 1870.
James M. Buding and America Jane West, (MD) March 16, ----.
John L. Kemp and Editha A. Thomas, (MD) October 19, 1863.
Samuel N. Steel and Vashti Graves, (MD) May 10, 1853.
John T. Watts and Martha E. Kessler, (MD) October 15, 1864.
Simpson Crump and Mary Jane West, (MD) August 12, 1830. (ED)
M. P. Wills.
David Allen and Ann Boone, (MD) August 9, 1829, (MG) Jabez
Ham, Groom is from Montgomery County, Missouri.
Jesse Combs and Virginia Cobb, (MD) January 24, 1867.
William O. Johnson and Mary Ann Carter, (MD)November 9,1848,
(MG) Noah Flood.
Jefferson Powel and Manerva Carlton, (MD) December 3, 1865.
James A. Smart and Mary S. Glover, (MD) December 24, 1845,
(UK) J. C. D. Hatcher.
Matthew W. Gathright and Mary Bryant, (MD) April 27, 1853.
Isaac M. Loyd and Catharine Adair, (MD) June 12, 1870.
Andrew J. Mosely and Marcy C. Larch, (MD) May 29, 1866.

Allen W. Gutherie and Elizabeth Ann Young, (MD) September 16, 1838, (UK) Jno. T. A. Henderson.

James Little and Fannie Adkinson, (MD) April 9, 1863.

William Pace and Hester Kidwell, (MD) June 24, 1836, (UK) Jno. Pace.

Richard Rennols and Nancy Chapel, (MD) September 28, 1836, (UK) John F. Young.

James H. Gregory and Mary Ann Scholl, (MD) September 29, 1842, (MG) James Love.

Jesse Allen and Nancy Davis, (MD) January 13, 1831, (MG) William Coats.

William A. Comer and Martha A. Frazier, (MD) October 25, 1866, (JP) Absalom Hughes.

Christian Fisher and Eliza Kayser, (MD) December 25, 1851, (MG) --- Robertson.

Henry Keaton and Cyan (sic) Reed, (MD) March 21, 1833, (UK) Robert Younger.

John Moseley and Sophia McMahan, (MD) September 24, 1833, (UK) Jones Stewart.

Abner Brandon and Sarah Zumwalt, (MD) July 22, 1866.

John B. Peters and Catharine Driskell, (MD)January 26, 1854.

Edward Reeves and Susanna Jones, (MD) October 8, 1863.

Joseph T. Bryan and Margaret A. White, (MD) November 18, 1860.

Ransom Morgan and Nancy Gray, (MD) March 24, 1853.

John Rogers and Margaret Grazier, (MD)December 14, ----, (UK) R. J. Ferguson.

Calvin S. Shepherd and Rebecca M. Spencer, (MD) January 1, 1856.

Charles S. Wells and Virginia L. Dam, (MD) July 31, 1854, (JP) W. J. Jackson.

Thomas I. Harper and Libbie Wills, (MD) February 17, 1857.

Nathaniel Berry and Margarett Cartwell, (MD) April 21, 1869.

James S. Conner and Catharine Burget, (MD)February 23, 1870.

C. W. Rutherford and Eliza W. Newlon, (MD) January 9, 1852.

William S. Clatterbuck and Mary E. Curry, (MD) February 28, 1867.

William Morris and Nancy McMurty, (MD) October 27, 1853, Groom is from Audrain County.

William Wallace and Hester Ann Freeman, (MD) September 1, 1867.

Robert Campbell and Mary Ann Allen, (MD) May 14, 1845, (JP) A. Northphen.

James F. Gray and Louisa J. Oliver, (MD) January 31, 1869.

Martin H. Ridgway and Nancy Wilburn, (MD) April 13, 1852.

John W. Shaw and Martha G. Young, (MD) November 5, 1866.

Martin R. Janery and Elizabeth Nicholson, (MD) January 8, 1846.

Joseph W. Coons and Amanda A. Duncan, (MD)December 12, 1860.

William Green and Larceney Smith, (MD) March 8, 1830, (JP)
Robert Davis.
Zadok Hook and Isabelle P. Barker, (MD) September 2, 1867.
James D. Sanders and Matilda G. Spillers, (MD) August 14,
1864.
William L. Vaughn and Mariah Blithe, (MD) March 14, 1844,
(UK) John E. Nevins.
Sinon (sic) Kelby and Martha G. Roy, (MD) April 27, 1859.
Miller Jones and Mary Ann Scholl, (MD) June 18, 1846, (MG)
James Love.
Charles E. Jackson and Ann Eliza Anderson, (MD) December 1,
1867.
Robert C. Hansard and Emily M. Turner, (MD) April 2, 1851,
(UK) O. J. VanDeventer.
Isaac F. Coons and Angie Duncan, (MD) December 22, 1868.
William L. Callaway and Sarah Jane Rankin, (MD) November 15,
1866.
Capt. Archibald Allen and Nancy Hamilton, (MD) February 4,
1858.
T. L. Baskett and Elizabeth A. Dawson, (MD) November 11,
1869.
Frances Eno and Jane Goff, (MD) August 18, 1850, (UK) M. S.
Coats.
Stephen R. Gilbert and Martha A. Pemberton, (MD) February
18, 1849, (MG) Absalom Rice.
John A. Gutherie and Elizabeth Butler, (MD) September 30,
1869.
Christopher C. Ivijer and Mahala S. Davis, (MD) December
27, ----.
Hamilton Smith and Amanda F. Finly, (MD) December 19, 1850.
James W. Humphreys and Susan Bennett, (MD) May 21, 1862.
John Galwith and Catharine B. Sitton, (MD) June 26, 1850.
Thomas N. Evans and Sallie C. Huston, (MD) October 30, 1855,
Groom is from Boone County, Missouri.
Benjamin F. Davis and Sarah Jane Davison, (MD) January 6,
1859.
Harvey T. Howe and Sophia M. Crooks, (MD)September 20, 1859.
James C. Johnson and Mary Epperson, (MD) October 9, 1870.
George B. Moore and Frances D. Wise, (MD) March 5, 1856.
William H. Spillers and Mildred L. Stull, (MD) September 2,
1856.
John Dickson and S. E. Scott, (MD February 23, 1863, (MG)
George W. Penn.
William E. Garrett and Sally Ann Calvin, (MD) October 10,
1850.
Harvey B. Hawkins and Sallie Snell, (MD) October 14, 1857.
Edward S. Herndon and Ann M. Craig, (MD) December 24, 1840.
Cabel G. Tate and Mary Ann Nichols, (MD) January 21, 1868.
John W. Thompson and Catharine Wilson, (MD) March 4, 1857.

William S. Allen and Katherine Boise, (MD)January 17, 1856.
James V. Callaway and Margaret Brown, (MD) January 9, 1850,
    (UK) Marshall S. Coats.
Jesse Farmer and Susan Bull, (MD) February 26, 1852.
William A. Harding and Mattie J. Holt, (MD) December 19,
    1868.
James Bailey and Mary Manning, (MD) April 23, 1841, (MG)
    Jabez Ham.
James S. Moore and Mary E. Brite, (MD) January 20, 1861.
John S. Dicus and Laura Henderson, (MD) January 3, 1866.
Thomas Stewart and Elizabeth Nichols, (MD) January 20, 1853.
Henry Ferguson and Ann McCarty, (MD) February 19, 1863,
    Bride is from Osage County, Missouri.
Benjamin Moseley and Mrs. Eliza Little, (MD)April 16, 1856.
Nathan Todd and Sarah J. Ham, (MD) June 6, 1847, (UK) George
    K. Ham.
Charles S. Watson and Rebecca Shobe, (MD) June 19, 1847,
    (UK) George K. Ham.
Henry Rector and Eliz. L. Allen, (MD) October 26, 1833, (MG)
    Theo. Boulware.
Walter A. Davis and Mary A. Hiller, (MD) February 29, 1852,
    (MG) Noah Flood.
Levi T. Blount and Mary A. Hinton, (MD) April 23, 1856.
George W. Smith and Elizabeth R. Baskett, (MD) February 9,
    1834.
Samuel Hardin and Lucinda Selby, (MD) August 10, 1842, (MG)
    B. R. Johnson.
David Eastwood and Julean Quarels, (MD) March 22, 1868, (MG)
    Absalom Rice.
Caswell Snell and Drusilla Craig, (MD) January 20, 1857.
James Brandenburg and Nancy Hall, (MD) January 6, 1853.
james S. Hill and Lizzie Fletcher, (MD) November 19, 1863.
Reuben Tatum and Cinderella Forbush, (MD) December 17, 1868.
William A. Wainscott and Lucinda J. Sanders, (MD) February
    23, 1861.
Stephen L. Scott and Sarah Jane Kemp, (MD) November 6, 1851.
Lycurgus (sic) Miller and Lucy Moss Jones, (MD) November 14,
    1866, Groom from Nodaway County, Missouri.
William Hunt and Sophia Jane Keele, (MD) September 5, 1835,
    (UK) John A. Burt.
John T. Dill and Margaret F. Steele, (MD) February 1, 1838,
    (MG) R. L. McAfee.
James Myers and Mary Susan Swepton, (MD) December 27, 1849,
    (MG) John Green.
Nathaniel E. Branham and Sarah Hobson, (MD) April 20, 1842,
    (UK) John H. Tuttle. Groom is from California (State or
    California, Moniteau County, Missouri)
Mark A. Craghead and Caroline C. Payne, (MD) February 19,
    1856.

Nicholas Foy and Susan Roy, (MD) June 23, 1839, (JP) A. K. Bell.

George W. E. Johnson and Permelia C. Baker, (MD) April 10, 1867.

James H. Moore and Elizabeth Congor, (MD) March 23, 1870.

Benjamin Sheley and Precilla Ann Reno, (MD)December 6, 1858.

James Spiller and Lenora A. Stull, (MD) June 24, 1856.

J. L. K. Peyton and Nancy Callison, (MD) December 18, 1851.

Joseph S. Hernderson and Maria L. Garrett, (MD) September 29, 1858.

John Dearing and Louisa Crump, (MD)March 7, 1841, (MG) James Love.

Peter H. Kemp and Martha A. Kemp, (MD) December 4, 1851, (MG) William F. Bell.

Epaphrotitus Smith and Elizabeth M. Davis, (MD) October 29, 1846.

James Herring and Eliza R. Congo, (MD) April 11, 1857.

John French and Isabella Dillard, (MD) May 11, 1837, (MG) William B. Douglass.

William Rogers and Eliza Jane Harris, (MD) April 2, 1846, (JP) B. Matthews.

Isaac Ruttes and Ruth Ann Thomas, (MD) May 18, 1851.

Fred Hopkins and Mary Bagby, (MD) May 24, 1865.

George T. Berry and Jane Humphries, (MD) December 12, 1833, (MG) William W. Redman.

Napoleon Martell and Susana Davis, (MD) July 4, 1860.

Peter Rice and Jane Frances Thomas, (MD) November 21, 1856.

Geo. D. Toll and Martha J. Stafford, (MD) May 2, 1850.

John L. Clatterbuck and Lucy F. Reynolds, (MD) March 21, 1862.

Joseph J. Grant and Sarah W. Grant, (MD) February 6, 1840, (MG) J. L. Yantis.

Washington Padget and Rebecca Jones, (MD) April 7, 1833, (JP) Geo. Bartley.

German B. Drinkard and Mary J. Hughes, (MD) March 29, 1855.

William G. Bennett and Lucinda Walton, (MD) July 10, 1851, (MG) Zacariah Jones.

Willis Derring and Elizabeth Jane Murdock, (MD) February 8, 1848.

Elias B. Martin and Mary Frances Jones, (MD) June 3, 1862.

Benjamin F. Rogers and ELizabeth Jamieson, (MD) November 30, 1863.

William Coons and Eleanor P. Robinson, (MD)January 29, 1846, (MG) W. W. Robinson.

Jeremiah Everhart and Sallie E. Maupin, (MD) December 18, 1866.

Samuel H. Kester and Sarah Simpson, (MD) February 11, 1838, (MG) Jabez Ham.

London Snell and Mary F. Hynes, (MD) January 10, 1860.

John B. Gregory and Isabel Scholl, (MD) May 11, 1846, (MG)
James Love.
Alexander P. Moore and Mary J. Guthrie, (MD) July 23, 1851,
(UK) James B. Mitchell.
Eli Rogers and Mary H. Scrogins, (MD) February 20, 1861.
Dr. Thomas Allen and Mrs. Sarah H. Scott, (MD) September 29,
1848, (MG) W. W. Robertson.
Newton Jones and Amanda Board, (MD) September 26, 1849, (UK)
William B. Douglas.
Henry Neal and Martha Ann Sampson, (MD) February 10, 1853.
Charles Riggs and Martha Ivins, (MD) November 14, 1861.
William S. Robinson and Mary F. Fisher, (MD) January 10,
1861.
Richard H. Vaughter and Elizabeth V. Swan, (MD) February 16,
1848.
Henry Oliver and Martha E. Stokes, (MD) September 17, 1868,
Francis Schweighouser and August Kraft, (MD) September 17,
1857.
John J. Baker and Elizabeth McClellan, (MD) October 24,
1853, (JP) M. S. Addison.
Benjamin S. Griggs and Catherine Ramsey, (MD) October 22,
1865.
Grant F. Langdon and Angeline T. Jimerson, (MD) July 20,
1848, (JP) Chas. A. Ming.
Edward Sinclair and Maggie Smith, (MD) October 6, 1868.
George W. Matox and Eliza Jane Lawrence, (MD)March 10, 1853.
William Blythe and Mariah N. Gilman, (MD) August 2, 1849,
(MG) Jacob Coons, Groom is from Boone County, Missouri.
John King and Narcissus Conger, (MD) October 29, 1835, (MG)
Jas. Suggett.
Samuel Sapp and Sophia S. Watson, (MD November 2, 1858,
Groom is from Boone County, Missouri.
David Wagoner and Mrs. Margery Trigg, (MD) May 31, 1855.
William Sanford Langley and Mrs. Jane McDaniel, (MD) Decem-
ber 23, 1865.
William K. McCall and Margaret A. Coats, (MD) December 15,
1863.
William Arthur and Nancy Ann Coons, (MD) August 22, 1850,
(ED) Jacob Coons.
David O. Hall and Susan E. Tharp, (MD) February 4, 1864.
George W. Smith and Mary Jane Dawson, (MD) October 5, 1868.
William T. Wise and Martha E. Moore, (MD) January 10, 1858.
Woodford Sheley and Arvenia Sheley, (MD) April 27, 1848,
(JP) D. M. Whyte.
John Goff and Elizabeth Clatterbuck, (MD) December 7, 1865.
Robert Muir and Margaret J. Gibney, (MD) January 12,1856.
George G. Bartley and Harriet Fitxhue, (MD)January 21, 1847,
(MG) Absalom Rice.
J. S. Dunnavant and Matilda F. Renoe, (MD) January 23, 1864.

---- James and Mary Boyd, (MD) January 17, 1839, (MG) James
    Suggett.
Robert McClanahan and Frances Gilbert, (MD) December 17,
    1858.
J. W. Wallace and Mrs. Jessie Ryley, (MD)September 19, 1855.
Richard Murphy and Sarah E. Bess, (MD) December 10, 1864,
    (UK) James A. Drennan.
James H. Jameson and Mary Ann Ennet, (MD) March 9, 1852.
Benjamin Goodrich and Harriet H. Thomas, (MD) October 8,
    1822, (UK) Robert Baker.
Daniel Atterberry and Mrs. Mary J. Camp, (MD) September 3,
    1854, From is from Monroe County.
Fielding Stubblefield and Ophelia McKee, (MD) February 1,
    1865.
Frederick Zumwalt and Mary Jones, (MD) March 3, 1853.
Duvall Nichols and Elizabeth Myers, (MD September 9, 1847.
Benjamin F. Berry and Eleanor Simpson, (MD) October 6, 1842,
    (JP) W. J. Gilman.
George K. Ham and Nancy S. Watson, (MD) July 19, 1846, (UK)
    Stephen Ham.
William Meredith and Lucinda Turner, (MD) December 15, 1841,
    (UK) William Martin.
William Watson and Mary Wood, (MD) May 7, 1851.
Francis Marion Jenkins and Louiza Burros, (MD) March 25,
    1869, (JP) W. A. Brite.
James Goodrich and Fannie McCall, (MD) October 6, 1868, (MG)
    S. L. Woody.
James Fowler and Sarah C. Stephenson, (MD) August 11, 1858.
matthew D. Boggs and Martha J. Kennett, (MD) August 2, 1838,
    (MG) J. L. Yantis.
William H. Hallowell and Mary F. Smoot, (MD) November 12,
    1860.
Gabriel A. Keeling and Adela H. Stokes, (MD) January 27,
    1853.
J. R. Yancey and Parmelia Stubblefield, (MD) April 25, 1866.
David Jawan and Amy Phillips, (MD) May 30, 1833, (UK) Robt.
    S. McAfee.
Abner Harrison and Nancy Harrison, (MD) November 11, 1834,
    (MG) Andrew Monroe.
Hiram T. Greenway and Charlotte Emmons, (MD August 13, 1857.
G. A. Craig and Nancy Board, (MD) November 23, 1854.
George Smith and Nancy Melvins Coons, (MD) May 11, 1853.
Thomas Wilson and Deborah A. Long, (MD) November 22, 1837,
    (UK) Thomas M. Allen.
Thomas F. Moore and Mildred V. Hughs, (MD)December 30, 1869.
Andrew McLaughlin and Jane Grazier, (MD) 1848 (sic), (JP)
    Nathan Young, Bride is from Osage County.
Archibald Langley and Mary Ann Muldrow, (MD) March 31, 1858.
Samuel Early and Elizabeth Sparks, (MD) February 10, 1867.

John H. Ellis and Sarah E. Dyer, (MD) February 27, 1844.
Pleasant Branch and May Falla, (MD) September 1, 1842, (JP)
N. B. Ferguson.
Lewis W. Hewer and Maria Christiany, (MD) April 3, 1862.
Rufus Hornbuckle and Amanda Davis, (MD) April 2, 1839, (UK)
George B. Hopkins.
Richard Oscar Jones and Nancy Ellen Wright, (MD) May 24,
1860.
Henry C. McGowen and Marriam Boone, (MD) November 17, 1847,
(JP) Joseph Scholl, Groom is from Warren County.
John Neal and Nancy Griffith, (MD) December 10, 1846, (UK)
W. W. Robertson.
William Yancey and Emily Nashum, (MD) December 24, 1863.
James D. Dillard and Sally Ann French, (MD)October 28, 1841,
(UK)William B. Douglass, Groom is from Montgomery County.
James L. Lynes and Bettie Hyten, (MD) November 16, 1864.
Peter McLane and Susan Shelly, (MD) January 24, 1854, (UK)
Thomas M. Finny.
Martin A. Miller amd Jane Miller, (MD) February 4, 1830,
(ED) M. P. Wills.
C. A. Robbins and Kiturah (sic) V. Overfelt, (MD) April 28,
1835, (MG) John Rennie.
Spencer C. Wright and Eliza E. Ecton, (MD) September 19,
1861.
Benjamin W. Alexander and Anna M. Cason, (MD) December 1,
1870.
John W. Blackwell and Jane Davis, (MD) August 1, 1839, (MG)
Jacob Coons.
Edward Booker and Mary Lomax, (MD) January 6, 1836, (JP) A.
G. Boone.
Martin B. Edge and Mary Jane Gardyer, (MD)November 26, 1857.
John R. Ferrell and Susan J. Jameson, (MD) May 9, 1865.
James Hamilton and Ann Callison, (MD) October 31, 1839, (MG)
Jabez Ham.
James K. McClelland and Martha Jane Linville, (MD) October
10, 1864.
Marcus F. Roberts and Lydia A. Carlton, (MD) March 24, 1867.
George C. Bowden and Drusilla D. Stokes, (MD) October 29,
1863.
William T. Chappell and Abigail Y. Waggoner, (MD) March 8,
1853.
Henry Dillon and Nancy Jano, (MD) January 20, 1842, (UK)
Matthew Davis.
Joseph P. Hampton and Nancy Gee, (MD) November 21, 1855.
Isham McMahan and Louisa Love, (MD) October 12, 1865.
Patrick Richerson and Luceina Wood, (MD) July 17, 1864.
Hillard Crump and Liniza Estes, (MD January 13, 1858.
Charles Marshall and Caroline Allen, (MD) February 14, 1856.
David B. Rice and Mary E. Davis, (MD) February 19, 1860.

John Allen and Martha J. Hansard, (MD) May 16, 1855.
James Bourn and Mariah I. Cosby, (MD) October 3, 1867.
William A. Brite and Mary Ann Scott, (MD) May 2, 1839, (JP)
William J. Gilman.
Joseph Callaway and June E. Craghead, (MD) April 28, 1839,
(MG) Jno. Pace.
Truman Day and Virginia P. C. Namer, (MD) January 29, 1846,
(JP) James Stewart.
Peter Duby and Kitty Quinn, (MD) April 4, 1845, (JP) Charles
A. Ming.
Thomas I. Marlow and Mary E. Hockaday, (MD) May 31, 1855.
James A. Nichols and Nancy E. Snell, (MD) February 22, 1848,
(MG) Noah Flood, Groom is from Boone County, Missouri.
George Dailey and Martha E. Newton, (MD) March 22, 1870.
Samuel G. Mason and Ann Eliza Dyer, (MD) January 6, 1835,
(UK) Isaac S. Houser.
Richard Oldham and Emily F. Reed, (MD) October 28, 1847.
Samuel Rhoads and Sarah Pace, (MD) June 24, 1824, (JP) Jas.
Nevins.
Jesse B. Wainscott and Eliza Langley, (MD) August 16, 1838,
(UK) John T. A. Henderson.
Abner Dickson and M. A. Boyd, (MD) December 25, 1862.
Joseph W. Coons and Mary Arthur, (MD) November 29, 1842,
(MG) Joseph Coons.
John T. Baker and Nancy Devore, (MD) December 29, 1831, (MG)
David M. Kirkpatrick.
J. A. Dearing and Emily S. Ferguson, (MD) February 24, 1864.
William Mask and Mary Andres, (MD) February 22, 1839, (UK)
Joseph T. Bryan.
Thomas Walton and Sarah Darieux, (MD) December 21, 1848,
(UK) Zachariah Jones.
Benjamin Rader and Margaret McCafferty, (MD) March 27, 1859.
John A. Allen and Elizabeth F. Pratt, (MD) December 18,
1856.
Henry Bailey and Elizabeth Glover, (MD) September 29, 1834,
(MG) Tho. Boulware.
Marshal Coats and Artemesia Duncan, (MD) October 16, 1844,
(MG) James Love.
George W. Dooley and Amanda Wilkerson, (MD) September 26,
1850.
Samuel F. Flemmin and Mary Ann Moore, (MD)September 9, 1854.
James Galbreath and Elizabeth Galbreath, (MD) October 18,
1821, (UK) Solomon Thomas, Groom is from kentucky.
William C. Ham and Susan H. Hawkins, (MD) January 25, 1866.
Samuel Maycock and Sarah Ann Overton, (MD) July 27, 1859.
Matthew Ray and Mary S. Owen, (MD) January 14, 1868.
John C. Thornton and Mary Ann Phillips, (MD) December 25,
1857.
Jacob Zumwalt and Nancy Zumwalt, (MD) January 31, 1850.

W. H. Alexander and Mattie C. Humphreys, (MD) February 9,
----.
T. M. W. Alfrey and Mary J. Gibbs, (MD) December 27, 1855.
Samuel Ashlock and Sarah D. Hunt, (MD) may 31, 1838, (UK)
    Thomas M. Allen, Groom is from Boone County, Missouri.
William B. Baker and Lucy M. Adkins, (MD) January 29, 1862.
David D. Barnes and Sallie Selby, (MD) March 3, 1870.
William W. Bartley and Frances A. Mosley, (MD) January 15,
    1852.
John Bellows and Margaret Brown, (MD) May 25, 1837, (MG) R.
    L. McAfee.
Robert M. Berry and Emily Ann Scholl, (MD) October 9, 1864.
James R. Blackmore and Hattie R. Nevins, (MD) October 11,
    1866.
Dr. G. G. Bolton and Lucy Agnes Thornhill, (MD) April 29,
    1866.
Marshall P. Boswell and Nancy J. Shepard, (MD) November 28,
    1854.
Samuel L. Breckbill and Martha Jane Freeman, (MD) September
    18, 1860.
Robert F. Bryant and Mary Elizabeth Gee, (MD) October 12,
    1866, (JP) John Vinson.
James R. Burnett and Bartena J. Yount, (MD) August 13, 1862,
    (UK) James H. Tuttle.
William A. Douglass and Julia A. Romans, (MD) February 23,
    1870.
C. W. Major and Sarah A. Wallace, (MD) May 31, 1862, Groom
    is from Henry County.
Joseph Lynes and Mary Branham, (MD) September 13, 1855,
Andrew Hamilton and Elizabeth Callison, (MD) September 17,
    1835, (MG) Jabez Ham.
William Gregory and Amanda J. Morrison, (MD) December 26,
    1870.
Joseph Gordon and Matilda Henderson, (MD) August 22, 1822,
    (JP) Adam Hope.
Alford A. Longley and Francis A. Clatterbuck, (MD) March 4,
    1858.
Bernard Maupin and Rosette Manners, (MD) November 24, 1859.
James Clarence Renshaw and Nannie M. Bragg, (MD) June 13,
    1861.
John M. S. Smith and Caddee D. Cowles, (MD) January 15,
    1868.
Sam. B. Thompson and Margaret J. Bright, (MD) September 2,
    1853, (UK) Stephen Scott, Groom is from Mexico, Missouri.
Bluford Hopper and Nancy J. Tucker, (MD) July 31, 1843, (JP)
    A. Northphen, Bride and Groom are from Boone County.
James A. Henderson and Mrs. Eliz. Vaughn, (MD) February 5,
    1867.
Eli Harmon and Lucy Watson, (MD) December 16, 1857.

Lewis J. Hilton and Sasann M. Langley, (MD) September 17, 1863.

George T. Howard and Nancy Irvin, (MD) January 6, 1867.

Oliver Little and Jane Trimble, (MD) December 7, 1833, (MG) Jabez Ham.

Jesse E. McCampbell and Lucinda Congo, (MD) May 9, 1824, (JP) James Nevins.

Joel McConnel and Julia Hughes, (MD) June 10, 1841, (MG) Theo. Boulware.

Isaac M. McGirk and Margaret Hockaday, (MD)November 7, 1848, (UK) W. W. Robertson.

Thomas Nesbitt and Sarah Duncan, (MD) June 16, 1842, (MG) J. Coons.

William Callaway and Tabitha Coats, (MD) April 9, 1829, (MG) William Coats.

George H. Craghead and Sarah Craghead, (MD) April 15, 1830, (UK) D. M. Kirkpatrick.

J. P. Harrison and Fnnie C. Bernard, (MD October 26, 1858.

Silas Hudson and Annie A. Callison, (MD) November 23, 1869.

James McGuin and Fannie Bell, (MD) May 14, 1868.

Willoughby and Mary Ann Ferguson, (MD) April 2, 1848, (JP) Geo. B. Hopkins.

William Mason Farrow and Mrs. Martha J. Frazier, (MD) November 29, 1866.

David W. Craig and Louisa Glover, (MD) February 10, 1848.

Henry Covington and Nancy Arnold, (MD) November 14, 1839, (UK) Joseph Scholl.

John W. McKinney and Elizabeth Jane Taylor, (MD) April 14, 1864.

Smith G. Thomas and Lucy J. Moore, (MD) August 2, 1868.

Samuel Thorp and Emily Langley, (MD) January 31, 1841, (UK) George B. Hopkins.

Charles A. Yates and Sarah L. Roman, (MD) December 9, 1869.

B. F. Bailey and Melcena Thrialkeld, (MD) January 20, 1848, (UK) W. W. Kemp.

Albert Bradford and Nancy Ferrier, (MD) December 12, 1844, (MG) William H. Hopson.

Justinian Cave and Mary E. Gathright, (MD) November 8, 1855.

William Cole and Elizabeth Owens, (MD) September 7, 1851.

Thomas A. Culbertson and Sarah J. Meredith, (MD)February 24, 1858.

Samuel H. Gilbert and Sarah Gregory, (MD) November 22, 1849, (MG) Jas. H. Tuttle.

Coello (sic) Glover and Eliza Patton, (MD) April 2, 1854, (MG) D. Coulter.

William Mortz and Mildred G. Kemp, (MD) September 13, 1855.

George Ogan and Louisa Hunter, (MD) December 29, 1857.

James C. Read and Tilly Fones, (MD) November 19, 1857.

William Rickey and Izabel Sinclair, (MD) January 23, 1862.

John Stapleton and Kitty Davis, (MD) March 19, 1970, (JP) H.
C. Oliver.
John Harding and Mahala Peyton, (MD) September 11, 1845,
(UK) W. B. Douglas.
James R. Galbreath and Sarah Petty, (MD) November 17, 1836,
(MG) Theo. Boulware.
James Fletcher and Margaret L. Thomas, (MD) May 16, 1844,
(MG) Noah Flood.
Snellon E. Dillon and Mrs. Eliz. McGee, (MD)August 17, 1864,
(JP) Thomas H. Breeding.
Henry Dickmann and Ann Elizabeth Thomas, (MD) August 18,
1860.
James Crump and Sally Ratekin, (MD) Novmber 1, 1832, (UK)
David Kirkpatrick.
Thomas G. Coons and Frances B. Garrott, (MD) November 22,
1860.
Robert Cowell and Eliza Ann Gregory, (MD) February 17, 1857.
James Clatterbuck and Emily Forsee, (MD) March 5, 1857.
Henry Smith and Nancy Davis, (MD) October 15, 1845, (MG)
Theo. Boulware.
Thomas Stark and Eliza Jane Rily, (MD) October 6, 1847.
Robert W. Miller and Mary J. Paten, (MD) March 3, 1837, (UK)
Elizah (sic) E. Chrisman.
James McMurty and Serelda Hays, (MD) October 10, 1832, (JP)
Enoch Fruit.
William Ramey and Mary Ann Copley, (MD) February 24, 1843,
(UK) Joseph T. Bryan.
Rev. H. H. Dodd and Nancy Allen, (MD) May 10, 1834.
Jas. Davithy (sic) and Eliza Zumwalt, (MD)February 16, 1855.
John G. Carter and Matilda Hering, (MD) September 7, 1842,
(MG) Noah Flood.
Samuel Carrington and Lydiann Bowen, (MD) May 14, 1840, (MG)
Absalom Rice.
James P. Burks and Martha Newman, (MD) August 31, 1831, (UK)
J. C. Berryman.
John W. Brasher and Elmira Lyons, (MD) April 18, 1861.
Robert M. Boyd and Elizabeth A. Woolery, (MD) February 18,
1857.
Albert G. Boone and Ann Read Hamilton, (MD) July 9, 1829,
(MG) T. N. Durbee.
Erminie Wayne and John Bowdoin, (MD) October 11, 1854.
B. P. Bailey and Mary Addie Allen, (UK) January 27, 1869.
Samuel H. Hudson and Louanna E. Duane, (MDD) December 2,
1868.
Thomas G. Maddox and Sephsona Davis, (MD) March 17, 1859.
Fenton M. Slaughter and Nancy Thomas, (MD)November 25, 1848,
(MG) Noah Flood.
Samuel P. Wilson and Amanda C. Stewart, (MD) June 25, 1866.
Lewis Hord and Mollie B. Gant, (MD) November 10, 1858.

James G. Allen and Mary E. Jones, (MD) December 1, 1859.

Thomas J. Barnett and Mary Johnson, (MD) January 25, 1848.

John Baswell and Mary Martin, (MD) October 9, 1869.

Henry Battie and Dorothy Gradavene, (MD) October 29, 1835,
(MG) William Coats.

William H. Boggas and Susan E. F. Adkins, (MD) March 11,
1862.

James O. Boone and Mrs. M. Cleveland, (MD)November 17, 1858.

Thomas H. Bradley and Mary Martha McCall, (MD) May 23, 1861.

J. N. Brandon and Ann Jennie Flemming, (MD)December 3, 1869.

David H. Brownfield and Sarah E. Sublett, (MD) September 28,
1870.

William Bryant and Louisa Scott, (MD) August 17, 1842, (MG)
Noah Flood.

William H. Davis and Emily B. Nichols, (MD) September 8,
1864.

James Harry Dinsmoore and Nancy Thomas, (MD) December 19,
1849, (JP) W. J. Jackson.

John Rosson and Margaret Daniel, (MD) June 25, 1839, (MG)
Joseph Coons.

David H. Hubbard and Sallie Jane Duncan, (MD) December 15,
1869, Groom is from Boone County, Missouri.

Joseph Crump and Mrs. Nancy Calvin, (MD) December 28, 1853,
(UK) Berryman Wren, Groom is from Boone County, Missouri.

George W. Douglass and Anna M. Bowman, (MD) September 4,
1870.

William T. Edg (sic) and Sarah E. White, (MD) April 4, 1851.

Joseph Farmer and Martha Samuel, (MD) November 25, 1835,
(MG) Jas. Suggett.

Samuel Ferrier and Alice Shannon, (MD) November 22, 1827,
(UK) J. Y. L. Verrejot.

Joseph Foda and Susan Anderson, (MD) August 31, 1856.

Francis J. Foy and Divinity P. Daffron, (MD) March 14, 1869.

James E. Furby and Mary Nesbitt, (MD) April 20, 1856.

William Harrison and Jane Harrison, (MD) February 10, 1841,
(UK) R. C. Mansfield, Groom is from Pulaskie County.

Turner R. Hayden and Sarah Ann Loyd, (MD) October 28, 1847,
(MG) T. M. Allen.

Dr. James Head and George Ann Harris, (MD) July 20, 1868,
(UK) John W. Montjoy.

John B. Henderson and Mary Ann McPheeters, (MD) September 1,
1841, (MG) Theo. Boulware.

Crowder Holloway and Mary Irvine, (MD) October 10, 1833,
(JP) B. A. Ramsey.

James Livily and Sarah Eliz. Estes, (MD) March 30, 1858.

Adam Mead and Sally Clay, (MD) April 25, 1832, (JP) William
Martin.

Benjamin F. Sitton and Rebecca Austin, (MD) January 7, 1823,
(JP) Thomas Fisher.

James W. Smart and Celina S. Smith, (MD) August 10, 1863, (MG) Geo. Fenton.

Thomas Vandever and Milly Leonard, (MD) May 8, 1855.

William A. Zumwalt and Delia A. Thurmond, (MD) December 15, 1869.

Will H. Wood and Sarah J. Jackson, (MD) April 24, 1853.

Benjamin Wheeler and Margaret Fleming, (MD) June 5, 1842.

Galbreath Wilson and Clarissa Ann Foxworthy, (MD) October 31, 1839, (MG) J. L. Yantis.

Rev. Tiler Williams and Susan Maria West, (MD) October 16, 1844, (MG) Asa McMurty.

Moses Wilkerson and Amanda Duncan, (MD) August 9, 1838, (UK) Jacob Coons.

Samuel Watson and Mrs. Margarette Ward, (MD) May 1, 1864, (MG) J. A. Hollis.

Rusell Ware and Melinda Ann Dorsey, (MD) March 8, 1840, (JP) J. B. Grant.

Charles Velte and Elizabeth Russ, (MD) April 23, 1870.

George C. Thompson and Eleanor Leeper, (MD) July 29, 1830, (UK) David Kirkpatrick.

George H. Thomas and Nancy P. Kemp, (MD) May 25, 1870.

James Thaxton and Polly Stoker, (MD) September 12, 1839, (MG) Jacob Coons.

Loren Swearingen and Mary Elizabeth Ford, (MD) September 25, 1870.

Wesley F. Swift and Joan Elizabeth Dillion, (MD August 12, 1866.

William Stewart and Amy Yager, (MD) October 1, 1845, (MG) James Love.

Ambross R. Tompkins and Eliza I. Snell, (MD) October 10, 1855, Groom is from Randolph County.

William Taylor and Lucy Ham, (MD) September 29, 1831, (MG) William Coats.

Rheuben Standley and Luthy (sic) Pulliam, (MD) March 18, 1835.

James H. Smith and Clarinda Gooch, (MD) December 24, 1865.

John W. Phillips and Fannie Dudley, (MD) March 25, 1863, (UK) E. R. Childers.

Martin Sitton and Harriet Allen, (MD) August 24, 1826, (MG) William Coats.

James Sheley and Mary Ann Smart, (MD) November 8, 1837, (MG) Theo. Boulware.

Joseph Sallee and Elizabeth Thornhill, (MD)January 11, 1859.

Benjamin F. Oliver and Celestia Wilson, (MD) November 1, 1866, (MG) E. Brookman.

William F. Hawkins and Catherine Sheley, (MD) February 2, 1843, (UK) Samuel D. Gilbert.

George W. Harris and Telitha Ann Lawrence, (MD) January 7, 1841, (UK) M. S. Coats.

George Green and Mrs. Jane Wayne, (MD) April 16, 1861.
Jefferson McMahan and Jane A. Brooks, (MD) January 31, 1854, (UK) D. Coulter.
Washington Padgett and Martha Carter, (MD) June 24, 1838, (UK) George W. Morris.
Elias Spicer and Mary Adaline Robinson, (MD) December 19, 1849, (UK) M. S. Coats.
William Tooles and Emily Morgan, (MD) October 11, 1856.
Thomas Truitt and Italia Baker, (MD) February 6, 1867, (MG) G. D. Tole.
William M. Estis and Laura A. Collicott, (MD) January 17, 1867.
Samuel A. Burnett and Cordelia Coonce, (MD) September 1, 1867.
Benjamin F. Jones and Lucinda Humes, (MD) August 17, 1841, (MG) Joseph Coons.
William Metcalf and Narcissa Jones, (MD) October 27, 1842.
Asa N. Overall and Mary T. Anderson, (MD) October 21, 1856.
Reuben Tatum and Sallie Blythe, (MD) November 23, 1859.
James W. Terrell and Elizabeth W. Bradley, (MD) April 30, 1867.
Nimrod A. Wilkerson and Elizabeth A. Watts, (MD) March 20, 1856.
Henry B. Williams and Sarah Minerva Landers, (MD) November 6, 1850, (MG) Absalom Rice.
Isham McMahan and Elizabeth Duncan, (MD) January 6, 1831, (MD) Jabez Ham.
George Ferrier and Elvira Jane Stark, (MD) September 2, 1847, (UK) Moses Phillips.
David C. Chatham and Amanda Rice, (MD) April 15, 1845, (MG) Jacob Coons.
James Jesse and Margaret Price, (MD) October 5, 1833, (UK) Thomas Stephens.
Jefferson Jones and Sally Ann Jamerson, (MD) March 6, 1844.
David Myers and Lucretia D. Jones, (MD) March 2, 1830, (UK) D. M. Kirkpatrick.
Yearless (sic) Turner and Margaret Perry, (MD) August 17, 1851.
Isaac Zumwalt and Matilda Blythe, (MD) June 10, 1826, (UK) Christopher Zumwalt.
John W. White and Amelia R. Heron, (MD) April 11, 1855, Groom is from Boone County.
Adam Wolf and Bettie Jane Griffins, (MD) February 21, 1861.
Thomas W. Williamson and Eliza Jane Stewart, (MD) July 30, 1848, (UK) John R. Craighead.
Henry B. Williams and Mary Ann Dearing, (MD) February 6, 1868.
James Tharp and Matilda Ann Goodrich, (MD) July 16, 1857.
Francis Murphy and Sarah C. Hall, (MD) February 20, 1860.

David Newsom and Mary Ann Dunham, (MD) April 26, 1855.

William Spillers and Nancy E. Miller, (MD) June 10, 1866.

William M. Stewart and Nancy W. Wright, (MD) March 11,
1841, (JP) W. J. Gilman.

Ambros D. Tharp and Martha A. James, (MD)September 26, 1861.

James Vest and Mary Jane Oslin, (MD) March 3, 1836, (JP)
J. M. Doan.

John Allen and Martha Sheley, (MD) September 15, 1836, (MG)
Theo. Boulware.

Pleasant Arnold and Caroline Scholl, (MD) July 20, 1843,
(MG) James Love.

Samuel Atterberry and Rachel Scarbury, (MD) December 29,
1842, (MG) James Love.

Theodrick Boulware and Ann Young, (MD) September 6, 1865,
(MG) S. A. Mutchmore.

Robert M. Berry and Pamelia Martin, (MD) April 3, 1854,
(JP) Joseph Scholl.

Andrew J. Cable and Mary E. Oxendine, (MD) March 20, 1851,
(MG) George R. Hams.

Benjamin Miller and Eva Blevins, (MD) April 29, 1827, (UK)
James Henderson.

Robert Jones and Tellacinda Sympson, (MD) June 10, 1830,
(JP) John A. Burt, Groom is from Montgomery County.

Lewis Griffith and Nancy Lampkins, (MD) April 15, 1827,
(JP) Solomon Thomas.

Meritt Y. Duncan and Mary Baskett, (MD) October 25, 1854.

Austin B. Corley and Ann Eliza Day, (MD) January 1, 1845,
(MG) Absalom Rice.

John F. Fletcher and Judith Sinnco, (MD) August 29, 1839,
(MG) Theo. Boulware.

William Wildhagen and Mary Flalker, (MD) December 22, 1868,
(UK) Reynold Kalmback.

David M. Willett and Margaret Davis, (MD) February 10, 1845,
(JP) Jos. Fisher.

George R. Terry and Elizabeth Terry, (MD) November 20, 1866,
(UK) John R. Ferguson.

Hiram R. Philips and Emily T. Wilkerson, (MD) November 10,
1836, (JP) James Stewart.

Perry Pollard and Bettie Henderson, (MD) October 17, 1834.

B. Smith and Sarah Ferguson, (MD) September 19, 1833, (MG)
Theo. Boulware.

John Sitton and Sally Jamison, (MD) November 11, 1825, (MG)
William Coats.

Henry M. Shobe and Mary Belcher, (MD) July 30, 1846, (JP)
William Gilman.

James B. Mosely and Mary Ann Carrington, (MD) November 22,
1866.

A. A. Moore and Bettie Annette, (MD) March 10, 1870.

Preston Milliken and Sally R. Allen, (MD)September 20, 1865.

John K. Allen and Mary S. Sparks, (MD) March 21, 1853.
Samuel Alkire and Lamenta Gibson, (MD) December 10, 1840,
(JP) W. J. Gilman.
R. E. Baker and Lucy Hume, (MD) November 25, 1863, Groom is
from Audrain County, Missouri.
John G. Barger and Fanny A. Road, (MD March 28, 1858.
James W. Barry and Mary J. Kilgore, (MD) February 11, 1866,
(UK) David Anderson.
James W. Bell and Martha J. Bogue, (MD) July 26, 1866.
Willis D. Bennett and Sarah C. Moon, (MD) May 3, 1855.
James H. Birch and Sallie A. Davis, (MD) November 3, 1870.
Rugus Clark and Eliza Graves, (MD) November 4, 1852, Groom
is from Danville (no other location given)
James F. Foster and Mildred F. Long, (MD) January 10, 1860.
Linneus B. Garrett and Nancy Crump, (MD) August 31, 1853,
(UK) E. M. Marvin.
Joseph H. Logan and Elizabeth Stignol, (MD) April 27, 1853.
Robert McClure and Sophie E. Brown, (MD) November 17, 1853.
Richard Miller and Mary McClelland, (MD) April 5, 1840, (MG)
Joseph Coons.
Will Turner and Martha T. Adams, (MD) August 16, 1848.
Thomas Yates and Kate Langtry, (MD) September 16, 1869.
Blagden (sic) Wood and Talitha Muldor, (MD) May 27, 1852.
Robert White and Mary E. Rice, (MD) August 10, 1859.
William R. Wilson and Jane McConathey, (MD) November 26,
1867.
Reuben Williams and Evaline Moore, (MD) May 17, 1836, (UK)
Jno. Pace.
Harry S. Wilcockson and Rosa M. Crowson, (MD) December 18,
1838, (MG) Theo. Boulware.
George L. Towner and Frances V. Robion, (MD) June 7, 1851,
Groom is from Macon County.
John Taylor and Sarah Ellen Wilson, (MD) August 2, 1857,
Groom is from Samans County, Texas,
Hiram A. Stevens and Sarah Ann Garritt, (MD) January 25,
1844, (UK) William B. Douglass, Groom is from Boone
County.
William T. Smith and Mary T. Derreux, (MD) March 13, 1870.
James Whitesides and Susan H. George, (MD)November 26, 1845,
(UK) W. W. Robertson.
James Logan and Elizabeth Talbott, (MD) May 12, 1836, (UK)
John F. Young.
Thomas Lowery and Sarah Jane Nicholson, (MD) July 22, 1846,
(JP) B. Matthews.
William C. Leeper and Lucy J. Bourn, (MD) March 22, 1854.
William J. Kidwell and Winey Nevel Reed, (MD) April 6, 1858.
William Scroghem and Mrs. Eliz. Selby, (MD) November 16,
1840, (UK) Joseph Coons.
E. B. Gladden and S. A. Chapin, (MD) October 6, 1864.

John Selby and Lavina Glover, (MD) February 16, 1843, (UK)
Absalom Rice.

Isaac Miller and Sarah Elizabeth Finley, (MD) June 8, 1843,
(JP) N. B. Ferguson.

John Moss and Mary Hunt, (MD) September 28, 1826, (UK)
Anderson Woods.

Ira P. Nash and Ann Smith, (MD) December 18, 1827, (JP)
Enoch Fruit.

Zenas Smith and Nancy Hinton, (MD) November 11, 1847, (UK)
Franklin Jenkins.

Reuben Stewart and Nancy Stewart, (MD) May 29, 1831, (JP)
John A. Burt.

Joseph A. Taylor and Mrs. Georginna Wood, (MD) December 6,
1868, (UK) William M. Hersman.

Benjamin Suggett and Elizabeth F. Branham, (MD) November 1,
1848, (UK) W. W. Kemp.

W. C. Via and Betsy Kemp, (MD) November 1, 1859.

A. P. White and Francis H. Woody, (MD) November 2, 1865.

Jeremiah Sanders and Matilda Estill, (MD) December 30, 1852.

Baxton S. Nevins and Sallie A. Dozier, (MD) March 20, 1860.

Ulysses T. Miller and Nancy F. Larimore, (MD) September 18,
1855, (UK) Absalom Rice.

George B. Maughs and Ann Anderson, (MD), March 12, 1845,
(MG) Richard Bona.

Samuel S. Keene and Harriet Holt, (MD) May 13, 1849, (MG)
Jacob Coons.

J. M. Johnson and America Martin, (MD) December 20, 1866.

Newton Jameson and Pamela Smith, (MD) January 21, 1836, (MG)
Jas. Suggett.

James Holt and Nannie Armstrong, (MD) August 31, 1865.

William L. Holliday and Lucy A. Randolph, (MD) April 20,
1869, (UK) Theo. J. Marlow.

William D. Harrison and Affiah G. Brown, (MD) July 2, 1855,
Groom is from Audrain County.

Hugh Hamilton and Nancy William Read, (MD)February 10, 1848,
(UK) Wm. B. Douglass.

Robert E. Guthrie and Elizabeth Butler, (MD) September 30,
1869.

Franklin Hall and Martha Ann Shamblon, (MD) May 16, 1859.

Cyrus C. Griffin and Feley Ann Sloan, (MD) August 25, 1870.

Jerome Goodman and Theodocia Hosman, (MD) June 17, 1857.

Thomas B. Gilbert and Bettie M. Smith, (MD) February 27,
1868.

Samuel Fletcher and Judith Heinny, (MD) January 31, 1856.

Thomas Estes and Jane Calvin, (MD) January 8, 1835, (MG) Wm.
Coats.

Jerome Duncan and Mary George, (MD) July 24, 1851.

David W. Craig and Frances Garnes, (MD) September 9, 1852.

Isaac Foy and Maggie Jane Johnson, (MD) February 12, 1863, (UK) Thomas J. Ferguson.

Samuel Gibs and Jane Davis, (MD) July 4, 1850, (MG) Theo. Boulware.

William Gilmon and Charlotte Williams, (MD) February 25, 1830, (MG) Wm. Coats.

James Glover and Sophronia Hall, (MD) January 26, 1843, (MG) James Love.

Bailey Lathlin and Salina Agee, (MD) December 3, 1835, (MG) Jabez Ham.

Absalom Lewis and Sarah Ann Peyton, (MD) October 5, 1852.

Jerroam (sic) J. Maddox and Nancy Coats, (MD) October 4, 1855.

Oty T. Martin and Eliza V. Kennett, (MD) July 1, 1852.

William McIntire and Linda Walker, (MD) December 21, 1865, (MG) R. S. Symmington.

Clarion Longe and Parthena Kelly, (MD) September 15, 1867.

Samuel G. Myers and Lyda M. Bell, (MD) December 20, 1860.

Joseph Nesbit and Harrietta Frank, (MD) March 2, 1847, (MG) Jacob Coons.

James Organ and Mary J. Barker, (MD) March 6, 1865.

James Walker Redden and Sarah Jane Hays, (MD)March 5, 1871, (MG) Thomson Penn.

Bedford Reynolds and Elizabeth Callaway, (MD) October 14, 1847.

Allen White and Sarah E. Masters, (MD) March 25, 1869, Groom and Bride are from Boone County, Missouri.

Thomas Williams and Elizabeth Todd, (MD) January 20, 1834, (MG) Jabes Ham.

John S. Wilfley and Lucy B. Combs, (MD) December 7, 1870.

William Willing and Eliza C. Parker, (MD) March 8, 1838, (UK) Jno. Pace.

Thomas Webbert and Lucretia Potter, (MD) November 16, 1837, (JP) John Burt.

William Joseph Ward and Elizabeth Calicott, (MD) January 8, 1865, (UK) M. M. Williams.

Abraham Vier and Mary McDonald, (MD) August 23, 1853.

Joseph Thompson and Patsy Baker, (MD) January 13, 1831, (UK) (UK) Theo. Stephens.

Hugh Tincher and Marcella Jones, (MD) November 22, 1860.

Thomas Thephonto and Elizabeth Nichols, (MD) January 23, 1870.

Volney Suggett and Mary H. Shortridge, (MD) March 23, 1836, (MG) Jas. Suggett.

Isaac Tarr and Bettie W. Young, (MD) February 27, 1867.

Judson G. Stewart and Lucinda Wright, (MD) November 3, 1842, (JP) W. J. Gilman.

Thomas E. Stucker and Lutitia H. Coats, (MD)October 6, 1870.

John Trimble and Mary Jane Miller, (MD) April 19, 1853.

John A. Taylor and Nancy Woods, (MD) October 18, 1864.
Joel Tharp and Susannah Hough, (MD) October 17, 1833, (MG)
Theo. Boulware.
Zephaniah Spier and Elizabeth Allen, (MD) August 8, 1849,
(UK) T. O. Stephens.
John Stewardson and Martha Hawkins, (MD) May 7, 1869, (UK)
Thos. McLaughlin.
George W. Smith and Amanda Carter, (MD) September 28, 1857.
John Snell and Lucy Craig, (MD) August 6, 1868.
James Philips and Ala Ann Gilbert, (MD) November 10, 1853,
(MG) John Green.
John Pomi and Mollie Adair, (MD) February 17, 1870.
Joseph T. Sitton and Preciller May, (MD) May 17, 1821, (UK)
Wharton T. Moore.
Ennis Smart and Elizabeth Whittington, (MD) November 30,
1848.
Willia Shelton and Nancy Elston, (MD) August 30, 1821, (UK)
Solomon Thomas.
James A. Simpson and Sarah E. Arnold, (MD)December 28, 1869.
Frederick Sanman and Sophia Baker, (MD) July 18, 1857.
Bernard Schefers and Rebecca Day, (MD) April 2, 1857.
James Rose and Deleria Zumwalt, (MD) October 30, 1824, (JP)
George King.
John W. Russell and Mary Wiggs, (MD) November 23, 1858.
Daniel Robertson and Patey VanCleane, (MD)September 3, 1828,
(MG) Jabez Ham.
Lenoir Riggs and Elizabeth Lampton, (MD) December 24, 1826,
(JP) George King.
Joseph Rice and Sally Davis, (MD) November 6, 1840, (UK)
Absalom Rice.
Samuel S. Riley and Jane D. Armstrong, (MD) April 21, 1869.
John Reynolds and Sarah F. Clatterbuck, (MF) February 15,
1866.
Elisha Radican and Cena King, (MD) Marchh 2, 1837, (UK) Jas.
Suggett.
J. W. Potts and Dulcena Dulin, (MD) September 24, 1854.
Cyrus Price and Adeline Dickerson, (MD) November 2, 1837,
(MG) Tho. Boulware.
Harrison Pauly and Mara B. Dodds, (MD) August 4, 1842, (MG)
James Love.
John Petty and Patsy Dunch, (MD) April 16, 1833, (JP) John
K. Barry.
James A. Padgett and Susan A. Corley, (MD) March 4, 1868.
Minor Pate and Sayys Mays, (MD) December 12, 1833, (UK) Theo
Stephens.
James W. Overton and Mary A. Overton, (MD) September 23,
1856.
Isaac Nickell and Isabel Humphreys, (MD) April 25, 1844.
C. H. Olde and Amanda J. Nevins, (MD) December 29, 1868.

James F. Night and Kinville J. Crook, (MD) December 2, 1841, (UK) Absalom Rice.
Luther S. Newman and Mary A. Bartley, (MD) June 11, 1861.
Robert R. Nichols and Fannie J. Fisher, (MD) February 9, 1870.
Washington Neff and Vitula Winn, (MD) September 25, 1870.
Andrew R. Murray and Nancy Sheley, (MD) December 28, 1837, (MG) R. L. McAfee.
Alfred Nash and Miss Conger, (MD) January 11, 1831, (UK) Beverly A. Ramsey.
Thomas Morrow and Seleta Agee, (MD) January 26, 1837, (JP) James Stewart.
William Morgan and Sarah Langley, (MD) January 27, 1848.
Isaac Moore and Amelia Pauly, (MD) May 26, 1846, (UK) Franklin Jinkins.
Jeremiah Miller and Mary Baker, (MD) May 21, 1843, (MG) Jos. Coons, Groom is from Boone County.
Josiah Moody and Emily Jane Price, (MD) January 2, 1854, Groom is from Boone County.
Peter White and Elizabeth Cheatham, (MGD) June 3, 1840, (MG) Absalom Rice.
Moses Wilkerson and Martha A. Callison, (MD) September 24, 1857.
William H. Smith and Fannie Rankin, (MD) May 15, 1862.
Thomas Sheperd and Polly Ann Nichols, (MD)December 12, 1867.
Cyrus Scott and Elizabeth E. Scott, (MD) July 7, 1852, (UK) David Coulter.
Michel Roberts and Sarah F. Vandiver, (MD) March 4, 1858.
Robert McPheeters and Annie Hamilton, (MD) March 28, 1869.
John Meadows and Eliza P. Lawrence, (MD) October 21, 1858.
Charley T. Martin and Lucy J. Jourdon, (MD)October 26, 1848.
John W. Love and Eliza Susan Humphreys, (MD) March 29, 1868.
Josiah Layson and Mary Young, (MD) December 13, 1832, (MG) Theo. Boulware.
James W. Kemp and Mary A. Huffmaster, (MD) February 6, 1868.
John Kelison and Margaret B. Lochridge, (MD) April 8, 1830, (JP) John K. Berry.
Thomas Jones and Margaret Duley, (MD) June 8, 1837, (UK) Wm. Martin.
Woodson A. Johnson and Mary Vier, (MD) October 24, 1849, (UK) Elijah E. Christmand.
Emanuel James and Susan Belama, (MD) November 22, ----, (UK) Jno. Pace.
John W.Selby and Mary M. D. Burn, (MD) September 23, 1852.
G. H. Hudson and Nancy Yates, (MD) April 25, 1869.
James Holt and Nannie Armstrong, (MD) August 31, 1865.
Silas Hickerson and Jane Allen, (MD) February 3, 1841, (JP) John Young.
Marshall Gibson and Sarah C. Wren, (MD) May 6, 1852.

Hiram Shaw Galbreath and Sarah Ann Allen, (MD) February 16, 1864.

B. F. Garrett and Elizabeth Ellis, (MD April 28, 1864.

Napoleon Foy and Alesey Foster, (MD) May 24, 1856.

Elias B. Walker and Hester A. Nichols, (MD) February 25, 1859, (MG) G. Hudson.

Lewis W. Turner and Mary J. Davis, (MD) April 14, 1853.

Armstead L. Vandever and D. D. Stevenson, (MD) July 4, 1850, (UK) James M. Wright.

William L. Yancey and May Mavid Bowles, (MD) January 12, 1854, (JP) U. L. Ramsey.

Wm. T. Wood and Maria H. Payne, (MD) February 23, 1841.

William P. Wright and Sally A. Price, (MD) May 11, 1853, Groom is from Boone County.

William Wheeler and Sarah V. Smith, (MD) July 15, 1845, (MG) Richard Bona.

William B. White and Mary Jane Day, (MD) July 22, 1846.

Edward Wilson and Leeny Burket, (MD) October 13, 1825, (UK) Chris. Zumwalt.

Cary Williams and Nancy Bull, (MD) April 25, 1850, (JP) J. D. McGary.

Joseph Wilfey and Sally Newland, (MD) September 27, 1838, (MG) Theo. Boulware.

William West and Margery Miller, (MD) December 21, 1834, (MG) William Duncan.

John Wilburn and Jane Morris, (MD) February 17, 1853.

Griffin Walker and Sally Roberson, (MD) February 3, 1831, (MG) William Coats.

Dr. J. E. Thompson and Elizabeth A. Turner, (MD) March 9, 1854.

Ferdinand Tincher and Elizabeth A. Jones, (MD) June 4, 1857.

Oliver P. Thomas and Pricilla Davis, (MD) August 24, 1853.

Volney Suggett and America Ann Holeman, (MD) March 2, 1847, (UK) Franklin Jenkins.

Zachariah Tate and Elizabeth Richardson, (MD)March 17, 1853, (MG) Stephen Ham.

John B. Stewart and Martha Williams, (MD March 4, 1863.

Charles Strum and Serilda Bagby, (MD) September 19, 1869, (UK) WM. S. Patterson.

John M. Allen and Martha Ann Smart, (MD) September 5, 1833, (MG) Jas. Suggett.

William J. Baker and Susan O. Bullard, (MD) October 7, 1869.

William A. Brooks amd Eliza J. Thomas, (MD)February 7, 1860.

Richard M. Carter and Mary F. Tuttle, (MD) March 25, 1858.

John Coil and Caroline Taylor, (MD) September 12, 1860.

John G. Conger and Jane Herring, (MD) October 22, 1857.

John Day and Eliz. M. Claskey, (MD) January 31, 1850.

M. D. Dunn and Martha Vincent, (MD) March 10, 1858.

William D. Gardner and Sarah J. Donald, (MD) March 20, 1861.

John Y. Gilbert and Nancy Pratt, (MD) January 27, 1842,
(UK) Samuel D. Gilbert.
George Gray and Eliz. C. Hot, (MD) November 16, 1837, (UK)
John T. A. Henderson.
William R.Herndon and Mary C. Kemp, (MD) November 11, 1852.
Wm. Harris Martin and Sophronia McLanahan, (MD) December 26,
1835, (MG) R. L. McAfee.
William H. McCartey and Sallie M. Foxworthy, (MD) January
24, 1856.
John M. Allen and Martha Q. Baker, (MD) March 6, 1870.
John F. Bagby and Margaret Forbes, (MD) September 30, 1869.
Thomas J. Barnes and Sarah L. McCray, (MD) April 28, 1836,
(UK) Theo. P. Stephens.
Ambrose Griggs and Isabella Evans, (MD) March 2, 1837, (JP)
H. S. Turner.
William Hamilton and Jane Board, (MD) June 10, 1847, (MG) R.
S. Symmington.
John S. Harris and Sallie Bell Herndon, (MD)October 5, 1869,
(UK) D. M. Grandfield.
T. J. McMahan and Susan A. Samuels, (MD) October 25, 1868.
Bayliss C. Renoe and Eliza Jane Nevins, (MD) December 1,
1853.
James A. Tate and Martha Watkins, (MD) July 23, 1843, (UK)
Joseph Coons.
James G. Smith and Isabel Gray McCredie, (MD) August 25,
1858.
William J. Hays and Nancy E. Booth, (MD) December 6, 1855.
C. H. Harland and Mary A. Hord, (MD) May 20, 1863.
George A. Coil and Elizabeth Roman, (MD) June 26, 1864.
John Burnett and Sarah Ann Foster, (MD) December 1, 1863,
(MG) W. H. Burnham.
William A. Pledge and Mary J. Davis, (MD) July 28, 1861.
Benjamin D. Suggett and Frances J. Conger, (MD) December 22,
1864.
Benjamin F. White and Margaret Burnett, (MD) March 21, 1862.
Israel Robinson and Catharine Wells, (MD) January 6, 1870.
William Eli Maden and Christian F. Hatyman, (MD) October 22,
1867.
Johan Leopard and Henrietta Moon, (MD) September 6, 1849.
Silas Larimore and Polly Ann Coats, (MD) September 17, 1848.
Patrick Day and Caroline Boyd, (MD) February 2, 1845, (MG)
Jas. Criswell.
J. P. Crossthwaite and Sarah Herron, (MD) January 27, 1853.
George W. Creed and Eliza Miller, (MD) November 6, 1834,
(MG) William Duncan.
William Quim and Eliz. J. Spraddle, (MD) May 14, 1865.
G. W. Waters and Barbara Ruloff, (MD) January 6, 1870.
D. M. Bartley and P. E. Neil, (MD) February 24, 1864.
John T. Kirby and Sarah Ann Lyons, (MD) April 11, 1855.

George W. Aubert and Mary Ann Bentley, (MD) August 19, 1869.
Floyd Baker and Rachel Bell, (MD) September 23, 1830, (JP)
  Henry Neill.
John W. Bailey and Mary Gregory, (MD) December 2, 1858.
George Bartley and Elizabeth Moore, (MD) July 8, 1827, (MG)
  William Coats.
William Belama and Ann Tharp, (MD) March 9, 1836, (MG) Theo.
  Boulware.
John Bently and Harriet Ansel, (MD) February 1, 1844.
Norman Bolin and Louisa Suggett, (MD) June 23, 1857.
Alonzo Boon and Mary Jane Jackson, (MD) January 2, 1834,
  (MG) William Coats.
Wharton H. Boyd and Mary E. Blackmore, (MD) April 28, 1870.
Russel W. Martin and Mary E. Scott, (MD)March 15, 1854, (UK)
  Dudly C. Julow.
Drury A. Maupin and Martha Norris, (MD) April 3, 1865, (MG)
  William A. Taylor.
Samuel T. Moore and Emma L. Ferguson, (MD)February 18, 1867,
  (MG) Absalom Rice.
Shadrick Reynolds and Nancy Wood, (MD) April 15, 1835, (MG)
  H. J. M. Doan.
John R. Davidson and Ann Taylor, (MD) June 22, 1847, (MG)
  Jas. Criswell.
William Davis and Minerva Vanbibber, (MD) December --, 1850,
  (JP) W. J. Jackson.
William Blythe and Terilda Ann Dorton, (MD)November 6, 1845,
  (UK) Benjamin Wren.
William Collier and Harriet Bullard, (MD) April 19, 1848.
R. D. Craghead and Mary Finley, (MD) February 21, 1858.
Bright K. Crews and Hannah E. Miller, (MD) July 6, 1854.
James Hamilton and Cornelia O. Bernard, (MD) May 15, 1844,
  (ED) Ricard Bona.
George Harris and Mary M. Sims, (MD) May 4, 1864.
David R. Morris and Sarah M. Adkins, (MD) January 25, 1858.
Harvey Newsom and Miranda Griggs, (MD) July 8, 1852.
Selby Clark and Virginia Jones, (MD) September 27, 1849,
  (MG) William B. Douglas, Groom is from Audrain County.
Levi R. Kemper and Nancy C. Morgan, (MD) October 13, 1864.
John Kilgore and Patsey Williams, (MD) December 11, 1835,
  (JP) H. J. M. Dean.
George E. Thomas and Sophronia A. Fidley, (MD) December 14,
  1859.
James A. Wood and Mary Jane Burditt, (MD) August 25, 1850,
  (JP) Marshall Coats.
George Nicholson and Anna Zumwalt, (MD) December 11, 1824,
  (JP) John Ferguson.
John Cochran and Eliz. M. Davis, (MD) June 28, 1868.
Richard Branch and Malinda Pulliam, (MD) November 3, 1853,
  (JP) Thos. J. Ferguson.

Preston Reed and Mary Tate, (MD) March 17, 1841.
John B. Richie and Ann Shields, (MD) September 30, 1841,
    (MG) Noah Flood.
Isaac Stites and Susan Williams, (MD) June 19, 1825, (JP)
    Thomas Fisher.
Robert Arnold and Elvira Allen, (MD) August 13, 1867, (MG)
    W. J. Mason.
Martin L. Dawson and Penelope Hackley, (MD) March 10, 1852,
    (MG) Noah Flood.
William Townsend and Eliza Anderson, (MD) February 27, 1834,
    (MG) William Duncan.
James R. Smith and Mary Bruskill, (MD) April 3, 1869, (JP)
    D. P. Railey.
Ellis R. Sloan and Nancy Armstrong, (MD) August 7, 1834,
    (MG) Horace Sheley.
John B. Moore and Mrs. Abigail Forsythe, (MD) October 22,
    1863, (UK) S. M. Harrison, Bride is from Franklin County.
John D. Maupin and Jane Dickinson, (MD) June 6, 1858.
Elizah Solomon Martin and Caroline M. Ishman, (MD) August
    20, 1868.
George W. Lovelace and Mary E. Wright, (MD)January 23, 1868.
Smith Lawson and Sarah E. Holt, (MD) April 14, 1850.
Ambrose Kizer and Mary Brown, (MD) February 2, 1868.
George Jordan and Cora Ann Humphries, (MD) June 2, 1847,
    (UK) Jas. S. Whittington.
J. T. Jesse and Sarah J. Scott, (MD) October 25, 1854, (UK)
    J. E. Hughes.
Winthrope H. Hopson and Caroline H. Gray, (MD)March 9, 1848,
    (ED) M. P. Wills.
William Holland and Alay Walls, (MD) May 28, 1846, (UK) Jas.
    Criswell.
John H. Stone and Catharine R. Grant, (MD)February 22, 1838,
    (MG) Theo. Boulware.
James F. Wilson and Sally Callison, (MD) September 30, 1852,
    (MG) S. Scott.
Joseph Price and Elizabeth Renfro, (MD) December 13, 1841,
    (UK) Thos. P. Stephens.
Joseph D. Nevins and Martha Ann Comer, (MD) March 26, 1856.
Joseph James and Eliza Adair, (MD) September 17, 1854.
George A. Hamley and Mary A. Blackburn, (MD) July 19, 1863.
Charles A. Day and Nancy Walker, (MD) May 27, 1835, (MG) Wm.
    Coats.
George Davis and Polly Freeman, (MD) April 19, 1840, (JP) H.
    S. Turner.
Samuel Crump and Elizabeth Baker, (MD) January 7, 1830, (ED)
    M. P. Wills.
Jas. Mosby Wills and Martha A. Roberts, (MD) December 25,
    1870.
William D. Turley and Laura Wood, (MD) March 28, 1869.

W. Edmonston and M. Ficklin, (MD) December 17, 1846, (MG)
   Theo. Boulware.
Absalom Ferguson and Francis M. Bagby, (MD) April 8, 1857.
Beverly Allen Fields and Louisa West, (MD) August 11, 1836,
   (JP) George L. Smith.
Bird Moore and Sarah Blackwell, (MD) March 11, 1841, (MG) J.
   Coons.
John W. Noble and Hannah S. Felkner, (MD) December 14, 1869.
F. M. Tourdan and Patrick Doyle, (MD) January 19, 1861.
Henry H. Stokes and Sarah L. Hughes, (MD) February 14, 1867.
John P. Allen and Alice West, (MD) January 14, 1845, (MG)
   Jacob Lighter.
James Dorsey and Sarah W. Willing, (MD) March 20, 1862.
Henry Miller and Emily Payton, (MD) February 8, 1854, (UK)
   W. B. Douglad.
George W. Kemp and Ellen Carrington, (MD) January 2, 1870.
William Johnson and Ellen Kennett, (MD) July 11, 1848, (UK)
   James M. Green.
M. M. Huddleston and Ann Hall, (MD) February 11, 1858.
Samuel H. Day and Margaret A. Fitzgerald, (MD) December 23,
   1866, (UK) Will Walthall.
William T. Craghead and Mary Gilbert, (MD) October 28,
   1858.
Isaac Langley and Mary Daffron, (MD) April 14, 1867.
William A. Powell and Mary C. Cheatham, (MD) November 6,
   1870.
Wm. Harvey Smith and Mary Flood, (MD) September 30, 1865,
   (MG) Noah Flood.
Elisha Vinson and Mrs. Sarah Adair, (MD) December 12, 1867.
William Pratt and Polly Eaken, (MD) April 18, 1822, (MG)
   Robert Baker.
Robertson Woodson and Ann N. Strother, (MD) May 26, 1859.
Moses Stanley and Mrs. Eliza Dorton, (MD)September 27, 1848,
   (MG) J. Criswell.
Frances M. Brown and Mary P. Howe, (MD) October 11, 1851,
   (MG) W. W. Robertson.
Joseph Grady and Ann Eliza Smith, (MD) January 30, 1845,
   (UK) Robt. A. Younger, Groom is from Boone County.
Samuel Martin and Judith Wright, (MD) May 21, 1829, (MG)
   Theo. Boulware.
Joseph Proctor and Mrs. Narcissa Medcalff, (MD) February 18,
   1852.
Robert J. Alexander and Lavina W. Sheley, (MD) November 10,
   1851, (UK) T. M. Allen.
Isaah Davis and Patsey C. Jones, (MD) December 23, 1864.
Silas Rambaugh and Mrs. Sarah Widdle, (MD)December 31, 1863.
Daniel White and Virginia Covington, (MD) December 11, 1851,
   (JP) Jos. Scholl, Groom is from Montgomery County.
James Lewis and Ann Dougherty, (MD) May 6, 1866.

David Leiper and Martha Scott, (MD) January 25, 1832, (UK)
Benjamin Hoxey.
John A. Moore and Sallie Ann Davis, (MD) December 18, 1861.
John Thos. Griggs and Catharine Wiley, (MD) April 9, 1856.
Francis James and Isabelle Williamson, (MD) April 24, 1856.
Wm. Taylor Ramsey and Sarah Doda Miller, (MD) May 20, 1849,
(MG) David Coulter.
Isaac Roy and Victoria Holt, (MD) May 4, 1854.
William H. French and Virginia Harrison, (MD) November 17,
1852.
W. C. Davis and Harriet E. Smart, (MD) January 15, 1868,
(UK) W. M. Burnham.
Bollinger Crump and Susan May, (MD) February 2, 1830, (ED)
M. P. Wills.
John W. Kemp and Anna S. Wood, (MD) August 11, 1840, (JP) R.
B. Jackson.
Felix G. Nichols and Eliz. Ann Renoe, (MD)February 12, 1833,
(MG) Theo. Boulware.
Richard Robertson and Mary Francis Logston, (MD) September
19, 1861.
Robert A. Sanders and Susan J. Straw, (MD)February 22, 1866.
Samuel Grant and Martha V. Yates, (MD) January 17, 1856.
William J. Aau (sic) and Priscella McGirk, (MD) August 6,
1846, (MG) Absalom Rice.
John Hall and Winifred Newman, (MD) February 15, 1860.
Joseph Mead and Levina Thomas, (MD) September 27, 1832, (JP)
Arthur Neill.
Jesse Farmer and Elizabeth E. King, (MD) December 4, 1833,
(MG) Robt. McAfee.
William F. Schifker and Mary J. Haynes, (MD) February 2,
1854, (MG) Theo. Boulware.
William Rice and Susan Thomas, (MD) August 5, 1847, (ED) M.
P. Wills.
John Sampson and Nancy Emmerson, (MD) July 29, 1846.
William W. Findley and Margaret J. Campbell, (MD) October
25, 1838, (MG) Robt. C. Hill.
Tyn (sic) H. Jones and Martha Bass, (MD) December 23, 1852,
(UK) B. Wren.
Elias Lewis and Darley Philips, (MD) April 6, 1834, (MG) Wm.
Coats.
W. Taylor Maupin and Sarah Ann Miller, (MD) December 20,
1856.
Samuel R. Saterfield and Margarette Loveet, (MD) October 20,
1863.
John Simco and Frances Smith, (MD) October 15, 1851.
George Allen and Mrs. Catherine V. Martin, (MD) April 27,
1853.
James G. Armistead and China R. Newman, (MD) December 10,
1867, (PM) Home of Capt. Jos. Price of Callaway County.

Samuel Brown and S. M. Kemp, (MD) December 7, 1843, (MG)
Theo. Boulware.

James Hanna and Lydia Ann Potts, (MD) February 24, 1853,
(UK) Joel Palmer.

Jacob Kenida and Ann R. Smith, (MD) January 7, 1841, (MG)
Theo. Boulware.

Tilman Agee and Charlotte Townsand, (MD) December 17, 1835,
(MG) William Coats.

Levi Jackson and Sally Ridgway, (MD) March 18, 1841, (MG) J.
Coons, Groom from Boone County.

James B. McIntire and Rachel M. Baker, (MD) June 30, 1842,
(MG) W. W. Robertson.

William P. Coonce and Mary Basinger, (MD) April 18, 1863.

Marcus B. Bullard and Eliza C. Spry, (MD) June 18, 1862.

Robert Martin and Ann Baker, (MD) February 22, 1827, (UK)
Thos. P. Stephens.

Charles McKinney and Mary Ann Craig, (MD) February 10, 1830,
(MG) Theo. Boulware.

Dr. W. J. Yeates and Mary Eliza Floyd, (MD) September 11,
1867, Groom is from Versailles, Morgan County, Mo.

John Smith and Sarah Waggoner, (MD) September 10, 1847, (JP)
Chas. A. Ming.

John C. B. Guy and Amanda M. Green, (MD) February 3, 1852,
(MG) W. H. Wood.

Matthew Edwards and Margaret Ferguson, (MD) May 24, 1827,
(UK) Ninian Ridgway.

William Langley and Mrs. Cithy Gordon, (MD) February 28,
1866.

Samuel C. McCall and Eliz. A. Linville, (MD) December 13,
1860.

Silas B. Pugh and Emmeline Davis, (MD) June 16, 1825, (MG)
William Coats.

Christopher Turner and Serena Boaz, (MD) April 18, 1860.

R. C. White and M. A. Hughs, (MD) February 28, 1866.

John Wilkerson and Sally Wells, (MD) September 13, 1860.

William M. Nevins and Anna E. Davis, (MD) December 4, 1867.

Charles W. McIntire and Margaret Harrison, (MD) January 10,
1828, (MG) Theodore Boulware.

Samuel Hudson and Eliz. P. Bennett, (MD) January 5, 1864,
(UK) J. H. Tuttle.

Frances Dodd and Nancy Thompson, (MD) May 3, 1860, Groom is
from Gasconade County.

David Custard and Catharine Grey, (MD) April 4, 1869.

Bryon S. Hite and Virginia Allen, (MD) November 20, 1859.

Franklin Samuel and Julian Snell, (MD) November 26, 1843.

Wm. Harvey Vivion and Rebecca M. Grant, (MD) February 6,
1867, (MG) John F. Cowan.

Caleb W. Tate and Ora A. Hamblin, (MD) March 23, 1848.

Lewis Fred and Catharine Gibbs, (MD) December 25, 1853.

John T. McClaim and Iby J. Whittey, (MD) October 9, 1836,
(JP) James Stewart.
James J. Shepard and Nancy J. Todd, (MD) January 20, 1844,
(UK) John R. Barry.
George Gilman and Maggie Bowlin, (MD) January 28, 1869.
Francis R. Davis and Mary F. Holt, (MD) September 7, 1848,
(MG) Noah Flood.
Ira Thomas and Malisa Fox, (MD) May 18, 1824, (JP) Enoch
Fruit.
Dr. M. M. Maughs and Eliz. C. S. Offutt, (MD) November 10,
1858.
Stephen Guerrant and Lucy Ann Hardin, (MD) March 2, 1837,
(MG) Theo. Boulware.
Hiram S. Kemp and Ann Ross, (MD) August 11, 1867.
Calvin H. Tate and Eliz. H. Allen, (MD) February 11, 1835,
(MG) Robt. McAfee.
William Vivion and Mary Caroline Shaw, (MD)October 28, 1852,
(MG) D. Coulter.
Samuel Haydon and Mary McClure, (MD) October 16, 1834, (MG)
Theo. Boulware.
Jeptha Yates and Jane Harrison, (MD) April 2, 1838, (MG)
Theo. Boulware.
Richard D. Gray and Ellen S. Huff, (MD) October 4, 1868.
George W. Maxy and Elizabeth Bethal, (MD August 22, 1865.
Daniel H. Rice and S. J. Wright, (MD) January 1, 1851, Groom
is from Cole County.
William Longley and Mollie Murry, (MD) January 8, 1862, (MG)
Geo. W. Penn.
Fielding Kirtley and Emily Denius, (MD) July 6, 1852.
James Galbreath and Lavisa Branghton, (MD) october 22, 1846,
(MG) James Love.
James D. Martin and Martha A. Hall, (MD) June 21, 1858.
George W. Oliver and Edna Stuart, (MD) February 9, 1860.
James M. Hamilton and Rebecca Davis, (MD) December 9, 1856.
John McClanahan, jr. and Bettie S. Wiggs, (MD)June 15, 1869.
William G. Smith and Amelia Dearing, (MD) February 16, 1853,
(JP) M. S. Coats.
Samuel Wilfley and Nancy Ellis, (MD) July 15, 1824, (JP)
Jas. Nevins.
J. R. Collier and Mary Ann Dickinson, (MD) November 25,
1856.
James Love and Ann George, (MD) February 29, 1844.
William McClure and Nancy Carter, (MD) June 1, 1864, (UK)
John Robinson, Groom is from Boone County.
Hugh T. Richardson and Mary Jane Adkins, (MD) January 18,
1858.
Thomas Sallee and Margaret Games, (MD) July 9, 1834, (MG)
Theo. Boulware.
John B. Wade and Catherine E. Gay, (MD) September 20, 1863.

Willian H. Arnold and Lucia C. Wellbum, (MD) November 2,
1863.
T. W. Longley and Zerah Ann Chaney, (MD) April 25, 1867.
Benjamin Ola and Zerelda Kemo, (MD) March 15, 1842, (JP) N.
Norflet.
Andrew Rogers and Jane Dunlop, (MD) December 23, 1852.
Levi O. Day and Agnes E. CC. McGinnes, (MD) February 13,
1845, (UK) Winthrop H. Hopson.
Robert Freeman and Elizabeth Evans, (MD) January 16, 1861.
Joseph Kubezeck (sic) and Josepha Presschibik (sic), (MD)
February 12, 1856.
Garland Nichols and Sarah P. Jameson, (MD) January 7, 1841,
(UK) Berryman Wren.
Addison D. Saunders and Letice A. Gough, (MD) February 8,
1869, (UK) Barnabas Baker.
James M. Dunlap and Mattie E. Dawson, (MD) October 27, 1870.
George S. Brothers and Mary E. Sallee, (MD) April 23, 1845,
(MG) Theo. Boulware.
John Clatterbuck and Mary Tureman, (MD) March 31, 1847, (MG)
Noah Flood.
Decetine (sic) Lawrence and Permelia Taylor, (MD) February
12, 1852.
Samuel Newland and Mary W. Martin, (MD) December 12, 1839.
Dudley H. Overton and Virginia C. Barnett, (MD) October 13,
1856.
George D. King and Elizabeth Ramsey, (MD) September 2, 1858.
Samuel Collier and Susan Nichols, (MD) May 22, 1851.
Toliver Bryant and Sarah E. Hackney, (MD) January 26, 1837,
(JP) Jabez Ham.
William Coats and and Mattie E. Taylor, (MD) December 10,
1868.
William G. Duncan and Judith E. Sheley, (MD) November 11,
1846, (MG) S. McAfee, Groom is from Jefferson City.
Henry Hunter and Martha Allen, (MD) August 15, 1848, (UK)
R. S. Symmington.
Thomas E. Nunn and Mrs. Aletha Stinson, (MD)October 2, 1847.
Granville Reid and Nancy Black, (MD) February 21, 1837, (JP)
James Barnes, Groom is from Boone County.
Benjamin Kemper and Sary Langley, (MD) August 29, 1849.
William Haynes and Polly Louder, (MD) February 25, 1830,
(MG) Thos. Stephens.
William Fred and Catharine Gibbs, (MD) December 25, 1853.
Carey James Davis and Mrs. Martha Gilbert, (MD) April 18,
1864, (UK) John Cowan, Groom is from Kentucky.
James Callaway and Fanny Meadows, (MD) September 2, 1839,
(JP) W. J. Gilman.
Thomas A. Brooks and Mary M. Hutts, (MD) December 17, 1868,
(MG) Wm. B. Walthall.
Levi Frickas and Lavina Johnson, (MD) November 9, 1864.

Overton Hunter and Elizabeth Huff, (MD) December 21, 1837,
(MG) John F. Young.
James Pugh and Mrs. Julia C. Chaney, (MD) November 17,1868.
John Gilmore and Eliza Burgett, (MD) October 17, 1867.
Claybourne Cheatham and Nancy Smith, (MD) September 2, 1834,
(MG) Wm. Coats.
Calvin Criswell and Elizabeth Moon, (MD) February 10, 1853.
James M. Davis and Polly Ann Blount, (MD) July 20, 1851,
(MG) James Morrow.
Ezekiel Hutson and Catharine Landrum, (MD) April 19, 1849,
(JP) --- Ramsey.
Robert A. McClelland and Alice Ann Nesbit, (MD) January 19,
1843.
Berry Ola and Mary Meng, (MD) February 4, 1838, (JP) A.
Northphen.
James Lewis and Ann Dougherty, (MD) Mary 6, 1866.
John N. Baker and Serenas A. Baker, (MD) April 4, 1844, (ED)
W. W. Robinson.
John C. Baskin and Rebecca J. Neale, (MD)September 25, 1839,
(MG) J. L. Yantis.
Joseph Corley and Felicity Parue, (MD) September 10, 1822,
(UK) Jonathan Holliway.
Thomas W. Herring and Mary Jane Young, (MD) February 11,
1864.
John T. McClure and Eliza Jane Sheets, (MD) March 7, 1860,
(UK) Robt. C. Hatton.
James McVeigh and Sallie Ann Garrant, (MD) September 15,
1863, (MG) Theo. Boulware.
Edmond W. Ratekin and Susan Cheatham, (MD) May 8, 1838, (MG)
Absalom Rice.
W. P. Sullins and Sallie J. Betz, (MD) October 7, 1861.
Joseph W. Thompson Jewima Harland, (MD) October 23, 1857.
Robert S. Martin and Sarah C. Hudson, (MD)December 10, 1847,
(JP) Chas. A. Ming.
James Jones and Sarah Pemberton, (MD) May 20, 1866.
John W. Selby and Rachal M. Bedsworth, (MD) April 30, 1846,
(MG) Jacob Coons.
Zadok Hook and Mary E. Steinberger, (MD) September 15, 1863,
(UK) John M. Robinson.
Nicholas T. Clanton and Mrs. Diana E. Day, (MD) January 7,
1858.
John P. Barry and Rosanna Barry, (MD) September 30, 1846,
(UK) Ninian Ridgway.
William H. Holman and Sarah E. Guthrie, (MD) April 29, 1857.
Richmond Pearson and Eliz. Allen Brown, (MD) March 15, 1832,
(UK) James Banres.
George Britt and Susan Jane Clamins, (MD) March 26, 1845,
(MG) Oliver McEwan.
Cyrus C. Smith and Margaret Jane Wise, (MD)February 21,1855.

Jeffrey S. Austin and Elvira Gray, (MD) March 11, 1863, (ED)
March 11, 1863.
Morris Baker and Hily Haines, (MD) June 27, 1842, (JP) Pat-
rick Ewing.
John Bailey and Martha Overton, (MD) March 21, 1853, Groom
is from California (State or California, Moniteau Co.
Robert A. Longley and Clarissa Hinton, (MD) April 3, 1849,
(UK) Gro. B. Hopkins.
Harvey McClure and Mary Jane Davis, (MD) October 8, 1835,
(MG) Theo. Boulware.
John Barry and Virginia Garrett, (MD) June 5, 1851, (UK) W.
B. Douglass.
Mark Renfro and Nancy Ridgeway, (MD) September 18, 1825,
(MG) Thos. Stephens, Groom is from Boone County.
Isaac Tate and Jane Henderson, (MD) July 14, 1830.
Jewel Ramsey and Caroline Conger, (MD) January 31, 1828,
(JP) George King.
Thos. Johnson and A. E. Cobb, (MD) April 5, 1869, Groom is
from Clark County and Bride is from Montgomery County.
Robert J. Hord and Martha James, (MD) January 26, 1848, (UK)
Geo. B. Hopkeins.
Samuel Hannah and Susan Lowden, (MD) November 18, 1839, (UK)
James Barnes.
D. F. Huntington and Mary L. Grant, (MD) June 1, 1848, (UK)
W. W. Robertson.
Daniel Bagby and Sophronia Day, (MD) November 22, 1840,
(JP) A. R. Bell.
Walter W. James and Sarah Stoflet (sic), (MD) November 19,
1841, (MG) Jacob Coons.
William Crowson and Rachel Miller, (MD) May 2, 1839, (MG)
Theo. Boulware.
Thomas Kitching and Elizabeth Lenville, (MD) July 22, 1841,
(JP) W. J. Gilman.
Moses Payne and Mary White, (MD) June 25, 1829, (UK) Nathan-
iel M. Talbot, Groom is from Boone County.
Robert A. Bailey and Mary Ellen Jameson, (MD) October 19,
1852.
Francis Dyer and Mrs. Irmine Mosby, (MD) January 28, 1866.
Joseph Hays and Nancy Hays, (MD) March 18, 1825, (UK) Samuel
Crockett.
David Palmer and Nancy T. Lawrence, (MD) August 23, 1859.
John Staub and Eliz. Marvia Payne, (MD) December 20, 1854.
Elisha Vincent and Sophrona Frazier, (MD) January 5, 1863.
Henry Hudson and Elizabeth Holt, (MD) June 17, 1869.
James J. Gilbert and Mary J. Gilbert, (MD)December 24, 1840,
(UK) Samuel D. Gilbert.
James W. Bellama and Susan A. P. Jones, (MD) June 28, 1866,
Henry A. Paris and Amy J. Bull, (MD) September 16, 1852,
(JP) Jas. McGary.

64

Joseph C. Renfro and Elizabeth Scott, (MD) June 18, 1846,
(MG) Noah Flood.
John Bunkall and Elizabeth Simpson, (MD) December 27, 1846,
(MG) Oliver McEwan.
Josiah Burkett and Catharine Gilmore, (MD) May 7, 1857.
Edward T. Smith and Sarah T. Baker, (MD) January 13, 1858.
James O. Pope and Nettie Warren, (MD) November 5, 1867, (UK)
Sherman M. Williams.
William Morrison and Mary Ellen Bowen, (MD) June 10, 1841,
(UK) R. C. Mansfield.
John Marack and Lisa Patarka (sic), (MD) December 6, 1864.
James Love and Lucy A. Ward, (MD) November 5, 1846, (UK) W.
W. Robertson.
Nelson Lewis and Patheny Eakins, (MD) February 21, 1833,
(MG) William Coats.
C. H. Olde and Amanda J. Nevins, (MD) December 29, 1868.
J. F. Spamhorat and Mary Crosswait, (MD) May 18, 1859.
W. W. Turk and Amanda J. Turk, (MD) August 10, 1854.
John Barker and Ann E. Jones, (MD) November 2, 1866.
Barnabas C. Davis and Julia Ann Davis, (MD)February 1, 1832,
(JP) Henry Neill.
James M. Glover and Gennette Bright, (MD) November 13, 1862,
(MG) Jesse Forbrain.
Hugh Harryman and Christenny Zumwalt, (MD) May 10, 1827,
(UK) Christopher Zumwalt.
Wm. Ewing Johnson and Harriet M. Rawson, (MD) May 24, 1846,
(JP) Jos. T. Bryan.
Jordan Kemp and Mrs. Margaret Wells, (MD) November 17, 1842,
(UK) Matthew Davis.
James M. Tharp and Mary Todd, (MD) February 28, 1867, (UK)
W. J. Patrick.
James R. Baker and Eliz. Jane Finley, (MD)November 29, 1855.
Iram H. Dunham and Mary S. Newsom, (MD) July 26, 1855.
Willis Goodman and M. M. Penn, (MD) April 4, 1853, Groom is
from Montgomery County.
John H. Jameson and Mollie Henrdon, (MD) December 10, 1861.
John Pasley and Julina Keen, (MD) August 5, 1851, (MG) R. H.
Jordan.
John Ramsey and Elizabeth Bradner, (MD) March 23, 1857.
Franklin W. Phillips and Mary Ann Allen, (MD) February 2,
1854.
James P. Thurman and Mary Jane Leeper, (MD)January 18, 1860,
(UK) J. G. Smith.
Barthewel Ubank and Mildred Ann Miller, (MD) October 15,
1840, (JP) Geo. W. Morris.
Joshua W. Baitty and Sarah Jane Farmer, (MD) December 7,
1854.
Andrew Boaz and Elizabeth Manning, (MD) March 11, 1841, (MG)
Jabez Ham.

W. H. Grear and Rebecca Thatcher, (MD) July 22, 1831, (MG)
Theo. Boulware.
Nathaniel Knipp and Adra Eliz. English, (MD) May 15, 1862.
James M. McKamey and Elizabeth Murray, (MD) January 8, 1829,
(UK) David Kirkpatrick.
Dr. Sou-- Stephens and Sarah Jane Stephens, (MD) August 29,
1848.
Martin Turner and Debby Hornbuckle, (MD) February 24, 1825,
(JP) Geo. King.
Claggett Offutt and Pinkney J. Buckner, (MD) December 9,
1863, (UK) John T. Cowan.
Zimarman Nichols and Elizabeth Smith, (MD) August 14, 1844,
(JP) Joseph Scholl.
Henry R. Nevins and Mary J. Holt, (MD) March 20, 1860.
Henry P. Musgrove and Margaret Crags, (MD) January 14, 1858.
James McNear and Malinda J. Boyd, (MD) February 12, 1846,
(UK) James Criswell.
William R. McBride and Letha Jane Adams, (MD) January 30,
1866.
Charles Love and Catherine Martin, (MD) May 24, 1827, (JP)
Enoch Fruit.
Abraham Knoff and Lucy Hun, (MD) March 17, 1840, (JP) Jabez
Ham.
B. O. Austin and Eleanor S. Allen, (MD) March 27, 1855.
John Baker and Miss Sampson, (MD) June 30, 1846, (MG) R. S.
Symmington.
R. H. Blackburn and Mrs. N. E. Hays, (MD) April 1, 1869.
James R. Caldwell and Eliz. Jane Davis, (MD) February 25,
1847.
Silas Dudley and Martha F. Lawrence, (MD) November 29, 1868.
Augustus Fry and Mary Glendy, (MD) January 31, 1855.
Benjamin Jones and Martha Peters, (MD) March 1, 1849, (JP)
John A. Butt.
Reuben Mozuigo and Delpha Ann Mozuigo, (MD) September 12,
1847, (UK) John R. Craghead.
Louis Starke and Hellen R. Reimer, (MD) October 15, 1860.
William Biby and Eliz. M. Crook, (MD) November 25, 1848,
(MG) Noah Flood.
Randolph Eversoll and Hattie Erwin, (MD) November 28, 1867.
William T. Green and Charlotte Emmons, (MD) August 13, 1857.
Robert Irvine and Evalina Scott, (MD) March 10, 1836, (UK)
John F. Young.
Henry N. Langley and Mary Langley, (MD) February 28, 1866,
(UK) William F. Dunn.
Robert Muir and June Renoe, (MD) March 29, 1848.
Robert H. Smith and Martha Ann McCutcheon, (MD)May 25, 1843,
(UK) W. W. Robertson.
Henry Basinger and Lauseller (sic) A. Shaw, (MD) December
12, 1867, (MG) G. Fenton.

Robert Berry and Edward Jackson, (MD) December 23, 1868,
(JP) W. J. Gilman.
James A. Calvin and Mildred F. Callaway, (MD) December 23,
1862, (JP) J. O. Craghead.
Christopher T. Garner and Elizabeth Mosby, (MD) November 5,
1850, (UK) T. M. Allen.
David C. Harvey and Elizabeth J. Rossen, (MD) February 28,
1866.
Alfred B. Hays and Martha Collins, (MD) February 3, 1870,
Groom is from Jackson County.
R. D. Renoe and Jane Davis, (MD) August 9, 1838, (UK) Geo.
B. Hopkins.
Philip H. Blattenburg and Laura E. Turner, (MD) November 10,
1869.
John Campbell and Nancy Boyd, (MD) January 31, 1839, (MG) J.
L. Yantis.
John Curry and Jane Wilkerson, (MD) April 30, 1848.
E. B. Harndon and ELiz. A. Bradly, (MD) October 26, 1851,
Groom is from Platte County.
Legrand Jordan and Rebena A. Day, (MD) July 9, 1846, (MG)
Jacob Sigler.
Isaac Moore and Rebecca Hart, (MD) December 24, 1834, (MG)
B. A. Ramsey.
John Blackburn and Melvina Scott, (MD) April 22, 1845, (MG)
James Love.
John Bourd and Jane Callison, (MD) October 1, 1839, (MG)
Jabez Ham.
Samuel Ferguson and Nancy Humphreys, (MD) February 29, 1860,
(MG) Austin Warner.
Abraham Howard and Sally Alexander, (MD) March 1, 1826, (MG)
Wm. Coats.
David H. McKinney and Mary Tharp, (MD) December 13, 1842,
(JP) Wm. J. Gilman.
George Reanolds and Sarah Ann Harper, (MD)February 17, 1833,
(UK) Thos. Hornbuckle.
John Longley and Sally Curry, (MD) August 29, 1865.
Thomas Guin and Mary Graham, (MD) July 6, 1840, (JP) A. R.
Bell.
William Frazer and Frances Wallace, (MD) February 27, 1850.
James Johnston and Nancy Arnold, (MD) January 29, 1841.
Stephen Maddox and Emily C. Dudley, (MD) February 2, 1860.
Willian White and Amelia Moore, (MD) September 28, 1860.
William F. Ross and Elizabeth Callaway, (MD) March 24, 1842,
(JP) W. J. Gilman.
Alfred Kibbey and Cynthia Harrison, (MD) June 9, 1831, (JP)
Enoch Fruit, Groom is from Montgomery County.
John W. Blunt and Jane Thomas, (MD) January 2, 1831, (MG) M.
P. Wills.
John E. Coats and Mary Ann Blythe, (MD) June 15, 1865.

John Farmer and Emerald J. Major, (MD) November 12, 1829, (MG) Theo. Boulware.

R. S. Guy and Emily Green, (MD) October 22, 1846, (MG) R. S. Symmington.

Thomas Kelly and Malinda Ellis, (MD) May 30, 1844, (MG) Noah Flood.

Richard B. Owen and Annuline Walton, (MD) February 6, 1867.

William Reynolds and Polly Ann Day, (MD) January 1, 1835, (MG) James Baines.

Hamilton Steward and Sarah Patty, (MD) August 2, 1832, (JP) Robt. Davis.

Elizah P. Blankenship and Eliz. P. English, (MD) June 14, 1867.

James Brown and Catharina F. Holman, (MD) December 6, 1848, (MG) David Coulter.

Joseph P. Callaway and Miss Nancy Coats, (MD) December 12, 1822, (MG) Robert Baker.

Charles Glover and Mahala Davis, (MD) October 3, 1839, (MG) Theo. Boulware.

Richard Hays and Elizabeth Scholl, (MD) April 5, 1853, (MG) James Love.

Elijah Holt and Virginia Hisey, (MD) January 8, 1846, (UK) James Criswell.

Joseph Lenard and Sara Grant, (MD) December 10, 1826, (UK) Irvine Hockaday.

Frederick Nichols and Angeline Crump, (MD) January 11, 1832, (MG) Theo. Boulware.

Julius Blackly and Eliz. A. Payton, (MD) October 28, 1857.

Thomas Carlish and Polly Langley, (MD) July 31, 1843, (MG) Jas. Criswell.

James A. Dawson and Nanny Wise, (MD) August 10, 1842, (MG) Noah Flood.

John G. Ratekin and Mary Ewing, (MD) March 12, 1854, (MG) Theo. Boulware.

John Windland and ELizabeth Star, (MD) July 3, 1862, (UK) John Ferguson.

John Stanley and Martha Ann Pulliam, (MD) January 13, 1847, (UK) Wm. P. Nichols.

Samuel Saulsbury and Christianna Wilson, (MD) July 19, 1836, (JP) A. Northphen.

James Kemp and Sarah Kemp, (MD) August 19, 1851.

Zedekiah Hook and Mary West, (MD) July 21, 1842, (UK) J. Coons.

William H. Dorsey and Elizabeth Myers, (MD)January 28, 1841.

James A. G. Culberson and Sarah E. Selby, (MD) March 12, 1856.

Alexander Bleven and Emeline Zumwalt, (MD)November 21, 1833, (JP) Geo. B. Hopkins.

John Comer and Bettie Overton, (MD) January 11, 1866.

Mathew Ham and Elizabeth Gray, (MD) October 18, 1836, (JP)
A. Norflet.
William Boon and Maggie Moore, (MD) November 7, 1867.
Robert H. Colman and Sarah A. Moreland, (MD) February 5,
1845, (MG) Jacob Ligler.
Christopher B. Feribaugh and Rachel A. Galbreath, (MD) July
20, 1843, (UK) W. W. Robertson.
Matthew Hamilton and Roady Ann McKinney, (MD) May 26, 1857.
Joseph N. Holt and Amanda I. Randolph, (MD)October 31, 1860.
Graham Turner and Scithe Ann Meyers, (MD) May 14, 1836, (MG)
Theo. Boulware.
Joseph Baker and Sarah Ann Parks, (MD) March 21, 1863, Both
are of Boone County.
Richard H. Wise and Susan C. Clark, (MD) December 18, 1860.
Alexander Williams and Susan Wayne, (MD) December 19, 1848,
(JP) Geo. B. Hopkins.
William Boswell and Susan Harvey, (MD) March 7, 1848, (UK)
A. O. Hall.
John Doe and Martha A. Gee, (MD) August 31, 1852.
Frederic Elinch and Bertha Kaiser, (MD) August 14, 1867.
Thomas H. Renoe and Eliz. Jane Brandon, (MD) January 17,
1855.
Dr. Laurance Rootes and Sarah A. Whittingham, (MD) October
13, 1870.
Samuel S. Bugg and Sarah E. Logston, (MD) October 25, 1857.
Henry H. Degarnet and Mary Jane Criswell, (MD) October 13,
1857.
Abner T. Epperson and Amanda D. Oliver, (MD) November 3,
1868.
John Finley and Eliz. Jane Griffith, (MD)September 25, 1854.
Milton Jones and Nancy Wilkerson, (MD) November 24, 1854.
John Henry Knight and Mary C. Crooks, (MD) March 1, 1864.
Vincent Yates and Nancy Estes, (MD) September 9, 1827, (UK)
Cap. Vanquickenborne,
William Powel and Mary Fitzhu, (MD) November 12, 1846.
G. F. Burdet and Martha A. George, (MD) October 31, 1855.
Benjamin Cason and Ann E. Overton, (MD) January 29, 1840,
(MG) Theo. Boulware.
John W. Doubleday and Ann Maria Bradwell, (MD) October 26,
1847, (ED) W. W. Robertson.
Jesse Glover and Susan Williams, (MD) May 4, 1848.
James Harrison and Mary E. Maddox, (MD) November 8, 1848,
(MG) Noah Flood.
Isaac Miller and Nancy E. R. Davis, (MD) January 19, 1854.
John F. Nichols and Sarah Blythe, (MD) June 30, 1836, (UK)
David Doyle.
Stephen G. Boulware and Martha E. Boulware, (MD) May 11,
1848.
Samuel G. Collins and Elizabeth Kemp, (MD) March 27, 1856.

Asmuth Lath and Mary Bringwatt, (MD) August 30, 1866.
William I. Bills and Jane Morgan, (MD) December 14, 1858.
William Dunn and Sarah Patton, (MD) February 8, 1839, (UK)
John T. A. Henderson.
John S. Henderson and Mary Anne Allen, (MD) December 21,
1843, (UK) W. W. Robertson.
Allen Miller and Mariah Reed, (MD) October 22, 1828, (JP)
Wm. Martin.
John Nichols and Julia Lewis, (MD) October 10, 1839, (JP)
A. Noflet.
David Rouse and Malinda Ann Viers, (MD) October 28, 1845,
(UK) Thos. P. Stephens.
Thomas A. Scott and Juliam Pervis, (MD) May 15, 1845, (UK)
Oliver McEwan.
William Baly and Rebecca H. Baker, (MD) September 7, 1836,
(MG) Jas. M. Jameson.
John Yates and Ann Nichols, (MD) May 15, 1828, (MG) Theo.
Boulware.
Anderson Nunnelly and Mrs. Cyrithia Harrison, (MD) December
17, 1867.
Pinson J. Hendrix and Amanda Flood, (MD) November 6, 1863.
William M. Hatton and Cynthia Ellis, (MD September 22, 1842,
(UK) Geo. M. Effinger, Groom is from Boone County.
James T. Foster and Isabella Ellis, (MD) September 22, 1836,
(MG) R. L. McAfee.
Waddy Bagby and Margera Humphries, (MD) April 7, 1842, (MG)
Geo. Smith.
James M. Oliver and Sarah J. Jones, (MD) October 27, 1870.
John Fielding Martin and Lucretia Walter, (MD) May 1, 1868.
John W. Kelly and Nancy Ann Cason, (MD) March 11, 1855.
James Hamilton and Viema (sic) Wright, (MD) December 25,
1851.
Leonard Gurley and Salome Schueller, (MD) May 17, 1867.
Otho McCrackin and Mary M. McFarland, (MD) April 14, 1857.
Henry Neil and Sally A. Dozier, (MD) 1861, Groom is from
Audrain County.
Joseph G. Baker and Miss Almyre Taylor, (MD) ?, (UK) Tho. P.
Stephens.
Thomas Boles and Louisa Syms, (MD) January 27, 1848, (MG)
Noah Flood.
Ebenezer Corby and Harriet Smoot, (MD September 14, 1865,
(JP) Wm. B. Tucker, Groom is from Brunswick, Mo.
Lewis Hilborn and Sarah Zumwalt, (MD) May 17, 1849, (JP) C.
A. Ming.
James D. McGary and Louisa H. Bryan, (MD) November 18, 1860.
Elijah Creed and Rachel Miller, (MD) November 28, 1870.
Pearre (sic) L. Dye and Elizabeth Clemons, (MD) October 26,
1842, (MG) Oliver McEwen, Groom is from St. Louis County.
John Lewis and Jemima Thompson, (MD) April 10, 1858.

70

John H. Barry and Sallie A. Stephens, (MD) May 16, 1866,
    (MG) H. Craig, Groom is from Boone County.
Edward H. Bond and Eliz. G. Hughes, (MD) July 20, 1837, (MG)
    Jas. Suggett.
William Bowen and Matilda Willett, (MD) June 16, 1870.
John J. Bradley and Nancy Scott, (MD) April 30, 1846, (MG)
    Wm. N. Jepo.
John Broadwater and Caroline E. Jackson, (MD) February 28,
    1844, (UK) Richard G. Janes.
Henry N. Ewing and Carrie M. Martin, (MD) March 22, 1860.
William H. Fisher and Julia Ann Snell, (MD) May 24, 1841,
    (MG) J. L. Yantis.
Benjamin Nale and Ann Walker, (MD) November 14, 1830, (MG)
    William Coats.
George M. Waters and Mattie Dudley, (MD) November 25, 1858.
William T. Barker and Mary S. Sharp, (MD) March 11, 1868,
    (UK) N. L. Fish.
James P. Covington and Missouri C. Allen, (MD)April 5, 1870.
John W. Hensley and Lucy A. Sims, (MD) January 29, 1867,
    Groom is from Jackson County and the Bride is from Au-
    drain County.
Calvin Jomer and Nancy Davis, (MD) January 5, 1865, (MG) R.
    H. Hord.
Moses Lewis and Delilah Jamison, (MD) March 7, 1833, (UK)
    Horace Sheeley.
Richard Runols and Rachel Zummalt, (MD) April 24, 1823, (JP)
    George King.
David T. Boaz and Polly Brown, (MD) May 22, 1830, (MG) Theo.
    Boulware.
Joseph G. Crain and Martha Coward, (MD) December 13, 1852,
    (MG) H. J. Speed, Groom is from Williamsburg, Mo and the
    Bride is from Montgomery County.
Benjamin Estill and Mary McCall, (MD) November 26, 1858.
George W. Gravit and Catharine Filtrighorger, (MD) May 25,
    1860.
Thedore L. Harvey and C. B. Dyer, (MD) January 21, 1863.
Jeremiah Nichols and Susan J. Dawson, (MD) January 23, 1867.
Samuel Rohrer and M. Booker, (MD) May 17, 1853, Groom is
    from Osage County, Mo.
Daniel R. Boulware and Martha P. Smith, (MD) August 8, 1838,
    (MG) J. L. Yantis.
Joseph S. Craig and Mary Jones, (MD) April 9, 1856.
Andrew Jordan and Barberry A. Straw, (MD) January 14, 1857.
I. M. B. Neill and Evelin T. Nichols, (MD) April 14, 1858.
Shelton Wilkerson and Luisa W. Martin, (MD) February 16,
    1860.
Hugh L. Williams and Mary F. Hamilton, (MD) September 14,
    1856.
Daniel Baits and Mrs. M.A.B. Whyte, (MD) December 15, 1858.

Thomas Gylmare and Charlotte Coons, (MD) October 20, 1831.
Isaac H. Johnson and Jane Amanda Wilson, (MD) November 21,
1865, (UK) Ed. P. Cowan.
William D. Proctor and Martha M. Miller, (MD) November 12,
1840, (MG) J. L. Yantis.
B. S. Bigbee and Cynthia J. Renoe, (MD) December 15, 1853.
Thomas F. Brown and Magdalene W. Faber, (MD) November 13,
1866.
Wm. Joseph Buchanan and Samantha E. Clanton, (MD) July 31,
1860, Groom is from Linn County.
Robert A. Caldwell and Mary A. Holman, (MD) July 25, 1838,
(UK) R. L. McAfee.
John Carrington and Eliz. T. Randolph, (MD) December 21,
1837, (MG) Absalom Rice.
Wesley A. Crutchfield and Nancy H. Miller, (MD) October 27,
1859.
Samuel Ewens and Maria L. Hopkins, (MD) February 22, 1844,
(MG) Absalom Rice.
James M. Hall and Sarah E. Sanders, (MD) February 23, 1868.
James Hart and Nancy Ferguson, (MD) April 20, 1837, (UK)
Condley Smith.
John Kennon and Julia Sorrow, (MD) March 25, 1852.
Payton Langley and Matilda G. Langley, (MD) June 7, 1864,
(UK) S. M. Harrison.
Joshua Myers and Mary Ann Brooks, (MD) January 4, 1866.
Joseph Sloan and Irena Wilcockson, (MD) April 11, 1833, (JP)
Horace Sheley.
Erm (sic) J. Bethe and Abegail Stutz, (MD)September 11,1844,
(JP) Jos. T. Bryan.
James M. Davis and Alice Crigler, (MD) October 31, 1869,
Bride is from Audrain County.
John G. Douglass and Nannie A. Dudley, (MD) October 1, 1862.
Thomas J. Ferguson and Nancy Lewis Moore, (MD) February 14,
1833, (UK) Wm. W. Redman.
Edward Foster and Mary Ann F. Stewart, (MD) April 30, 1857.
James S. Gilbert and Caroline Read, (MD) January 30, 1851,
(MG) Noah Flood.
Jarret T. Harris and Mary Wilburn, (MD) December 3, 1840,
(UK) WM. B. Douglass, Groom is from Montgomery County.
William Blackburn and Mary A. Rich, (MD)July 29, 1869, Groom
is from Jefferson City.
Stephen Craghead and Nancy Blount, (MD) March 11, 1834, (MG)
Wm. W. Redman.
Charles Kreelow and Mrs. Sarah Wheeler, (MD) July 26, 1870.
David Henderson Leper and Sophia Race, (MD)January 28, 1841,
(UK) John Young.
Abraham Norflett and Margaret Campbell, (MD)August 16, 1832,
(UK) Geo. W. Teason.
Chas. M. Samuels and Eliz. F. Hart, (MD) December 6, 1854.

Levi O. Sabin and Mary Tennison, (MD) December 7, 1870.

William Bitner and Mrs. Amanda Bratton, (MD) February 23, 1868.

William Gordan and Livisa Meur, (MD) February 8, 1838, (JP) Arthur Neill.

William P. Greer and Lucy Jones, (MD) December 24, 1865.

R. F. Gregory and R. O. Oliver, (MD) February 26, 1857.

William S. Knight and Mary C. Crooks, (MD), March 1, 1864.

Robert P. Mosley and Addie Goff, (MD) December 2, 1869.

Jeremiah D. Ray and Nancy J. Baker, (MD) November 13, 1869, (JP) J. J. Railey.

Samuel S. Rossen and Sarah J. Hiller, (MD)December 25, 1860.

Isaac N. Sitton and S. J. Fletcher, (MD) September 22, 1870, (UK) E. R. Childers.

Thomas Baker and Ann Adair, (MD) January 10, 1833, (UK) Tho. P. Stephens.

Samuel M. Stokes and Carolyne Jeters, (MD) September 26, 1869, (UK) John E. Adkerson.

Jeff C. Thatcher and Mary B. Griffith, (MD) November 14, 1844, (MG) L. J. Simpson.

John Blunckall and Mary Hamblin, (MD) September 8, 1835, (UK) Jacob Ham.

James M. Bridges and Caroline Miller, (MD) August 28, 1848, Groom is from Osage County.

Aaron George and Julian Potter, (MD) January 8, 1857.

Henry L. Gray and Martha Gray, (MD) February 24, 1842, (JP) Robert Brandon.

Benjamin F. Hapey and Catharine Murphy, (MD) March 25, 1858.

Jesse C. Henderson and Nancy Hughart, (MD) April 5, 1827, (UK) James Henderson.

John M. Kelsoe and Mary F. Thomas F. Thomas, (MD) November 25, 1848, (MG) Noah Flood.

Philip T. Moore and Ray Board, (MD) September 3, 1857.

Robert Nichols and Mary Ann Ham, (MD) December 21, 1854, Groom is from Boone County.

Benjamin F. Overton and Juliett S. James, (MD)July 28, 1858.

David Parmer and Sarah Ann Hutchinson, (MD)October 28, 1847, (MG) R. S. Symington.

Henry C. Peterman and Elizabeth Pondexter, (MD)May 12, 1869.

John Scott and Catharine Dunn, (MD) April 25, 1846, (MG) Rich Bona.

Moses Smart and Pamelia Smart, (MD) November 28, 1847, (MG) Absalom Rice.

James Smith and Mary Ann Neal, (MD) July 14, 1847, (JP) Wm. J. Gilman.

Joseph B. Phillips and Eliza W. Allen, (MD)January 21, 1858.

Robert Wily and Margaret White, (MD) March 3, 1852.

Phillip Bode and Willmena Hans, (MD) August 11, 1861.

Elija Helm and Nancy G. Proctor, (MD) October 25, 1860.

73

William Kubajak and Mary Julia Ladman, (MD) December 26, 1864.

George M. Moss and Sarah J. Truitt, (MD) April 19, 1862.

John W. Blunt and Sintha Hays, (MD) September 13, 1838, (MG) John T. A. Henderson.

Jas. Madison Boone and Mary McMurty, (MD) April 7, 1831, (JP) Enoch Fruit.

William Boyes and Margaret A. Barry, (MD) September 8, 1831, (JP) John K. Barry.

Felix Briant and Maxey Boone, (MD) May 3, 1832, (MG) William Coats.

Robert S. Bruner and Ann Eliz. Nevins, (MD) September 30, 1858.

Robert Bryant and Galena Davis, (MD) February 22, 1844, (MG) Jacob Coons.

John T. Daily and Eliza Driscall, (MD) October 14, 1846, (JP) John A. Burt.

James Davis and Susan M. Bagby, (MD) January 7, 1841, (UK) R. O. Blaker.

William H. Gilmore and Moresey W. Baker, (MD) September 15, 1863.

Philip Love and Susan Love, (MD) January 6, 1854.

William T. Miller and Nancy Crowson, (MD) February 12, 1868, (MG) Noah Flood.

Eli Overfelt and Sarah Parker, (MD) November 18, 1833, (UK) Irvine O. Hockaday.

John Pratt and Amy Baker, (MD) January 11, 1821, (MG) Robert Baker.

William Simpson and Mary Harvey, (MD) March 1, 1867, (MG) C. R. Pittman.

George Smith and Susan Thomas, (MD) April 15, 1846, (MG) A. Rice.

Peter K. Straw and Mrs. Susan Plummer, (MD) November 20, 1853, (MG) H. Brown.

William Wilkerson and Cynthian Coons, (MD) August 8, 1846, (UK) Jacob Coons.

Robert Williams and Francis May, (MD) November 30, 1824, (UK) Felix Brown.

Thomas Winn and Roxalina Day, (MD) August 25, 1839, (UK) Joseph T. Bryan.

Turley Cheatham and Emily Fort, (MD) April 15, 1839, (MG) Jacob Coons.

Aaron J. Couts and Eliz. Lee Stephenson, (MD) January 18, 1855, Groom is from Boone County.

Henry Dinkman and Flora Thomas, (MD) November 6, 1862.

J. A. Henley and L. R. Hobson, (MD) December 22, 1868, (MG) George W. Penn.

Hal S. Mosby and Ermin A. Fullilove, (MD) July 21, 1859.

Chas. M. Peck and Susan E. Rodgers, (MD) August 16, 1855.

Robert Bogges and Lucrecy (sic) Jane Miller, (MD) December
8, 1832, (JP) J. W. Johnston.
R. T. Bond and Hannah McIlhaney, (MD) February 21, 1867,
(MG) George Smith, Both Groom and Bride are from Mont-
gomery County.
Col. John Boyd and Mary Ann Scott, (MD)April 15, 1828, (MG)
D. M. Kirkpatrick.
William Brockman and Agnes Hill, (MD) April 23, 1839, (MG)
Theo. Boulware.
James M. Bruner and Evaline Duncan, (MD) August 31, 1848,
(ED) Jacob Coons.
Colman Bullard and Fanny Bowen, (MD) June 28, 1847, (ED)
Jacob Coons.
William Hook and Nancy Newland, (MD) January 7, 1841, (MG)
J. L. Yantis.
Elihu Jones and Sarah Humphreys, (MD) September 22, 1869.
James Miller and Elizabeth Arthur, (MD) October 6, 1844,
(ED) Jacob Coons.
Isaac Smith and Keren H. Manner, (MD) January 14, 1847, (UK)
Ninian Ridgway.
Ashley Holt and Mary Frances Kirby, (MD) August 7, 1845,
(UK) R. L. McAfee.
R. A. Craig and Amanda Hensly, (MD) January 27, 1848.
Lewis French and Louisa Simpson, (MD) August 1, 1822, (JP)
Enoch Fruit.
Williard F. Harris and Mollie A. McCracken, (MD) January 4,
1870.
Albert G. Hubbard and Francis M. Austin, (MD) March 18,
1835, (MG) Theo. Boulware.
Singleton Sheley and Jane Christwell, (MD)February 18, 1834,
(UK) Jas. Suggett.
William S. Lambert and Nancy Ellen Fossee, (MD) March 26,
1856.
James M. Martin and Frances Callaway, (MD) July 3, 1847,
(UK) William J. Gilman.
Thomas Nevins and Kitty Randolph, (MD) September 26, 1835,
(UK) John T. A. Henderson.
John Boswell and Julia Ann Penn, (MD) April 25, 1860.
Stephen Foy and Hester A. Snethin, (MD) May 8, 1865.
Samuel M. Old and Elizabeth Nichols, (MD) May 26, 1847, (JP)
Chas. A. Ming.
Walter A. Robinson and Rachel E. Patterson, (MD) February 8,
1865, (MG) H. H. Craig.
Augustus Pickenny and Sarah Ann Roy, (MD) May 21m 1863, (UK)
Thos. J. Ferguson.
James Thomas and Didmay (sic) Pawley, (MD) October 18, 1849.
Robert R. Vivion and Eliz. J. Miller, (MD) May 27, 1858.
William Willing and Mary F. Fletcher, (MD) October 16, 1870.
James Rice and Mary Buckner, (MD) February 23, 1854.

Thomas J. Blumhall and Nancy E. Bentley, (MD) December 1, 1870.

Abraham Jimison and Mrs. Nancy Nichols, (MD) February 3, 1842, (UK) Berryman Wren.

George T. Johnson and Emeline Vier, (MD) October 25, 1849, (UK) Elijah E. Christman.

Samuel Nesbit and Polly Ann Meredith, (MD) June 14, 1838, (MG) Jacob Coons.

Samuel Nichols and Eliz. B. Moon, (MD) June 21, 1853, (UK) Thomas B. Haley.

Thomas Pratt and Lucinda Patty, (MD) September 19, 1839, (MG) Jabez Ham.

Calvin Pugh and Susan Galwith, (MD) March 16, 1854.

John Henry Boeje and Catherine Dickkoff, (MD) August 28, 1855.

William Musgrove and Lydia Culbertson, (MD) January 23, 1851.

Charles Cox and Nancy A. Freeman, (MD) December 11, 1856.

Thomas Duncan and Kitty Carr, (MD) October 31, 1842, (MG) Joseph Coons, Groom is from Platte City.

Robert M. Kemp and Nancy P. Craghead, (MD) January 22, 1839, (MG) Theo. Boulware.

William Markel and Alea Gingry (sic), (MD) March 10, 1870, (UK) Thos. W. Worley.

William H. Paw and Elizabeth Davis, (MD) March 25, 1845, (MG) Jacob Ligler.

William N. Peters and Harriet H. Horain, (MD) November 4, 1849.

Alexander Richardson and Lucy J. Shaw, (MD) September 27, 1837, (MG) Theo. Boulware.

Macky Smith and Mary Cheatham, (MD) October 10, 1833, (MG) Theo. Boulware.

Joshua Wade and Cynthia Collins, (MD) June 6, 1862, (UK) John R. Ferguson.

William H. Curtis and Nancy Jane Whaley, (MD) April 22, 1858.

Onslow Duncan and Julia Broadwater, (MD) September 14, 1843, (MG) James Love.

John Alfred Fentesche and S. McClelland Baker, (MD) September 12, 1839, (ED) M. P. Wells.

Thomas Jackson and Cor-- Hoalt, (MD) May 4, ----.

Wm. N. Peters and Elvira Jones, (MD) May 6, 1847, (UK) Wm. B. Douglas.

John J. Raymond and Margaret M. Kimbrough, (MD) October 16, 1860, Groom is from Clay County.

Allen Reynolds and Polly B. Martin, (MD) June 2, 1833, (UK) Robt. A. Younger.

Arthur C. Robinson and Kansas Bradford, (MD) December 19, 1839, (UK) Joseph T. Bryan.

John H. Sleeth and Louisa F..Johnson, (MD) August 16, 1863.

D. W. Snyder and K. L. Scott, (MD) May 27, 1860.

John Blythe and Polly Ridgway, (MD) February 16, 1854,Groom
is from Boone County.
Thomas B. Bradley and Mrs. Ann Craig, (MD) May 27, 1852,
(MG) G. D. Tolls.
William Derrit and Mrs. Magdaline Powell, (MD) October 23,
1842.
Joshua Ferguson and E. A. D. Paulsel, (MD) January 11, 1854.
(MG) H. Brown.
William C. Ham and Louisa Hickerson, (MD) February 6, 1857.
William Hans and Gertrude Van Straaten, (MD) March 25, 1860.
Henry Turner and Mary Hook, (MD) August 12, 1830, (UK) David
Kirpatrick.
James Wilfley and Elizabeth Kelso, (MD) August 19, 1830,
(JP) William Crain.
Marion Sweetzier and Margaret Anderson, (MD) November 12,
1863, Groom is from Boone County.
William Tate and Nancy Lane, (MD) May 21, 1856.
George W. Pitzer and Annie H. Bennett, (MD) November 10,
(MG) R. L. McAfee, Groom is from Pike County.
Owen Smith and Eliza P. Pace, (MD) June 16, 1836, (UK) John
F. Young.
Thomas Sloan and Sally Sherman, (MD) October 13, 1825, (UK)
Christopher Zumwalt.
John W. Ricketts and Frances Rodman, (MD) October 28, 1852,
(MG) Jacob Coons.
Charles W. Pratt and Sarah Vaughn, (MD) March --, 1854.
Thomas Nichols and Amanda Lewis, (MD) February 20, 1838,
(JP) A. Northphen.
Thomas McIntosh and Mary Penn, (MD) December 29, 1853, Groom
is from Montgomery County.
Geo. P. McCredie and Sarah Ann McKinney, (MD) October 12,
1830, (MG) Theo. Boulware.
James Langley and Matilda Hayner, (MD) January 22, 1824,
(UK) Jonathan Holliway.
Nathan C. Kouns and Bledsoe McRinney, (MD) October 18, 1859.
John H. Kilgore and Pamela D. Kilgore, (MD) February 25,
1836, (MG) Geo. L. Smith.
Richard Jordan and Sally Gill, (MD) October 29, 1867, Groom
is from Cole County.
John Frazier and Elizabeth Harrison, (MD)May 22, 1850, Groom
is from Jefferson City and Bride is from Boone County.
George F. Foster and Mrs. Harriet Ferguson, (MD) January 4,
1853, (UK) W. M. Woods.
John Evans and Eliz. Ming, (MD) April 2, 1846, (UK) Franklin
Jenkins.
David B. Dixon and Beveline R. Crawford, (MD)August 2, 1839,
(MG) Theo. Boulware.
John Brown and Jane H. Robinson, (MD) April 5, 1849, (ED) W.
W. Robertson.

William Burns and Miss C. H. Throckmarton, (MD) December 24, 1835, (UK) Robert A. Younger.

Jas. Vinson Callaway and Susan Kemp, (MD) February 9, 1832, (MG) Wm. Coats.

Christopher Chaney and Sallie Ferguson, (MD) June 24, 1863, (MG) Geo. W. Penn.

Isaac Child and J. R. Kellogg, (MD) October 9, 1862, Groom is from Dyersburg, Tennessee and the Bride is from Janesville, Wis.

Oliver Conningham and Hannah Ordway, (MD) October 31, 1843.

James F. Crockett and Susan Love, (MD) October 6, 1857.

Elisha Davis and Nancy Covington, (MD) January 19, 1840, (JP) H. S. Tunney.

David D. Finley and Belinda E. Johnson, (MD) February 21, 1869, (MG) Levi Shelby.

W. W. Gardner and Hannah McClaskey, (MD) August 20, 1845, (MG) Theo. Boulware.

Mastin Harris and Rachel Jane Akens, (MD) June 9, 1835, (MG) (MG) Wm. Coats.

Ely Shaon (sic) and Jane Seals, (MD) May 27, 1841, (UK) R. A. Ramsey.

William B. Miller and Minerva McClure, (MD)October 31, 1844, (MG) Jacob Lighter.

George Mires and Malinda MacDaniel, (MD) August 20, 1835, (MG) Jabez Ham.

Stephen Pugh and Rachel Sheets, (MD) November 13, 1862, (MG) John D. Gregory.

Nathan G. Chalfant and Melcena T. Lynes, (MD) February 18, 1858.

William Fish and Frances Bright, (MD) September 4, 1867.

Joseph Henderson and Lou A. McKamey, (MD) December 24, 1868, (MG) W. W. Trimble.

James Pemberton and Mildred Johnson, (MD) December 28, 1853.

Aaron Richardson and Catharine Clatterbuck, (MD) January 9, 1851, (UK) Zachariah Jones.

Sylvester J. Sailor and Lemina A. Larch, (MD) April 2, 1861, Groom is from Montgomery County.

David Smith and Mary Ann Nicholson, (MD) July 26, 1842, (UK) Geo. B. Hopkins.

Martin Baker and May Layson, (MD) May 22, 1854, (ED) D. Coulter.

Richard C. Tate and Elizabeth Hamblin, (MD)October 17, 1839, (UK) Joseph Scholl.

James Lawrence and Margaret Vaunter, (MD)September 14, 1840, (MG) Noah Flood.

James Kimbrough and Jane Price, (MD) December 17, 1846, (UK) Z. N. Roberts.

John D. Cason and Judy F. Hawkins, (MD) June 19, 1864.

Samuel G. Debo and Sarah Ann Martin, (MD) September 1, 1859.

Frederick Hess and Elizabeth Hess, (MD) September 10, 1848,
(ED) M. P. Wills.
John W. Hord and Annie F. Roots, (MD) October 10, 1866, (MG)
G. Fenton.
Greenbury C. Johnston and Mary C. Carter, (MD) January 29,
1851.
Franklin Peters and Catharine Miller, (MD) April 10, 1856.
Hezekiah Carlton and Judy T. Henshaw, (MD) May 6, 1866.
Henry Chilton and Mahala Edwards, (MD) March 29, 1869.
Madison Crawford and Teletha C. Wilson, (MD) April 14, 1842,
(MG) Noah Flood.
James Hereford and Rosy Vincent, (MD)May 24, 1832, (UK) Tho.
Stephens.
Alfred Petty and Synthia Howard, (MD) May 15, 1831, (JP)
John K. Barry.
Joseph Brandenburg and Amanda J. Hill, (MD) September 24,
1846, (JP) W. J. Gilman.
John L. Broadwater and Margaret Trimble, (MD) September 14,
1847.
William G. Brown and Mary Jane Martin, (MD) July 29, 1841,
(UK) Benjamin Wren, Groom is from Boone County.
Leroy Clatterbuck and Mary Gray, (MD) April 22, 1831, (MG)
Jas. Suggett.
James H. Comer and Nancy E. Overton,(MD) December 22, 1863,
(UK) John M. Robinson.
John Fant and Cassie Scott, (MD) October 25, 1865, (UK)
Squire Horde.
William Fowler and Lucinda Williams, (MD) December 25, 1844,
(MG) William Saughan.
David Harris and Mary McKinney, (MD) October 9, 1850, (JP)
Wm. J. Gilman.
John Hinskafer and Mary Jane Hamilton, (MD) September 30,
1853.
Stephen Homestead and Thirza J. Bell, (MD) March 5, 1867.
Richard S. Hornbuckle and Elvira Smart, (MD)October 1, 1838,
(UK) Milton Cleveland.
Jesse King and Nannie S. Davis, (MD) August 13, 1860.
Seth Martin and Mrs. Rhoda Potter, (MD) May 7, 1850, (MG)
Oliver McEwen.
James E. McCall and Angelina Gilbert, (MD) November 7, 1839,
(MG) Jabez Ham.
Jesse McKinney and Louisa V. Laurenia, (MD) December 12,
1861.
William B. Miller and Bathsheba Ewing, (MD) November 22,
1842, (MG) Joseph Coons.
William B. Moss and Nancy Jane Craig, (MD)December 28, 1859,
Groom is from St. Louis.
John H. Wilkerson and Eliz. Ann Nevins, (MD) February 26,
1862.

Lock Stephens and Nancy Renfro, (MD)April 5, 1834, (UK) Tho.
Stephens.

James S. Stevens and Amelia Hockaday, (MD) February 6, 1844,
(MG) Isaac Jones, Groom is from Boone County.

James W. Terrell and Araminta S. Bradley, (MD) May 23, 1861,
Groom is from Tarrunt (sic) County, Texas.

William B. Stone and Eliz. Va. Gray, (MD) August 10, 1837,
(UK) Thomas M. Allen.

Stephen Conger and Lucy Jane Gordon, (MD) March 8, 1835,
(MG) Jas. Suggett.

Nathan M. Gardner and Rachel Ann Smith, (MD)August 22, 1863,
(MG) A. C. McDonald, Groom is from Dade County.

Dennis M. Garvin and Mary Poindexter, (MD) November 1, 1850,
(MG) Theo. Boulware.

Timothy Holt and Nancy J. Gordon, (MD) January 14, 1829,
(UK) James Henderson.

Daniel Scroghem (sic) and Parmelia Beaven, (MD) November 3,
1842, (UK) Joseph Coons.

Amer (sic) Leopard and Nancy Jane Clatterbuck, (MD) June 4,
1862.

Bently Lewis and Nancy Garret, (MD) April 17, 1851, Groom is
from Montgomery County.

William McClure and Eliz. M. McClure, (MD) April 16, 1833,
(MG) Theo. Boulware.

James Moad and Sally Jane Stephens, (MD) November 2, 1865,
(UK) L. W. Stephens.

William M. Palmer and Sarah E. Hunter, (MD) December 23,
1858, (UK) S. T. McNeiley.

Thomas Terry and Nancy Jane Ewing, (MD) April 11, 1867,
(UK) John O. White

John Thatcher and Ann Hase, (MD) December 18, 1828, (MG)
Theo. Boulware.

Delona Willingham and Malinda Winscott, (MD)June 23, 1831,
(UK) James Barnes.

Eli M. Bass and Caroline M. Dozier, (MD) September 12, 1849,
(UK) A. E. Sears.

William T. Gilbert and M. D. Holland, (MD) May 31, 1870.

William E. Hale and Pocohontas Maddox, (MD) December 10,
1868, (UK) Wm. V. Douglass.

John Houston and Permelia Branum, (MD) September 3, 1829,
(UK) Wm. P. Cochran.

Geo. W. Kemp and Sarah Craghead, (MD) May 12, 1841, (MG) J.
L. Yantis.

William H. McKamey and Angelina Scott, (MD) June 17, 1836,
(MG) R. L. McAfee.

John Price and Louisa A. Leper, (MD) September 10, 1846,
(ED) W. W. Robertson.

William B. Baker and Pamela Lewis, (MD) December 16, 1836,
(JP) Andrew Alexander.

John W. Brandenburg and Elizabeth Harvey, (MD)July 25, 1867.
Amazon Collins and Isora Colbreath, (MD) February 2, 1870,
(MG) Charles Fuller.
Will H. Davidson and Mary A. Simpson, (MD) April 25, 1867.
William H. Dorsey and Jane Nevins, (MD) July 2, 1829, (UK)
David Kirkpatrick.
John T. Harrison and Mary Ann Baker, (MD) August 22, 1865,
(MG) John F. Cowan.
Francis M. Powel and Nancy J. Yancy, (MD) October 25, 1866.
George J. Key and Martha L. Hiller, (MD) December 18, 1860.
John William Wilson and Julia H. Emmons, (MD) January 21,
1869.
Joseph E. Rutherford and Elvina Miller, (MD) January 14,
1848.
Rev. George Penn and Mary A. Rennolds, (MD) April 2, 1861.
George D. Miller and Annie Baker, (MD) January 6, 1859.
Isaac Branham and Amanda Bailey, (MD) February 23, 1832,
(MG) Theo. Boulware.
John F. Jones and Mary A. Robison, (MD) August 27, 1867.
Seaton Owen and Mrs. Susan Hanna, (MD) October 24, 1864.
John G. Baynham and Elizabeth Jane Glendy, (MD) August 7,
1862, (MG) R. H. Baldwin.
William Ewing and Susy Ann Maupin, (MD) March 6, 1845,
(MG) Absalom Rice,
John Harris and Rhody Townson, (MD) July 23, 1835, (MG) Wm.
Duncan.
Joseph Darris Lorton and Nancy Williams, (MD September 10,
1835, (JP) John K. Barny.
Thomas A. McIntire and Sarah C. Sayers, (MD)August 29, 1865.
John Mead and Mintey Punnels, (MD) August 15, 1833, (JP)
Arthur Neill.
Banton G. Boone and Eliz. Copher Boone, (MD) June 26, 1828,
(MG) Jabez Ham.
Frank Finklang and Louisa Fahlbush, (MD) March 19, 1867.
Robert B. Price and Evelin I. Hockaday, (MD) May 1, 1860.
Charles A. Wood and Rebecca Ann McCowan, (MD) May 1, 1833,
(UK) Zacariah Jones.
William Dudley and Manerva Callaway, (MD) February 15, 1838,
(MG) Jabez Ham.
Joseph Fisher and Mary Criaghead, (MD) November 6, 1827,
(UK) David M. Kirkpatrick.
George Hatcher and Rebbecca Ann McClintic, (MD) February 18,
1863, (MG) Horace Brown.
John McDonald and Sarah Sloan, (MD) February 7, 1850.
William T. Whittington and Susan I. Murphy, (MD) October 31,
1867.
Robert P. Olde and Nancy Cooner, (MD) November 18, 1846,
(JP) Chas. A. Ming.
A. A. Holland and Sallie L. Dudley, (MD) December 20, 1870.

Asa Branson and Eliz. Ann Craig, (MD) February 16, 1860.
Calvin McMurty and Joicy M. Davis, (MD) August 13, 1846,
    (UK) John Gano.
--- Kibler and Mary Armstrong, (MD)April 4, 1828, (MG) Theo.
    Boulware.
Dr. Wm. W. McFarland and Mary E. Thurmond, (MD) November 5,
    1867.
Riley Sartor and Hinna Christ, (MD)May 13, 1870, (UK)Rudolph
    Shide.
Thomas Brooks and Isabel Fisher, (MD) November 2, 1843, (MG)
    James Suggett.
John E. Callaway and Elizabeth Taylor, (MD) May 26, 1867.
William Dudley and Laurian Coats, (MD) January 12, 1832,
    (MG) William Coats.
R. Jones and Mrs. Jane Scott, (MD) December 3, 1863.
Hamilton H. McGary and Rosetta H. Ewing, (MD) June 25, 1863.
Charles F. Rigg and Sophronia M. Maughs, (MD) April 12,
    1853, (MG) Daniel Penny, Groom is from Montgomery County.
Wm. Forbes Bristo and Anna Marie Swartwood, (MD)May 8, 1870.
Henry C. Douglass and Virginia F. Bowman, (MD April 7, 1867,
    (UK) Isaiah O. Craighead.
Seton O. Jordan and Kitty Hazelrigg, (MD) November 28, 1852,
    (JP) J. K. Allen.
William A. Rothwell and Sally C. Rothwell, (MD) April 3,
    1856.
Henry Scott and Elizabeth Kitchmings, (MD) March 27, 1851.
Albert Willet and Susan Emily Fletcher, (MD) January 17,
    1867.
Geo. Hibberts and Gladys Robinson, (MD) April 6, 1848, (UK)
    W. B. Douglass.
William G. Moore and Eliz. H. Long, (MD) May 1, 1838, (UK)
    Theo. M. Allen.
Reason Ridgway and Harriett Reede, (MD) September 17, 1835,
    (MG) William Duncan.
Jas. Stephens and Nancy Slow, (MD) 1840.
Geo. Thos. Cook and Lucy Ann Hockaday, (MD) January 3, 1868.
jacob Detweiler and Mary E. Gibson, (MD) September 4, 1855.
John Forbes and Rachel McDaniel, (MD) January 4, 1844, (JP)
    Chas. A. Ming.
Peter H. Kemp and Mollie E. Dudley, (MD) November 11, 1863.
M. S. Young and Dulcena Smart, (MD) September 27, 1854,
    Groom is from Audrain County.
Stephen Boulware and Mary Ratican, (MD)April 29, 1835, (MG)
    Jas. Suggett.
Frederick Duncan and Elizabeth Gibson, (MD)January 24, 1839,
    (MG) Jas. Love.
William C. Hawkins and Mary C. Overton, (MD) January 29,
    1840, (MG) Theo. Boulware.
W. F. May and Mary J. Riggs, (MD) July 11, 1870.

Robert M. McClanahan and Mary Jane West, (MD) June 3, 1862,
(MG) D. Coulter.

Thomas H. Culbertson and Sarah A. Meridith, (MD) February
25, 1858.

William H. Dunavant and Amanda J. Hyton, (MD) January 6,
1858.

Andrew Roy and Temperance Shivers, (MD) September 15, 1831,
(UK) George Bartley.

Fountain T. Letcher and Mary E. Wilson, (MD) March 7, 1846.

Henry Davis and Sarah E. Peyton, (MD) January 21, 1852, (MG)
Noah Flood.

Theodore Freize and Eliza Kemp, (MD) May 6, 1857.

Telmachus Harvie and Harriet Crowson, (MD) April 10, 1864,
(PM) Home of Richard Crowson.

Andrew J. Martin and Martha O'Daniel, (MD) November 8, 1857.

James T. Stewart and Laura A. O. Kemp, (MD) August 21, 1856.

D. W. S. Crump and Mary Love, (MD) December 5, 1831, (JP)
Enoch Fruit.

Alfred L. Brashear and Rosa Ames, (MD) April 2, 1860.

Nelson Cook and Lizzie Loyd, (MD) April 14, 1852, (MG) M. M.
Modisit (sic), Groom is from Virginia.

Hambleton Harris and Martha Day, (MD) August 9, 1847, (MG)
Absalom Rice.

Edward Lawrence and Evey Murdock, (MD) June 21, 1839, (MG)
Absalom Rice.

James M. McGhee and Rebecca J. Miller, (MD)January 13, 1869.

Augustus Moore and Catharine Matier, (MD)September 22, 1831,
(UK) David Kirkpatrick.

H. E. Stevens and Ann Ferreo, (MD) April 23, 1862.

Henry Barger and Phoebe Wilfley, (MD) February 26, 1826,
(JP) Wm. Barger, Groom is from Boone County.

William A. Bratton and Idy Wade, (MD) January 26, 1854, (UK)
Elijah E. Christman, Groom is from Boone County.

Moses B. Craft and Ann E. Adcock, (MD) July 15, 1846, (ED)
Jacob Coons.

Elijah Foster and Elizabeth Powell, (MD) July 12, 1827, (UK)
James Henderson.

Harvey Newsom and Jemina L. Caldwell, (MD) August 11, 1842,
(MG) John Young.

Henry W. Stambaugh and Catharine A. Barrick, (MD) February
17, 1868.

John Nicken and Rebeka Thoroughman, (MD January 31, 1850,
(UK) F. Jenkins, Groom is from Madsen (sic) County.

Shelton A. Oliver and S. Bishop, (MD) November 6, 1850,
Groom is from Montgomery County.

Joseph W. Jamison and Nancy C. Maupin, (MD) September 6,
1849, (UK) P. H. Steinberger.

Newton Hockensmith and Jennie Watson, (MD) November 1, 1866.

M. J. Feel and Miss J. Mallory, (MD) October 13, 1867.

83

Henry Martin and Ogden E. Martin, (MD) December 25, 1867, (MG) S. Beauchamp.

Rice F. Stuart and Frances Nichols, (MD) November 15, 1859, (JP) W. J. Jackson.

Presly E. Thomas and Sarah Galbreath, (MD) November 2, 1854.

John Wadley and Sophiah Doyel, (MD) December 7, 1828, (JP) Robert Davis.

Josiah Burgett and Mary Zumwalt, (MD) February 5, 1846, (JP) Chas. A. Ming.

John C. Carawell and Eliz. S. Young, (MD) December 28, 1862.

Lienden Fowler and Sarah Osten, (MD) January 19, 1832, (UR) David Kirkpatrick, Bride if from Boone County.

Larkin Craig and Anne Ficklin, (MD) June 7, 1831, (MG) Theo. Boulware.

Wm. J. Herring and Rebecca Ann Knight, (MD) September 14, 1848, (MG) Noah Flood.

David C. Cheatham and Martha Ratekin, (MD) July 4, 1838, (MG) Absalom Rice.

Robert S. Mosely and Susan Bagby, (MD) January 20, 1859.

Asn (sic) B. Chapman and Elizabeth Zumwalt, (MD) March 13, 1870, (UK) Wm. Stephens.

Charles Dougherty and Elizabeth Wallace, (MD) January 10, 1843, (MG) R. S. Reynolds.

Sterling P. Holt and Sarah F. Vaughn, (MD) December 17, 1868.

Robert H. Hudson and Sophia M. Meng, (MD) September 16, 1869.

John Newton and Evaline Longley, (MD) June 10, 1846, (UK) Geo. B. Hopkins.

Joseph D. Humphries and Rebecca C. Early, (MD) April 10, 1845, (JP) B. Matthews.

William H. Smith and Diana E. Curd, (MD) August 19, 1862, (MG) Thomas Marlow.

B. F. Thomas and Virginia S. Calbreath, (MD) November 18, 1859.

Otho McCrackin and Sarah C. Wilson, (MD) August 24, 1843.

Samuel Brandenburg and Alverda Pow (sic) Murray, (MD) October 17, 1861.

A. F. Brewer and Mary A. Allen, (MD) October 22, 1857.

Henry M. Gilbert and Martha Ann Driskall, (MD) February 26, 1860.

John R. Larue and Harriet Jane Austen, (MD) March 11, 1863.

Nat. G. McGwin and Mary J. Miller, (MD)March 31, 1843, (MG) Jacob Coons.

John Scoby and Polly Haynes, (MD) December 25, 1832, (UK) Thos. P. Stephens.

John Simco and May Fletcher, (MD) November 17, 1842, (MG) Noah Flood.

Nathan Young and Malissa R. Coates, (MD) December 29, 1842, (MG) W. W. Robertson.

James I. Bartley and Mary E. Berry, (MD) March 11, 1858.

William Nichols and Hannah Jane Muir, (MD)October 22, 1829,
(MG) Theo. Boulware.

Robert M. McClanahan and Catharine S. Strother, (MD) September 20, 1868, (UK) John F. Cowan.

William A. Brown and Rachel Dareycee (sic), (MD) February 3, 1870, (UK) Fourson Gee.

Georgo (sic) Coons and Sallie Bell, (MD) December 29, 1833, (MG) Samuel Day.

--- Crump and Mary J. Jones, (MD) October 14, 1863, Groom is from Boone County.

Samuel W. Gilbert and Martha E. Steele, (MD) December 1, 1868, (MG) W. B. Walthall.

Joseph T. Hoxey and Elizabeth Day, (MD) December 25, 1866, (UK) John G. Carter.

Andrew Jordan and Sarah A. Longley, (MD) March 25, 1863.

Hiram A. Masten and Nancy S. E. Ishmeail (sic), (MD April 4, 1861.

Oscar L. Meng and Annie L. Dougly, (MD) October 21, 1869.

William Miller and Nancy Ann Mateer, (MD) January 15, 1845, (UK) R. S. Symington.

Joseph Thomas and Rachel Ham, (MD) March 9, 1837, (JP) A. Norflet.

William Wells and Elizabeth Smart, (MD) November 25, 1836, (MG) Jas. Suggett.

Samuel Tucker Boone and Mrs. Eliza Ann Simpson, (MD) January 6, 1852, (MG) Jas. H. Tuttle.

Philip Bury and Henrietta Backer, (MD) February 6, 1868, (MG) Peter Klein, Groom is from Herman.

Thomas Favier and Jane Phillips, (MD) August 2, 1821, (JP) Solomon Thomas.

James G. Hall and Elmira C. Majors, (MD) August 23, 1865.

Allen Caperton Humphrey and Margaret Jenkins, (MD) April 13, 1862.

John McClure and Amanda Thomas, (MD) December 20, 1849, (MG) Noah Flood.

James F. Nelson and Martha E. Caldwell, (MD) August 9, 1869.

Ezeriah Num and Harriet Stinton, (MD) July 14, 1842, (JP) A. K. Bell.

R. R. Proper and Rebecca Price, (MD) April 30, 1845, (MG) W. W. Robertson.

Hezekaah (sic) Belcher and Delila Carthmill (sic), (MD) May 30, 1851.

Francis Atterberry and Francis E. Kelsick, (MD) March 22, 1855, (UK) B. B. Black.

Wm. Richman and Mary Ann Lawrence, (MD) August 28, 1845.

George Perry and Elizabeth Smith, (MD) September 14, 1854, Groom is from Audrain County.

P. M. Morris and Sarah C. Fish, (MD) September 27, 1854, (MG) H. H. Craig.

Martin Butter and Emeline Pugh, (MD) March 8, 1847, (UK) P.
H. Steinberger.

Henry Cave and Fanny Craig, (MD) September 8, 1824, (UK)
Richard Cave, Groom is from Boone County.

Henry C. Chiles and Maggie J. Goff, (MD) June 6, 1869.

Charles Thos. Fenley and Cary Jane Baker, (MD)June 26, 1845,
(ED) M. P. Wills.

Sylvester F. Fowler and Susannah J. Woodson, (MD) February
14, 1861.

B. B. Hall and Mary H. Reed, (MD) May 21, 1835, (MG) Theo.
Boulware.

James H. Jameson and Amanda Worthington, (MD) September 11,
1848, (UK) James M. Green.

James Love and Matilda Scholl, (MD) March 4, 1836, (JP) Jos.
Scholl.

Signor (sic) Mays and Martha Ridgway, (MD) September 18,
1835, (MG) Wm. Duncan.

James A. Simpson and Eliz. C. Boone, (MD) December 6, 1841,
(UK) Robert C. Hill.

Nicholas D. Thurmond and Sallie F. Robertson, (MD) December
13, 1865, (ED) W. W. Robertson.

Didymus Buzz and Sarah Langley, (MD) March 10, 1839, (UK)
Geo. B. Hopkins.

Joseph Brown and Julian Pearson, (MD) April 19, 1836, (JP)
Jas. Harris.

Stephen Chapman and Nancy Wood, (MD) June 8, 1826, (JP) Wm.
Martin.

Joshua Davis and Isabella Blount, (MD) September 27, 1866,
Bride is the daughter of Capt. Lamb Blount.   .

John Dunnica and Betsey Ferguson, (MD) April 11, 1822, (UK)
Samuel Baskett.

Columbus Finly and Eliz. K. West, (MD) December 24, 1851,
(MG) D. Coulter.

Samuel P. Harrison and Lucy French, (MD) May 31, 1859.

William A. Hunter and Minerva Jones, (MD) November 23, 1843,
(MG) Wm. Sampson, Groom is from Montgomery County.

John Conrod Neukomn and Elizabeth Schepp, (MD) April 16,
1864.

Robert W. Randolph and Mariah M. Adams, (MD) February 9,
1868.

Robert Smith and Rucella Selby, (MD) July 25, 1869.

Edward G. Berry and Sally Ann Galbreath, (MD) February 14,
1833, (MG) --- Hoxsen.

Tandy Vaughn and Eliz. M. Bullard, (MD) November 7, 1850,
Groom is from Boone County.

Alphonso Boon and Nancy Boon, (MD) February 1, 1822, (JP)
Enoch Fruit.

Garner Quarels Foster and Manerva Pinkston, (MD) March 17,
1836, (MG) R. L. McAfee.

Langford L. Browning and Louisa M. Brown, (MD) September 10, 1866, Groom is from Boone County.

Thompson Bunch and Nancy Hays, (MD) August 26, 1826, (JP) Enoch Fruit.

Samuel Carter and Clarinda Hisey, (MD) January 30, 1845, (UK) John E. Nevins.

James Childers and Josephine Goodin, (MD) October 4, 1866.

James H. Claughton and Matilda F. Todd, (MD)January 3, 1849.

William S. French and Eliza Jane Bullard, (MD) September 20, 1855.

Elijah Harrison and Millender (sic) Rowland, (MD) July 28, 1831.

Presley Byers and Mary Eliz. Douglass, (MD) October 7, 1866.

Jacob B. Cumberland and Mary Gay, (MD) October 29, 1867.

Jackson Hensley and Rutha Gatrice, (MD) October 27, 1842, (MG) Absalom Rice.

Henry Tinch and Mrs. Lucy Fletcher, (MD) December 18, 1864.

David M. White and Martha Ann Allen, (MD)September 22, 1842, (MG) Theo. Boulware.

John P. Baker and Elvira Kemp, (MD) April 19, ----.

James F. Sebastian and Letsy H. Stevens, (MD November 1, 1866.

James Crump and Amanda S. Garrett, (MD) December 28, 1858.

William Day and Eliza Childress, (MD) November 15, 1832, (MG) Geo. T. Key.

Robert T. English and Amandy Bryant, (MD) November 30, 1857.

Harmon Hays and Minervia Scholl, (MD) March 29, 1832, (JP) Enoch Fruit, Groom is from Montgomery County.

R. A. Mayhall and Eliza Edmonston, (MD) December 16, 1868, Groom is from Ralls County.

John G. Riley and Sara Ann Guy, (MD) July 23, 1851.

William T. Baker and Sarah T. West, (MD) December 9, 1847, (MG) Jacob Coons.

Thomas H. B. Williams and Martha Ellen Fisher, (MD) December 23, 1869.

John J. Wells and Mrs. Susan Farmer, (MD) February 17, 1864.

Robert J. Symmington and Martha E. Scott, (MD) July 2, 1846, (MG) W. W. Robertson.

Marcus Ravenscraft and nancy Meredith, (MD)October 22, 1840, (MG) Joseph Coons.

Lockwood S. Nevins and Ellen Long, (MD) November 21, 1861.

Joseph R. Fowke and T. A. Shealey, (MD) July 24, 1854.

David H. Duncan and Eliza Ann Morrison, (MD)January 6, 1836, (MG) Theo. Boulware.

Cary Hawkins and Fannie A. Newland, (MD) December 16, 1869.

Bartley Nichols and Mrs. Margaret Ray, (MD) January 8, 1865.

George W. Sons and Bettie V. James, (MD) December 7, 1865, (MG) C. Babcock.

Robert F. Davis and Eliz. W. Bagby, (MD) July 3, 1864.

87

T. Bugby and J. Deering, (MD) October 17, 1861.

Robert S. Carter and Melvina E. Scott, (MD) April 4, 1869.

James E. Chapman and Sarah Jane Smith, (MD)January 19, 1860,
(UK) Wm. B. Douglass.

Thomas B. Clark and Lucy T. Hockaday, (MD) October 28, 1852.

John Holt and Sarah Brandon, (MD)November 4, 1835, (MG) Jas.
Suggett.

Samuel Hunter and Elizabeth Dysart, (MD) January 15, 1839,
(UK) J. F. Young.

Richard W. Selby and Sarah E. Price, (MD) March 10, 1870.

Morgan Kyger and Malinda Powell, (MD) January 23, 1867.

James M. McClintock and Elizabeth A. Jefferies, (MD) october
13, 1842, (MG) W. Robertson.

James F. Overton and Harriet A. Baynham, (MD) October 11,
1832, (UK) William Duncan.

Andrew B. Dorsey and Mary Wiley, (MD) June 21, 1835, (UK)
John F. Young.

Levi Crump and Louisa Calvin, (MD) December 16, 1857.

William Comer and Mrs. Henrietta Leopard, (MD) March 17,
1864.

James Kimbrough and Elizabeth Anderson, (MD) November 25,
1869.

William McAarty (sic) and Eliz. Ann Miller, (MD) March 5,
1843, (UK) John E. Nevins.

Samuel S. McCue and Clarinda P. Tate, (MD)February 20, 1868,
(UK) John P. Cowan.

William McIntire and Julia Ann Harper, (MD) December 21,
1865.

Robert Randolf and Amanda J. Humphries, (MD) January 14,
1836, (MG) Jas. Suggett.

Robert J. Richarson and Sarah M. Marrow, (MD) November 18,
1858.

James Ross and Anna Nicholson, (MD) December 24, 1845.

Bethel A. Smith and Elizabeth C. Ewing, (MD) March 24, 1840,
(MG) J. L. Yantis.

Thos. D. Conger and Moniza McCampbell, (MD)October 18, 1827,
(JP) John Conger.

James M. G. Howe and Annie C. Baker, (MD) November 20, 1834,
(MG) Wm. Duncan.

William S. McCowan and July Ann Wood, (MD) March 23, 1853.

Boston W. Shobe and Mary E. Nunley, (MD) June 20, 1863, (JP)
Wm. Penn.

Milton Cleaveland and Susan Beavan, (MD) April 16, 1830,
(ED) Wm. Crain.

John C. Rice and Mrs. Eliz. Coonce, (MD) August 16, 1860.

David Straw and Anna Jan Hornbuckle, (MD) August 27, 1843,
(UK) Milton Cleveland.

Beqra (sic) Williams and Elizabeth W. Chiles, (MD) November
25, ----, (MG) Jacob Ligler.

William McCray and Nancy Carroll, (MD) September 29, 1842,
(UK) J. Coons.
Calvin Niccle and Sophy Thomas, (MD) February 2, 1854, (MG)
Theo. Boulware.
Richard D. C. Smith and J. Elizabeth Scott, (MD) August 25,
1847, (MG) P. C. Pinkard.
Martin Baskett and Margaret Jane Bartley, (MD) January 17,
1855.
Joshua M. Duncan and Mrs. Eliz. Ann McAfee, (MD) May 18,
1842, (MG) R. S. McAfee.
Joseph Erno and Ogela Foy, (MD)February 22, 1849, (JP) Isaac
Langley.
Edward Herndon and Sarah J. Griffin, (MD) October 31, 1849,
(UK) Alexander Irvine,
Padfield N. Kemp and Margaret L. Steele, (MD) December 3,
1868, Groom is from Pettis County.
William McGee and Sally Price, (MD) January 2, 1843, (UK) W.
W. Robertson.
Daniel Pasley and Harriet Walker, (MD) January 16, 1840,
(JP) W. J. Gilman.
John D. Ridgway and Saphira Wigginson, (MD) June 9, 1831,
(UK) Theo. P. Stephens.
Wm. M. Pledge and Isabel C. Leper, (MD) September 12, 1844,
(UK) W. W. Robertson.
Cantley W. Stewart and Lucy Ann Davis, (MD) July 7, 1844,
(MG) Jas. Suggett.
James H. Tullock and Sarah J. Scott, (MD) February 9, 1853,
(MG) W. M. Woods.
Lewis B. Thomas and Polly Robertson, (MD) August 26, 1823.
Oscar F. Thurmond and Malvina O. Weems, (MD) June 23, 1861.
William White and Catharine Covington, (MD) April 17, 1860,
Groom is from Montgomery County.
Jefferson Benson and Sally Hays, (MD) March 15, 1838, (JP)
Joseph Scholl.
Thomas N. Underwood and Mary W. Patton, (MD) August 10,
1848, (MG) R. S. Symmington.
Thomas D. Bogie and Virginia D. Maughas, (MD) January 8,
1863.
James Wren and Mariah Williams, (MD) December 5, 1870.
William Coats and Cena McLaughlin, (MD) January 29, 1837,
(UK) Andrew Alexander.
John Buckley and Eva Berkett, (MD) April 26, 1837, (JP) C.
Zumwalt.
Capt. Thomas Campbell and Martha West, (MD) September 25,
1839, (UK) Thos. P. Stephens.
John J. Fowler and Elizabeth Carr, (MD) June 18, 1840, (MG)
--- Robertson.
William W. Robinson and Hannah A. Layson, (MD) December 18,
1851, (MG) --- Spencer.

Dr. Church Brooks and Ann Fisher, (MD) June 12, 1851.
Mangram J. Bull and Mary Harvey Williams, (MD) December 14,
    1841, (JP) R. Brandon.
Edward T. Button and Mary Edge, (MD) December 21, 1852.
Albert G. L. Carruth and Parthena Jones, (MD) September 13,
    1838, (MG) Absalom Rice.
Henry Cave and Sarah B. Allen, (MD) March 20, 1849, (MG) J.
    Criswell.
John W. Christian and Julia A. Bllythe, (MD) December 24,
    1866, Groom is from Henry County.
William Ellis and Susan Sampson, (MD) October 26, 1854, (UK)
    W. W. Robertson.
James L. Jamison and Barbara L. Ellis, (MD) October 6, 1861,
    Groom is from Pike County.
William McCormack and Eliz. L. Jones, (MD) January 3, 1822,
    (JP) Enoch Fruit.
Charles A. Riley and Oretto Railey, (MD) February 18, 1869,
    (MG) S. A. Beauchamp.
John Wise and Milly Beeding, (MD) September 6, 1849, (MG)
    Noah Flood.
William Young and Sally Linvelle, (MD) April 18, 1831, (MG)
    Wm. Coats.
John F. Bush and Madelene L. Finley, (MD) February 27, 1865.
Joseph Hudson and Martha Ann Old, (MD) June 27, 1849, (JP)
    C. A. Ming.
Alexander Jamson and Caroline M. Clatterbuck, (MD) December
    23, 1856.
William Pastel and Celia B. Dyer, (MD) November 20, 1850,
    (UK) Thomas T. Ashby, Groom is from St. Louis.
Junius Robertson and Sarah H. Grant, (MD) June 17, 1857.
Wayman C. Sheets and Mary Ellen Duncan, (MD) September 13,
    1865.
Hescott H. Brown and Mary A. Mateer, (MD November 16, 1869.
Abram Cook and Duleeny Peek, (MD) April 11, 1868, (UK) John
    Douglass.
William Douglass and Lucy Chick, (MD) March 29, 1832, (JP)
    Enoch Fruit.
Alexander T. Ferguson and Pamelia E. Gilbert, (MD) November
    30, 1852, (MG) John Green.
Charles Huff and Catharine Martin, (MD) February 20, 1870.
Robert Selby and Artimesia Selby, (MD) April 22, 1847, (MG)
    Wm. D. Cave.
James Wm. Kelso and Virginia C. Rodgers, (MD) January 7,
    1869.
John May and Delea Boon, (MD) February 20, 1834, (MG) Wm.
    Coats.
Wikelif (sic) Miller and Louisa Jones, (MD) February 19,
    1834, (MG) Jabez Ham.
W. H. Woods and Mrs. Mariah Walters, (MD) October 20, 1868.

Charles H. Brown and Amanda McKinney, (MD) March 9, 1837,
(UK) R. L. McAfee.

Carter T. Craig and Mary S. Garner, (MD) October 14, 1836,
(MG) James Barnes.

Thomas J. Davis and Loutesia V. Swan, (MD)September 1, 1829,
(UK) David Kirkpatrick.

James Dougherty and Jan Eliz. Cliff, (MD) October 24, 1849,
(JP) Wm. T. Ramsey.

Joseph Driscal and Mary Shepherd, (MD) March 10, 1853.

John G. Self and Martha Davis, (MD) September 7, 1862.

Samuel Mackafee and Caroline Suggett, (MD) October 29, 1857.

Wharton H. Moore and Mariah Ferguson, (MD) June 16, 1831,
(UK) J. C. Berryman.

Samuel Boles and Susannah Muir, (MD) June 6, 1849, (MG) Noah
Flood.

James S. Wright and Mary Ann Ingersoll, (MD) May 30, 1840,
(MG) Theo. Boulware.

Elisha J. Rhodes and Martha A. Clarby, (MD) January 1, 1842,
(MG) Geo. T. Key.

Joseph Perkins and Sarah Raulins, (MD) July 14, 1864, Groom
is from Putman County.

John Warden Miller and Louisiana Coons, (MD) November 3,
1836, (MG) Joseph Coons.

John B. Broughton and Sheeloth (sic) A. Crag, (MD) May 1,
1854.

George Ely and Mary Jane Malony, (MD) November 3, 1852, (MG)
Theo. Boulware.

Joseph McDonald and Jane Cragg, (MD) December 5, 1833, (UK)
Robert Younger.

Boston Shobe and Martha Jane Watson, (MD) September 9, 1847,
(JP) Wm. Gilman.

Benjamin Winn and Ann Hunter, (MD) November 12, 1867, Bride
is from Portland, Mo.

Tarlton Barnes and Rebecca K. Wilkerson, (MD) January 24,
1850, (JP) W. J. Jackson.

Peyton J. Dudley and Harriet Gilbert, (MD)November 27, 1845,
(UK) John Green.

Benjamin Sexton and Louisa Ridgel, (MD) February 2, 1843,
Thos. P. Stephens.

Collet (sic) Langley and Thursy (sic) Langley, (MD) August
16, 1843.

Henry Mattock and Matilda Cox, (MD) July 19, 1835, (UK)Robt.
A. Younger.

Francis Withurington and Polly Parker, (MD)October 31, 1827,
(UK) Edward J. Ellis.

Robert Brooks and Elizabeth Rhour (sic), (MD) September 28,
1839, (JP) Robt. Brandon.

William D. Frazier and Angeline F. Betz, (MD)March 23, 1870,
Groom is from Boone County.

Marion Bryant French and Lucia Bert, (MD)May 4, 1848, (UK)
W. B. Douglass.
George W. Hendrix and Sadona C. Wilkerson, (MD) October 10,
---- (No Year Given).
William Selby and Julian Turley, (MD) September 19, 1832,
(UK) William Duncan.
Thomas McCulloch and Rebecaa M. Craft, (MD) December 11,
1836.
John Baskett and Lucinda Muir, (MD) May 12, 1841, (MG) Absa-
lom Rice.
George W. Dunham and Louisa M. Steel, (MD) March 4, 1847,
(MG) Theo. Boulware.
Jess Farmer and Nancy N. Reed, (MD) March 31, 1846.
Joseph Kemp and Lucy M. Medoe, (MD) December 11, 1866, (UK)
R. S. Symmington.
Akexander McPheeters and Juerusha Edmonson, (MD) January 30,
1856.
John A. Riggs and Mrs. S. E. Scott, (MD) August 11, 1853,
Groom is from Cabell County, Virginia.
Robert Shields and Lucy Thurmond, (MD) November 26, 1863.
Winfield S. Brunchbill and Mrs. Eliza J. Tompkins, (MD)
February 10, 1870.
James L. Dunn and Hattie Cousby, (MD) January 29, 1868.
James N. McClanahan and Louise A. Selby, (MD) January 9,
Flail (sic) P. Payne and Eliz. Cath. Richie, (MD) December
19, 1854.
Mark C. Rupert and Mary B. Moon, (MD) January 17, 1856,.
Isaac Rush and Catharine Pruitt, (MD) January 25, 1853.
Joseph M. Fort and Mary Ann Canterbury, (MD) September 7,
1853.
Solomon P. Foust and Lucretia Sacre, (MD) November 26, 1856.
William S. Duncan and Helen Cave, (MD) February 21, 1867.
Samuel Kelly and Caroline ----, (MD) January 1, 1868.
Samuel Blount and Jane Pemberton, (MD) September 17, 1863.
William M. Bradley and Nancy A. Crow, (MD) March 30, 1848.
Russell Lawrence and Lucy E. Falqueran (sic), (MD) February
6, 1862.
William McClelland and Nannie H. Holiday, (MD) November 19,
1861.
Archibald N. Williams and Maria Broughton, (MD)June 7, 1841,
(JP) James Scholl.
Thomas D. Boles and Amanda B, Smart, (MD) February 17, 1857.
Wm. John Threlkild and Elizabeth Schroyock, (MD) December
19, 1865.
Nicholas Sitton and Martha A. Fourt, (MD) September 8, 1854,
(UK) Jonathan Kemper.
Richard Menifee and Bettie Via, (MD) November 27, 1866.
Harrison A. Fleishman and Louisa Jane Crowson, (MD) May 8,
1851, (MG) W. W. Kemp.

Francis R. Foy and Eliz. Jane Williams, (MD) October 23,
    1853.
Hiram Harkins, jr. and Jane Cooley, (MD) May 31, 1842, (JP)
    B. A. Ramsey.
Stephen P. Brooks and Julia F. Hutts, (MD)February 25, 1869.
Robert Burnell and Martha Betz, (MD) October 15, 1865.
Joseph Scholl and Eliza Broughton, (MD) February 24, 1831,
    (JP) J. W. Johnston.
James N. Langley and Ruth A. Newton, (MD) August 9, 1838,
    (UK) John Henderson.
John McKinney and Anna E. Hill, (MD) September 21, 1837,
    (MG) Theo. Boulware.
Samuel Patton and Jane Wisley, (MD) January 16, 1849, (UK)
    Geo. B. Hopkins.
C. Shepherd and Ellen Jones, (MD) December 9, 1869.
Jesse Vincent and Jane Baker, (MD) August 11, 1825, (UK)
    Thos. Stephens.
John R. Williams and Amanda Simons, (MD) December 16, 1869.
Lewis Bolton and Anne Chandon, (MD) September 19, 1848, (UK)
    Martin D. Noland.
Howel F. Christopher and Permelia F. Taylor, (MD) February
    21, 1861.
John Duncan and Nanny Soia, (MD) June 20, 1847, (MG) Jacob
    Coons.
Patrick E. Ferree and Martha E. Cooper, (MD) October 23,
    1870.
Charles W. Baynham and Sallie Glendy, (MD September 5, 1866.
Philip Whooper and Eliz. Ann Baker, (MD) March 13, 1855,
    Groom is from Chariton County.
Fleming Watson and Catharine Albin, (MD) March 4, 1863, (UK)
    Absalom Hughes.
James G. Roberts and Lucy Ann Berry, (MD) January 13, 1853.
Robin Petty and Sarah Kemp, (MD) January 2, 1848, (UK) Wm.
    J. Gilman.
William McIlwrath and Ann E. Switzer, (MD) January 29, 1861.
Collett Langley and Therissa Evans, (MD) December 25, 1834,
    (UK) Geo. B. Hopkins.
Welton Hull and Martha Tucker, (MD) September 1, 1842, (MG)
    James Love, Bride is from Osage County.
James B. Burt and Martha A. Truitt, (MD) May 28, 1862.
James Coonce and Louisa Warfield, (MD) May 17, 1866.
Josphus Dunnavant and Malissa R. Nevins, (MD) March 1, 1864,
    (MG) Noah Cate.
Lorenzo D. Hultz and Melissa Vanbibber, (MD) January 12,
    1837, (UK) Jabez Ham.
Bascom Selby and Mary Stul, (MD)December 9, ----, (UK) Jacob
    Coons.
Thomas G. Kemp and Juley Ann Tate, (MD) May 16, 1861.
W. R. Moore and E. D. Smith, (MD) February 20, 1862.

Thomas Page and Jerusha Gregory, (MD) December 23, 1847.
John E. Comer and Nancy McGary, (MD) October 8, 1832, (MD)
    Theo. Boulware.
Francis M. Davis and Frances Saunders, (MD)November 2, 1848,
    (JP) W. J. Jackson.
John Dyer and Evalina H. Warren, (MD) February 19, 1824,
    (MG) Wm. Coats.
William P. Holt and Polly Bly, (MD) October 24, 1839, (MG)
    Jas. Suggett.
Theodore Lacoff and Josephine Horner, (MD) October 23, 1870.
Jeremiah Sanders and Mary J. Argabinte (sic), (MD) February
    13, 1845, (UK) J. R. Craghead.
Dr. J. J. Brown and Mollie M. Adams, (MD) October 26, 1870.
John Gibony and Parky Wood, (MD) January 4, 1846, (JP) J. R.
    Craghead.
Henry Holman and Nancy Nash, (MD) September 19, 1847, (UK)
    Franklin Jenkins.
William T. Kemp and Mary T. English, (MD) December 8, 1853.
james S. Lawrence and Margaret Swan, (MD August 15, ----,
    (UK) J. C. Renfro.
Robert J. Link and Lavinia Rennolds, (MD) October 20, 1870.
Thomas J. Baker and Ann West, (MD) March 1, 1865.
David Woods and Sarah Reynolds, (MD) October 9, 1831, (UK)
    Thos. P. Stephens, Groom is from Monroe County and the
    Bride is from Boone County.
George W. Bruner and Louisa W. Dillion, (MD)October 9, 1859,
    (MG) Absalom Rice.
John H. Crow and Elizabeth Gray, (MD) December 9, 1847, (UK)
    Geo. B. Hopkins.
Thomas Fisher and Martha Nichols, (MD) February 9, 1854.
Amos Sampson and Mrs. Nancy A. Fox, (MD) April 21, 1846,
    (JP) Joseph Scholl, Groom is from Montgomery County.
James Welch and Mary Lawrence, (MD) July 26, 1857.
William T. Burnett and Margaret S. Bullard, (MD) October 30,
    1851, (JP) H. B. Barger.
James Londer and Armenta D. Wilcoxen, (MD) January 8, 1846,
    (UK) Thos. P. Stephens.
Pleasant Robinet and Catharine Hunt, (MD) February 10, 1829,
    (UK) Anderson Woods, Groom is from Boone County.
Nicholas Phye and Margaret Roy, (MD) October 7, 1827, (JP)
    John Conger.
John A. C. Arthur and Rebecca Coons, (MD) December 21, 1841,
    (JP) Joseph Coons.
James Ellis and Mary J. Baynham, (MD) September 28, 1870.
Lewis Hockins and Claudia Thomas, (MD) January 31, 1828,
    (MG) Wm. Coats.
Philip T. McAfee and Mary Ann E. Selby, (MD) May 27, 1834,
    (MG) R. L. McAfee.
Edward W. Scott and Ellen Offett, (MD) October 7, 1869.

James Bruton and Julia T. Jackson, (MD) April 12, 1861,
Groom and Bride are both from Boone County.
Thomas Duncan and Polly McClure, (MD) January 21, 1836, (MG)
Wm. Duncan.
Henry Elley and Syntha Syms, (MD) June 15, 1847, (UK) Thos.
P. Stephens.
Joel T. Fisher and Mary E. Houf, (MD) December 20, 1870.
George S. Gallop and Sarah Stone, (MD) April 12, 1846, (ED)
Jacob Coons.
Benjamin F. Harris and Lucy Hensley, (MD) March 11, 1857.
Joseph Goodrich and Eliz. M. Payton, (MD) February 17, 1853.
William Nichols and Susan Bowles, (MD) April 5, 1855.
William J. Gillaspie and Eliz. Jane Loyd, (MD)March 4, 1858.
John G. Parvin and Eliz. Ann Coil, (MD) May 31, 1849, (UK)
Ninian Ridgway.
Zacariah Ausburn and Mary M. Atterberry, (MD) January 11,
1854.
Frank N. Baker and Mollie Ann Culberson, (MD) February 26,
1870.
Wm. T. Worsham and Samenta Ann Stokes, (MD) March 27, 1838,
(MG) R. L. McAfee, Groom is from Cole County.
John C. Fleming and Delilah E. Basinger, (MD) October 11,
1868.
Emanuel W. Ladman and Laura Polochich (sic), (MD) December
27, 1865.
John Magus and Elizabeth Roberson, (MD) February 7, 1865.
William B. McKinney and Turecy V. Brashears, (MD) September
11, 1866, (UK) W. M. Williams.
Wm. N. Peters and Lucy Newbolt, (MD) December 5, 1844, (MG)
Wm. B. Douglas.
N. W. Mauk and Ann E. Hayes, (MD) October 7, 1858.
William R. McCalister and Ella McIntosh, (MD)April 25, 1867.
James May and Nancy C. Craghead, (MD) October 27, 1850.
Henry H. Hunt and Francis A. McKinney, (MD)January 12, 1865.
Wm. W. S. Brooks and Virginia Meteer, (MD)December 16, 1841,
(MG) David Coulter.
Thomas Davis and Margaret Glendy, (MD) January 7, 1859.
Gilpin Hughes and Isabella Todd, (MD) December 2, 1870, (MG)
S. L. Woody.
Michael Klein and Caroline Seppett (sic), (MD) August 16,
1856.
William W. Miller and Elizabeth Baker, (MD) May 6, 1840,
(MG) Joseph Coons.
William H. Saunders and Susan A. Willing, (MD) November 22,
1868.
Thomas F. Bush and Martha E. Powell, (MD) December 3, 1857.
James G. Horn and Mary Z. Thatcher, (MD) May 7, 1856.
James Kemp and Sarah Kemp, (MD) August 19, 1851.
James O. Boon and Sallie E. Sims, (MD) November 12, 1861.

John M. Bryan and Charlotte M. Windsor, (MD) March 31, 1850,
  Benjamin J. S. Ashly.
William Humphries and Frances Muir, (MD) March 3, 1835, (UK)
  Theo. Boulware.
Madison Davis and Mary Ella, (MD) December 8, 1836, (MG)
  Theo. Boulware.
Duke Hults and Margaret Love, (MD) October 23, 1827, (JP)
  Enoch Fruit.
Nicholas J. McCubbins and Ruth Ann McCubbins, (MD) March 15,
  1866, (MG) R. S. Symington.
William Moseley and Jane Kimbrough, (MD) October 19, 1853,
  Groom is from Boone County.
Thomas R. Calvin and Mary Garret, (MD) October 10, 1850.
John Langley and Elizabeth Rose, (MD) May 25, 1829, (JP)
  Henry Neill.
Daniel Mahonny and Mainda Leach, (MD) November 1, 1835, (JP)
  John A. Burt, Groom is from Montgomery County.
William Cason and Sarah Overton, (MD) September 1836, (MG)
  Theo. Boulware.
James T. Clatterbuck and Mary Eliza Foster, (MD) February 8,
  ----, (MG) Jas. H. Tuttle.
Thomas Davison and Ann Harland, (MD) January 13, 1853.
Jefferson Doyal and Margaret A. Humphries, (MD) March 12,
  1857.
John Emmett and Rebecca Stansbury, (MD) August 26, 1847.
Thomas M. Gee and Hannah E. Potter, (MD) November 22, 1855.
John D. Howe, jr. and Malinda J. Howe, (MD) March 9, 1848.
James T. King and Jennie B. Goff, (MD) September 20, 1866.
William B. Monroe and Martha Ann Tuttle, (MD)April 30, 1838,
  (MG) Andrew Monroe.
Jeremiah Palmer and Martha O. Bowles, (MD)February 20, 1868.
Jeptha Thorn and Martha Walker, (MD) January 2, 1840, (JP)
  W. J. Gilman.
Milton M. Wigginton and Lizzie Marshall, (MD) February 2,
  1870, Groom is from Boone County.
Dr. Thos. J. Baskett and Mary Jameson, (MD) December 18,
  1867, (UK) D. M. Grandfield.
Charles W. Samuel and Ann E. Ferguson, (MD)January 13, 1858.
J. W. Morris and Sarah Baker, (MD) January 25, 1854.
William D. Love and George Ann Loy (sic), (MD) September 4,
  1864.
Samuel Hays and Rebecca Berry, (MD) September 23, 1845,
  (UK) John Greer.
Jacob W. Douglass and Serilda L. Ridgway, (MD) December 8,
  1870.
William Counce and Susan Hannah Pannell, (MD) November 22,
  1866.
Joseph W. Sallee and Mattie Jane McKim, (MD) March 21, 1867.
Andrew J. Barton and Sophia M. Love, (MD) February 17, 1848.

James Byers and Susan Day, (MD) July 9, 1857.
William A. Cannon and Mrs. Susan Groves, (MD) October 20,
    1869, Groom is from Saline County.
Barba (sic) Collins and Terelda McMurty, (MD) November 19,
    1844, (MG) Wm. B. Douglas.
Matthew K. Davis and Eliz. Ann Pannel, (MD) June 3, 1844.
Charles A. Emmons and Susan A. Vaughn, (MD) March 14, 1867.
Aaron Larue and Maria Sitton, (MD) August 31, 1834, (MG)
    Theo. Boulware.
Richard H. Nichols and Mollie F. Nichols, (MD)March 2, 1861.
William T. Newman and China R. Price, (MD) September 15,
    1863, (UK) Wm. E. Stephens.
Isaac Taylor and Nancy W. Kemp, (MD) December 1, 1867.
Ziby (sic) Pickering and Sarah Ann Taylor, (MD) January 11,
    1858.
Paschal F. Smidy and Elizabeth S. Olham, (MD) November 16,
    1847.
John M. Shock and Sarah A. Sheely, (MD) October 20, 1852.
William C. Robinett and Mary H. Nesbit, (MD) March 12, 1857.
John D. Parmer and Mary V. Woods, (MD) March 6, 1865.
Iccaton (sic) Owen and Martha Smith, (MD) January 16, 1852,
    (JP) J. Palmer.
Elkaman (sic) N. Lovelace and Sarah W. Gilbert, (MD) April
    1, 1841, (UK) Samuel D. Gilbert.
Samuel Lathlin and Franky Coats, (MD) October 22, 1829, (MG)
    Jabez Ham.
Andrew Hunter and Ann Rock, (MD) February 14, 1822, (UK)
    Solomon Thomas, Groom is from Montgomery County.
Isral (sic) B. Grant and Mrs. Miriam Pliage, (MD) May 1,
    1849.
John P. Gill and Rebecca A. Boone, (MD) February 4, 1857.
William Gilbert and Tabitha Phillips, (MD) March 4, 1847,
    (UK) Moses Phillips.
R. J. England and Susan Adams, (MD) May 11, 1854.
Joseph M. Duncan and Mrs. Judith Duncan, (MD) Septmber 23,
    1852.
E. R. Douglass and Jane Taylor, (MD) April 3, 1862, Groom is
    from Audrain County.
Francis Day and Virginia Day, (MD) June 9, 1853, (JP) Wm. J.
    Gilman.
John R. Bryan and Eliza M. Jones, (MD) November 25, 1867.
Nelson Freeman and Harriet J. Walker, (MD) July 18, 1849,
    (JP) J. K. Allen.
John Kenny and Lamira Yount, (MD) October 9, 1828, (JP) Geo.
    King.
Abram Miller and Mrs. Mary K. Wist, (MD) July 10, 1856.
John L. Taylor and Isabella James, (MD July 8, 1867.
Harry J. Bailey and Mary F. Gray, (MD) March 9, ----.
Charles M. Beavan and Frances I. Miller, (MD) March 8, 1860.

Marcus Bullard and Susannah Burnet, (MD) February 1, 1835,
(UK) John Selby.
Kato I. Burgess and Lucinda Holladay, (MD) July 1, 1856.
Charles W. Burk and Eliza Jane Longley, (MD)January 3, 1855.
Charles H. Fentum and Cyntha J. Longley, (MD) December 10,
----. (No Year Given)
Henry A. Graves and B. V. Hudson, (MD) March 25, 1869, (UK)
Davie Anderson.
John Gordon and Emaline Cason, (MD) January 3, 1870.
George King and Elizabeth Johnson, (MD) February 19, 1845,
(MG) Jacob Coons.
David Kiger and Mary Clardy, (MD) October 20, 1870.
Moses Henry McCue and Mattie D. Hockaday, (MD) June 2, 1868.
Richard McMahan and Louisa J. Love, (MD November 1, 1832,
(JP) James Stewart.
James C. McMurty and Eliz. M. McCubbin, (MD) February 15,
1870, Groom is from Jackson County.
John Mede and Polley Ellice, (MD) April 3, 1829, (JP) Wm.
Martin.
Armstrong Smith and Amanda B. Houf, (MD) February 15, 1860,
Groom is from Montgomery County.
Willis W. Snell and Susan A. W. Pledge, (MD) August 1, 1847,
(UK) Wm. P. Nichols.
Martin L. Soutman and Debara A. Davis, (MD) May 24, 1865.
Hiram Baley and Susan Boyce, (MD) April 26, 1858.
Richard M. Barnes and Sarah G. Fry, (MD September 22, 1858.
James Ellis and Martha Jane Glasgow, (MD) December 9, 1852,
Groom is from Boone County.
Abram S. Ellar and Mary E. Burt, (MD) March 23, 1864.
George W. Dunham and Mary Dawson, (MD) January 12, 1853.
Bilvard (sic) Orear and Margaret H. Branhan, (MD) October
16, 1861, Groom is from Saline County.
Jonathan Roberts and Synthy Chiles, (MD) December 23, 1858,
(UK) S. T. McNeiley.
Wm. A. Plunkett and Mary Jane Judy, (MD) November 23, 1869.
Will P. Porter and Nancy W. Robinson, (MD)November 30, 1851.
John H. Thomas and Nancy Herriman, (MD) December 18, 1864,
Groom is from Boone County.
Robert W. Thurman and Susan E. Leeper, (MD) August 21, 1838,
(MG) Theo. Boulware.
Samuel B. Tensley and Mary J. Longley, (MD) December 19,
1863.
Jeremiah Tharp and Mary W. Kelsoe, (MD) October 17, 1833,
(MG) Theo. Boulware.
John Wadley and Catharine Doyle, (MD) September 30, 1838,
(UK) Geo. B. Hopkins.
Daniel Witt and Rebecca Pratt, (MD) April 28, 1864.
Samuel Berry and Eliza M. Wells, (MD) December 23, 1841,
(MG) Mathew Davis.

Marcellus Vaughn and E. M. Yount, (MD) February 3, 1859.
John Bonald and Mrs. Eliz. Henrech, (MD) December 2, 1855.
David M. Carmack and Susanah C. Miller, (MD) April 2, 1848,
   (MG) Stephen Ham.
James A. Calvin and Mrs. Nannie Douglass, (MD) December 4,
   1870.
Creed R. Carter and Nannie S. McClanahan, (MD) December 5,
   1866.
Robert Craghead and Nancy Hughes, (MD) February 27, 1831,
   (UK) George Bartley.
John Dougherty and Rebecca Hatton, (MD) December 17, 1835,
   (JP) B. A. Ramsey.
H. H. Douglass and Eliza V. Jonson, (MD) July 16, ----.
William Estill and Margaret Larch, (MD) December 19, 1848,
   (UK) Stephen Ham, Groom is from Lawrence County.
Swan Ferguson and Mary F. Comer, (MD) March 25, 1857.
Richard D. P. Garner and Nancy Griffith, (MD) December 1,
   1842, (MG) Theo. Boulware.
George W. Gannaway and Mary E. Herring, (MD) February 14,
   1870.
Charles Guz and Mary Jane Thatcher, (MD) October 18, 1857.
Lewis B. Hall and Sallie B. Hall, (MD) September 22, 1870.
Henry Haltzman and Mrs. Catharine Scarborough, (MD) June 29,
   1865, Groom is from Chicago, Illinois.
Robert Humphries and Lucy Williams, (MD) February 12, 1824,
   (MG) Wm. Coats.
William Hutton and Sarah J. Thorton, (MD) December 25, 1850,
   (JP) M. Bright, Groom is from Boone County.
George Ingrams and Jane Ransoms, (MD) July 11, 1845, (UK)
   Walter Prescott.
Van Shealey and Nancy Overton, (MD) December 23, 1862.
J. A. Ryan and Nancy Hall, (MD) March --, 1840, (JP) A.
   Northphen.
James Sanders and Mary Ann Newsom, (MD) February 4, 1857.
John Sallee and Judith A. Robinson, (MD) July 17, 1842, (MG)
   Noah Flood.
George W. Sneathan and Eliz. Jane Nickell, (MD) October 20,
   1861.
Samuel E. Sparks and Mary Walker, (MD) December 31, 1845,
   (JP) J. K. Allen.
Aaron Swearingin and Christine Swearingin, (MD) December 13,
   1866.
Charles W. Whaley and Mary E. Hundley, (MD) March 5, 1861.
Archibald White and Rebecca Hall, (MD) October 22, 1842.
Robert Barker and Jane Blackburn, (MD) January 11, 1849,
   (MG) J. Love.
John Beeding and Melissa Guy, (MD) December 16, 1868.
James H. McRoberts and Harriet Harris, (MD) December 20,
   1846, (JP) W. J. Gilman.

L. Cheatham and Rebecca Fewell, (MD) December 6, 1870.
James D. Clasby and Cyntha Martin, (MD) January 7, 1842,
(UK) T. P. Stephens.
David C. Craghead and Sarah F. Hardin, (MD) February 14,
1865.
John Davis and Erma Pain, (MD) December 27, 1866.
James M. Dunlap and Mattie E. Dawson, (MD) October 27, 1870.
Eugene Ervin and Josephine Russell, (MD) July 10, 1853.
Archibald Gilmore and Majoicery (sic) Ferguson, (MD) Decem-
ber 28, 1837, (JP) B. A. Ramsey.
Thomas M. Glendi and Ellen Shields, (MD) January 15, 1833,
(UK) Benj. F. Hoxey.
Jeptha Hayton and Elizabeth Fulks, (MD) March 10, 1833, (JP)
Arthur Neill.
Alfred E. Heart and Nicy Pulham, (MD) January 17, 1833, (UK)
Robt. L. McAfee.
Seth Herndon and Augusta M. Shortridge, (MD) August 8, 1852.
Armstead Hickerson and Rhoda Bentley, (MD) April 12, 1832,
(JP) John A. Burt.
Bernhard Hinke and Agnes Shotterbaker, (MD) December 18,
1868.
John W. Longley and Nancy Umphreys, (MD) January 10, 1867.
John K. McDonald and Jane Burnett, (MD) July 11, 1833, (UK)
Robert S. McAfee.
Ashel Thomas and Lucinda Van Biber, (MD) October 15, 1848,
(JP) J. Palmer.
Berry Witt and Arementa Pratt, (MD) January 10, 1861.
Napoleon B. Barker and Sarah Ann Freeman, (MD) June 16,
1857.
Joseph B. Hereyford and Nancy J. Hereyford, (MD) October 2,
1866.
Andrew Jackson Lynes and Louise E. White, (MD) December 15,
1870.
George J. Cole and Jessie R. Grant, (MD) September 1, 1869.
William T. Day and Mary Syms, (MD) September 14, 1847, (JP)
J. K. Allen.
Liberty H. Giles and Sarah Ann Elly, (MD) December 21, 1848,
(UK) F. Jenkins.
John Henry Glenn and Mildred Ann Hall, (MD)November 7, 1865.
Alexander Irvine and M. Dunnica, (MD) March 19, 1833, (UK)
B. A. Ramsey.
Elisha McClelland and Betsey Ann West, (MD) March 20, 1834,
(MG) Wm. Duncan.
Calvin Pugh and Martha E. Guerrant, (MD) December 18, 1870.
Rev. S. S. Sams and Mrs. Ann M. Doubleday, (MD) January 19,
1860.
Caleb Warren Tate and Emily Hamblin, (MD) October 8, 1839,
(UK) Joseph Scholl.
James Wise and Rebecca E. Miller, (MD) March 30, 1854.

Jackson Combs and Sarah Gardner, (MD) November 9, 1858.
Daniel Carker and Ann Eliza Wilson, (MD) April 24, 1853.
Samuel R. Downy and Irene M. Oscley, (MD) April 20, 1870.
--- Estill and Mrs. Berry, (MD) November 8, 1867.
George A. Gilmore and M. J. Bryan, (MD) March 10, 1846,
    (UK) M. B. Douglass, Groom is from Warren County,
    Illinois.
Wesley C. Hall and M. E. Holt, (MD) March 19, 1868.
Schuyler B. Ham and Pamelia Ann Jones, (MD) February 21,
    1833, (UK) Wm. W. Redman.
John Hutcherson and Isabel Meteer, (MD) September 21, 1837,
    (MG) Theo. Boulware.
Y. R. Kidwell and Lucy D. Dyson, (MD) November 4, 1869.
Lewis Kiger and Angeline Crago, (MD) January 22, 1867.
James Riggins and Elizabeth Haynes, (MD) September 2, 1830,
    (UK) Theo. Stephens.
James Robnett and Sarah Ann James, (MD) March 17, 1840, (UK)
    M. P. Wells.
Mentor Suggett and Louisa Petty, (MD) December 21, 1837,
    (MG) Theo. Boulware.
Andrew M. Wiley and Jane H. Walker, (MD) March 31, 1842,
    (UK) Absalom Rice.
James A. Boyes and Mary A. Baker, (MD) October 24, 1867.
John Carrington and Nancy Hyten, (MD) February 7, 1855.
Willis S. Debo and Ann Maria Carew, (MD) February 18, 1868,
    (MG) W. A. Rothwell.
Amizon Hays and Agnes McMurty, (MD) October 21, 1841, (UK)
    Wm. B. Douglass.
William Hutts and Margaret A. Davis, (MD) August 25, 1864.
Asa Pulliam and Angeline Miller, (MD) January 7, 1837, (MG)
    R. H. Jordon.
Joseh W. Riggs and Sarah E. Maffett, (MD) December 23, 1858.
John Stewart and Martha J. Stewart, (MD) December 23, 1854.
James Belama and Zerelda Emerine Roberts, (MD) November 22,
    1838, (MG) Theo. Boulware.
Nathaniel Bradford and Polly Farrier, (MD) March 5, 1840,
    (JP) Joseph T. Bryan.
Aguiller (sic) Divers and Mary Cheatham, (MD) December 22,
    1858.
Armsted B. Gilbert and Mary Philips, (MD) March 27, 1856.
H. C. Harper and Rachel M. Yager, (MD) December 10, 1863.
Franklin Maden and Leanas (sic) Haw, (MD) April 25, 1844.
Uel (sic) Ramsey and Sarah I. Conger, (MD) February 4, 1857.
William Trimble and Martha Hughes, (MD) April 7, 1842, (UK)
    Jacob Coons.
Blanton Wray and Margaret Ann Hultz, (MD) July 5, 1837, (MG)
    James Love, Groom is from Warren County.
Benjamin Braham and Mary Ann Tucker, (MD)September 28, 1832,
    (MG) Wm. Coats.

Joseph Carr and Martha A. Martin, (MD) July 13, 1848.
John Drinkard and America Basinger, (MD) April 6, 1865.
John Ferguson and Elizabeth Smith, (MD) March 10, 1870.
Robert Maddox and Mary Keithler, (MD) April 10, 1856.
Woodson Lynes and Mattie B. Alexander, (MD) September 9, 1869.
Robert Samuel and Martha Overton, (MD) November 5, 1829, (MG) Theo. Boulware, Groom is from Palmyra.
Thomas Taylor and Lydia Dearing, (MD) March 5, 1837, (JP) Jas. Stewart.
James H. Bell and Sarah A. Bell, (MD) January 13, 1859.
James H. Bentley and Louisa F. Davis, (MD)September 8, 1870, Groom is from Montogmery County.
William Callison and Nancy Moore, (MD) April 26, 1832, (JP) John A. Burt.
William Charleton and Sarah Williams, (MD) November 5, 1841, (JP) Joseph Scholl, Groom is from Montgomery County.
James H. Cook and Grizella B. Caldwell, (MD) May 16, 1839, (MG) J. L Yantis, Groom is from St. Louis.
Francis Dodds and Mehaldy Coats, (MD) September 18, 1828, (MG) Jabez Ham.
Milton Saylor and Jane Lark, (MD) October 21, 1869, Groom is from Montgomery County.
Archibald R. Turck and Martha Renfro, (MD)December 10, 1854, Groom is from Montgomery County.
George Strickland and Jane Humphries, (MD) June 21, 1848, Groom is from Osage County.
Heinnih (sic) Vogel and Anna Baer, (MD) March 8, 1870, Bride is from Montgomery County.
John M. Berry and Jerusia (sic) Wright, (MD) May 28, 1850, (JP) M. S. Coats.
Ferdinand Tincher and Mahala M. Jones, (MD) November 14, 1850, (UK) C. J. VanDeventer.
Henry Stolle and Ann Stolle, (MD) September 20, 1864.
Elbert Smith and Julina Kemp, (MD) February 5, 1861.
John Chappell and Paralee Gillispy, (MD) June 5, 1848.
A. Evans and Sarah Jane Walton, (MD) October 28, 1859.
Richard McDonold and Hannah Harrison, (MD) April 27, 1851, (JP) W. J. Gilman.
Solomon T. Pasley and Mary E. Kemp, (MD) October 24, 1861.
Jacob Sigler and Elizabeth Hana, (MD) August 5, 1846, (UK) Z. N. Roberts.
J. L. Williamson and Rebecca Brown, (MD) October 19, 1859.
John T. Bradly and Martha Suggett, (MD) September 15, 1842, (UK) James Suggett.
Zepheniah Todd and Sally Stephens, (MD) September 5, 1839, (UK) Thos. P. Stephens, Groom is from Clay County.
William Truman and Letha Hudson, (MD) August 8, 1841, (JP) Joseph Scholl.

William Cave and Margaret Harrison, (MD) April 15, 1846, (UK) M. P. Wells.

Albin J. Dearing and Mary M. Harris, (MD) August 30, 1837.

Geo. W. Herring and Hester Ann Kemp, (MD) March 9, 1843, (UK) John R. Craghead.

Hiram Holt and Permelia Carrington, (MD) June 8, 1843, (UK) John E. Nevins.

Joseph C. McCracken and Nancy Crutsinger, (MD) September 18, 1864.

Christian Ostes and Mary Doerring, (MD) August 18, 1860.

Johann Vogel and Cumgrunde (sic) Spindler, (MD) March 8, 1870, Bride is from Montgomery County.

Ezekiel Williamson and Elizabeth B. Devore, (MD) October 14, 1847.

John Berry and Margaret Galbreath, (MD) March 25, 1830, (MG) Wm. Coats.

William H. Cox and Nani (sic) I. Gay, (MD) September 11, 1867.

William Duvall and Eliza Tully, (MD) February 27, 1827, (MG) Wm. Coats.

Robert Holt and Eliza Holt, (MD) July 30, 1846, (MG) James Criswell.

John Salor and Virginia Perkins, (MD) October 17, 1833, (MG) Jabez Ham, Groom is from Montogmery County.

Joseph Slaughter and Jane Artmen, (MD) September 16, 1860.

John Wills and Mary Hughes, (MD) December 1, 1837, (MG)Jabez Ham.

Napoleon B. Yancey and Sarah C. Oliver, (MD) September 5, 1867.

Joel D. Bennett and Mary M. McAfee, (MD) February 19, 1839, (MG) R. L. McAfee, Bride is from Kentucky.

Robert Cleveland and Eliz. A. Doyale, (MD)February 25, 1864.

David Duncan and Charlotte Powel, (MD) November 23, 1843.

Alexander Hord and Mary G. Janis, (MD) October 22, 1845, (UK) Jacob Ligler.

John McClintic and Elizabeth Tincher, (MD) April --, 1863.

T. R. Moore and N. F. Jones, (MD) September 25, 1861.

William N. Woods and Mary Dougherty, (MD) March 2, 1865, (UK) John Montgomery.

James F. Berry and Martha Jane Cartwell, (MD) February 10, 1867.

Tillman G. Vaughn and Eliza Ann Brandon, (MD) June 19, 1866.

Alexander Carter and Martha Thomas, (MD) November 1, 1843.

Robert Craig and Mary Huston, (MD) January 30, 1850, (MG) Noah Flood.

John Decker and Mary Nance, (MD) January 13, 1831, (UK) Geo. Bartley.

Clayton Frazour and Minerva E. Smith, (MD)February 27, 1862.

Ambrose D. Frye and Margaret Ellen Glendi, (MD)April 7,1858.

103

John Hodge and Louisa Meelor, (MD) October 30, 1832, (UK)
   Ninian Ridgway.
Levi McMurty and Catherine Scholl, (MD) December 6, 1855.
Samuel Meng and S. Calton, (MD) January 8, 1864.
Rev. Frank Savage and Nancy Givens, (MD) August 13, 1865.
Henry Tate and Drewshain (sic) Hall, (MD) January 14, 1864.
Richard Chamberlain and Minnie Birch, (MD) January 14, 1869.
Andrew Davis and Matilda May, (MD) October 3, 1844, (ED)
   Jacob Coons.
Jordan Dehaven and Nancy Callaway, (MD) October 29, 1857.
William Faris and Amanda Jones, (MD) May 24, 1868.
J. L. Porter and Amanda Ganig (sic), (MD December 8, 1848,
   (UK) W. W. Kemp.
Martain Basinger and Faney Basinger, (MD)September 12, 1869.
Josiah E. Wright and Jerusha (sic) Ann Pratt, (MD) January
   26, 1845, (JP) J. R. Craghead.
Joseph Witcher and Mildred F. Hall, (MD) November 22, 1867.
James Smallwood and Elizabeth Davenport, (MD) June 28, 1867.
William Hornbuckle and Sarah Allen, (MD)September 11, 1867.
Robert H. Gasper and Mary M. Sheets, (MD) December 17, 1869.
Levi Dudley Medders and Mary Ann Jackson, (MD) August 12,
   1857.
Wm. B. Patton and Naomi Johnson, (MD) October 5, 1845, (MG)
   Enoch Fruit.
Griffin P. Sanders and Eliz. A. Grant, (MD)January --, 1840,
   (MG) J. L. Yantis.
Ruben Tatum and July A. Stokes, (MD) October 3, 1869.
Irvin C. Vivion and Mollie A. Wallace, (MD)January 24, 1865,
   Groom is from Boone County.
Dr. Archilles Wilkerson and Larenda L. Baker, (MD) May 18,
   1865.
John R. Carter and Margaret Fletcher, (MD) January 30, 1868,
   (UK) W. M. Burnham.
Robert A. Crews and Sarah E. Cheatham, (MD) December 23,
   1868, (UK) D. M. Grandfield.
James Crump and Polly Ann Martin, (MD) September 22, 1842,
   (MG) James Love.
Robert Houchens and Harriet Stults, (MD) January 23, 1855.
Francis M. Scott and Marthy Pain, (MD) July 26, 1869, (UK)
   John E. Atkinson.
Elias J. Tharp and Elizabeth A. Darm (sic), (MD) July 31,
   1853, (UK) Daniel Penny.
W. E. Roberts and P. F. Berry, (MD)March 7, 1850, (MG) Theo.
   Boulware.
Geo. D. White and Mrs. Martha Vaughn, (MD) March 5, 1863,
   (UK) Jas. H. Tuttle.
William K. VanArsdall and Rosanna M. Curry, (MD) November
   19, 1829, (UK) D. M. Kirkpatrick.
Jas. R. Boyce, jr. and Bettie Fant, (MD) April 26, 1870.

John Carnes and Eliz. J. Ewing, (MD) March 6, 1853.
John Galdwell and Sarah Ann Faber, (MD) July 19, 1838.
Allen Lee Batts and Sarah Jane Linch, (MD) June 12, 1861.
John T. Harris and Lutitia Vandaver, (MD) March 31, 1867.
Timothy Holt and Elizabeth Clatterbuck, (MD) March 18, 1858.
Milton Scholl and Sally Hughs, (MD) March 16, 1848, (UK) Wm.
    B. Douglass.
Jas. Coffee Winscott and Ann Mary James, (MD)March 16, 1870,
    Groom is from Caldwell County.
Gideon S. Roberson and Mary F. Thomas, (MD) May 3, 1868.
Edward M. Sitton and Lucy A. Fletcher, (MD)January 11, 1870.
--- Garrett and Lucy Scott, (MD) August 13, 1835, (UK) Robt.
    A. Younger.
Richard T. Davis and Julian Cannungton (sic), (MD) September
    4, 1861.
William Darby and Francis Ann Neil, (MD) January 17, 1858.
Thomas Coen and Mollie Barnard, (MD) December 30, 1869.
Morgan Hill and Nancy Scrogham, (MD) July 28, 1846, (UK)
    Jacob Coons.
Abner Holt and Julian Gray, (MD) February 17, 1842.
William Mivis and Mildred E. Bell, (MD) July 7, 1853.
William Smidy and Malissa J. Martin, (MD) May 5, 1842, (JP)
    H. J. Turner.
John Wadley and Susannah Howard, (MD) December 29, 1825,
    (JP) Geo. King.
William J. Bellew and Chloe E. Stephens, (MD) May 16, 1866,
    Groom is from Boone County.
Louis Uno and Elizabeth Surrat, (MD) October 22, 1830, (JP)
    Henry Neill.
Wiley Maddon and Nancy Ann Goff, (MD) July 17, 1847.
Thomas M. Rutter and Violet C. Patton, (MD) November 24,
    1870.
Alexander Sloan and Mary J. Crago, (MD) May 12, 1861.
Andrew Williamson and Barbara S. Kyger, (MD) December 29,
    1868.
Trotter Bearn and Nancy Wilfley, (MD) March 12, 1837, (MG)
    John T. A. Henderson.
Henry Cartmile and Janava (sic) McClelland, (MD) December
    27, 1860.
Joseph Chick and Minerva Miller, (MD) January 7, 1847, (ED)
    M. P. Wills.
James Plunkett and Manery (sic) Ferguson, (MD)July 19, 1843,
    (UK) Jacob Coons.
John Tucker and Virginia Shyer, (MD) January 16, 1867.
Alfred Stout and Jane Pulliam, (MD) February 1, 1860.
David McCormic and Unice Jones, (MD) March 12, 1832, (JP) J.
    A. Burt.
Thomas McClelland and Sarah Robinet, (MD) May 1, 1832, (UK)
    Theo. P. Stephens, Bride is from Boone County.

Samuel W. Hickerson and Rebecca A. Harvey, (MD) January 28, 1858.

John H. Charlton and Nancy Carter, (MD) March 27, 1833, (UK) Geo. T. Keys.

Newman Clanton and Mariah P. Kelso, (MD January 2, 1840, (JP) T. G. Jones, Groom is from Montgomery County.

Thomas B. Howe and Zipparah (sic) Thatcher, (MD) September 14, 1842, (MG) Theo. Boulware.

John Hudson and Sarah Crank, (MD) November 17, 1852.

W. W. Miller and Martha Loyd, (MD) February 23, 1869.

Bennett Parmer and Pauline Thornton, (MD)September 15, 1868.

Dien (sic) Wilkerson and Harriet Dunham, (MD)August 2, 1831, (JP) J. W. Johnson.

James Chriswell and Jane Allen, (MD) October 15, 1835, (MG) Jno. Pace.

Richard W. Donell and Nancy Crosswaite, (MD) October 10, 1839.

Joseph H. Chang and Elizabeth Dozier, (MD) June 13, 1854, (UK) Martin D. Noland.

Lewis Hawkins and Claudia Thomas, (MD) January 31, 1828, (MG) Wm. Coats.

James Clingman and Salita (sic) Morgan, (MD) May 18, 1848, (JP) J. K. Allen.

Jacob Strode and Frances May, (MD) July 20, 1826, (MG) Wm. Coats.

James H. Bell and Semantha Swesater (sic), (MD) December 11, 1856.

John R. Craighead and Mrs. T. M. Patton, (MD) February 28, 1866, (JP) J. G. Carter.

James Delvin and Mary Y. Finley, (MD) February 2, 1854.

Patrick Ewing and Mrs. E. A. Fisher, (MD) June 15, 1851, (MG) Theo. Boulware.

James R. Scholl and Artmeisia McMahan, (MD) August 13, 1868.

Daniel Vincen and Susan Cryswell, (MD) November 15, 1864.

James M. Creed and M. M. Hill, (MD) July 13, 1853.

Drury Hall and Catharine Harris, (MD) September 26, 1854, (JP) M. S. Coats.

Milton Mercer Smith and Nanny West, (MD) February 25, 1869, Groom is from Cole County.

Joseph G. Wiley and Rosa Ann Guy, (MD) March 25, 1862, Groom is from St. Charles County.

Joseph D. Bartley and Saryann Wise, (MD) March 4, 1863.

Thomas G. Pledge and Liny Aje (sic) Edmonston, (MD) December 20, 1868.

George Cooly and Marthy (sic) Jane Waggoner, (MD) February 26, 1846, (UK) Chas. A. Ming.

James Drinkard and Eliza Ann Branch, (MD) November 21, 1855.

James L. Grant and Mariah Woodland, (MD) December 1, 1862, (MG) H. A. Bourland.

William C. Hile and Lucy J. Hall, (MD) November 22, 1860.
Shelton Moore and Sarah Bagby, (MD) April 27, 1848.
Thomas Pate and Ellen Craig, (MD) April 29, 1847, (MG) W. W.
    Robertson.
James Brackenridge and Martha Smith, (MD) December 23, 1846,
    (MG) J. R. Symmington.
David Bowen and Elizabeth Hays, (MD) December 9, 1866, (MG)
    Stephen Ham.
Charles Turner and Elizabeth Sacre (sic), (MD November 27,
    1858.
Wharton A. Bennett and Mary F. McKamsey, (MD) September 25,
    1849, (UK) D. Coulter.
Jacob Zumwalt and Sarah Zumwalt, (MD) August 18, 1836, (JP)
    A. Norflet.
Albert Woods and Mary Eliz. Howard, (MD) September 27, 1866.
Oliver Wright and Veany Pratt, (MD) November 28, 1839, (UK)
    John Fletcher.
David Thompson and Ann Dorting, (MD) July 12, 1827, (JP) Wm.
    Martin.
Samuel P. Riggs and Jane Owen, (MD) May 5, 1859.
John L. Rodgers and Virginia C. Berry, (MD) December 20,
    1860.
London Snell and Susan Snell, (MD) December 21, 1843, (MG)
    Theo. Boulware.
Carl Spencer and Nancy Freeman, (MD) April 7, 1870.
John W. Pierce and Manda Newsom, (MD) February 2, 1860.
John Smith and Mary Thomas, (MD) December 7, 1843.
Elisha J. Owens and Sarah Ann Magart, (MD) February 17,
    1870.
John P. Mosley and Pollie Ann Craig, (MD)September 16, 1858.
Morris Moore and Elizabeth Barry, (MD) April 27, 1841, (JP)
    John K. Barry.
Robert W. Miller and Eliza J. Crowson, (MD) October 5, 1864.
W. Magart and M. J. Payton, (MD) November 24, 1853.
John J. Sheely and Caroline A. Morgan, (MD) November 23,
    1855.
James T. Hutts and L. B. Crump, (MD) September 13, 1863.
John Howe and Nannie A. Turner, (MD) June 24, 1868.
Robert Hugh and Cordelia Sutton, (MD) September 28, 1863,
    (JP) W. B. Tucker.
John Clatterbuck and Martha -----, (MD) April 29, 1830, (UK)
    D. M. Kirkpatrick.
Samuel Bowman and Nancy Jane Tealy, (MD) August 15, 1849,
    W. L. Ramsey.
Joshua Wayne and Jane Straw, (MD) October 17, 1848.
James Ward and Mary Long, (MD) July 29, 1835, (MG) Theo.
    Boulware, Groom is from Boone County.
W. W. Thomas and Nancy Y. Nichols, (MD) January 29, 1861.
Rufus Hiss and Eliza J. Glendy, (MD) October 19, 1852.

John Carney and Sarah Ann Adair, (MD) March 22, 1859.
Seton E. Owen and Adaline Payton, (MD) April 23, 1865.
Monty Schleer and Caroline Christ, (MD) April 14, 1864.
John D. Cason and Judy F. Hawkins, (MD) June 19, 1864.
Thomas H. Robinson and Martha M. Potter, (MD) December 7,
    1854, (MG) G. K. Ham.
David M. Hill and Frances Hill, (MD) February 7, 1850.
Philip Cassidy and Catherine Jones, (MD) September 25, 1870.
John W. Moore and Elizabeth Windsor, (MD) February 28, 1867.
Nathaniel Truitt and America Hughs, (MD) March 27, 1845,
    (MG) Noah Flood.
Thomas Chandler and Mary E. Hall, (MD) September 1, 1870.
George Walker and Amanda Hays Collard, (MD) October 13,
    1867, (JP) Wm. Penn.
William D. Turley and Laura Wood, (MD) March 28, 1869.
Geo. W. H. Chase and Frances Ann Offutt, (MD) January 30,
    1844.
Jacob F. Sanders and Frances Child, (MD) January 15, 1857.
William Chasteen and Mary Jane Sissel, (MD) September 3,
    1869.
Morgan B. White and Mrs. Susan Hughes, (MD) August 18, 1858.
William H. Chiles and Selila Ann Davis, (MD) April 21, 1859.
Albert W. Howison and Mary B. Moore, (MD)September 10, 1866.
Jno. Coats and Sally Smith, (MD) August 16, 1821, (UK) Pat-
    rick Ewing.
Hans Patton and Sally Hatton, (MD) March 23, 1826, (JP) Wm.
    Martin.
Grave Cook and Soffrony Sublet, (MD) March 31, 1825, (MG)
    Wm. Coats.
David L. Whaley and Martha M. Divers, (MD) May 22, 1859.
Samuel Wilkes and Malinda Tate, (MD) June 1, 1839, (JP) Jos.
    Scholl.
Charles O. Strother and Mary E. Strother, (MD) January 28,
    1868.
George W. Trimble and Eliz. A. Gibbs, (MD)December 14, 1859.
Edwin Robinson and Amadetter I. Myers, (MD) January 6, 1859.
William Smith and Nancy Jane Coil, (MD) April 17, 1856.David
David Orsborn and Nancy Jane Thomlin, (MD) August 10, 1854.
John A. Moore and Lucy Jane McKinney, (MD) October 15, 1862,
    (UK) W. J. Jackson.
Henry B. Hornbuckle and Louisa J. Hinton, (MD) November 2,
    1848, (UK) Franklin Jenkins.
Francis M. Day and Amanda C. Dudley, (MD) June 4, 1857.
Isaac Clark and Eliz. Ann Everheart, (MD) November 6, 1845,
    (UK) W. B. Douglass, Groom is from Audrain County.
Samuel Humphries and Louisa G. Smart, (MD) March 3, 1833,
    (UK) Wm. W. Redman.
Irvin Wright and Rhoda Gordon, (MD) October 1, 1870, (MG)
    Jerome Bentley, Bride is from Polk County.

Columbus Winsdom and Mary Hendricks, (MD)November 19, 1867,
(MG) S. A. Beauchamp, Groom is from Audrain County.
George W. Poage and Sarah M. Wilson, (MD) March 14, 1853,
(MG) T. Scott.
John P. White and Georgeann Smart, (MD) September 28, 1870,
(MG) Absalom Rice.
Henry Tinnan and A. S. Robinson, (MD) June 2, 1869.
George W. Wylie and Jane Boaz, (MD) March 26, 1862, Groom is
from Ralls County.
John Sutter and Wilhelmine Stier, (MD) November 28, 1869,
Groom and Bride are from Bluffton, Mo.
Jefferson Owens and Polly Ann Adcock, (MD) August 26, 1855.
William H. Clanton and Laura A. Alkin, (MD) April 20, 1852,
(UK) W. Asbery Mayhew.
Greenup Snell and Sarah Ann Mackentire, (MD) December 14,
1837, (MG) James Barnes.
Maj. Thomas West and Mrs. Sally Smith, (MD) September 16,
1849, (UK) David Coulter.
James B. Sanders and Ann Eliz. Farmer, (MD) September 3,
1856.
John M. Ward and Margaret Hunt, (MD) December 27, 1839, (JP)
Geo. Morris.
Paul Pomi and Elizabeth Allen, (MD) July 22, 1869.
Jn. E. Overstreet and Mrs. Sarah Overfelt, (MD September 11,
1851.
John W. Moore and Margaret A. Davis, (MD) November 8, 1855.
William H. Chase and Margaret D. Offutt, (MD) January 14,
1846, (MG) Rich Bona.
John Iihaney and Mary Jane Offett, (MD) January 5, 1858.
Jesse Jacob Polly Ann Broughton, (MD) May 7, 1843, (UK)
James Thompson.
William Saia and Emeline Gee, (MD) July 28, 1842, (UK) Geo.
W. Morris.
--- Waldring and Rebecca Ransom, (MD) June 25, 1837, (JP) A.
Norflet.
Elijah M. Vandiver and Mary Cath. Curtis, (MD)June 10, 1858.
W. L. Williamson and Sarah Mattox, (MD) January 20, 1867.
Benjamin S. South and Emily A. Moore, (MD October 28, 1847.
Jerret Mapin and Mary E. Scholl, (MD) January 23, 1868,
Groom is from Montgomery County.
Hugh McGary and Susan Davis, (MD)February 9, 1837, (JP) Jas.
Stewart.
Henry Hudson and Mrs. Harriet Gibbs, (MD) January 19, 1848,
(UK) James Criswell.
James M. Creed and Martha J. Wilson, (MD) February 26, 1839,
(MG) J. L. yantis.
Thos. A. Howard and Louisa West, (MD) September 18, 1843,
(UK) J. D. N. Thompson.
James Miller and Martha S. Baker, (MD) May 2, 1855.

John Thomas and Sarah Nichols, (MD)March 2, 1848, (MG) Theo.
   Boulware.
Julias Walls and Alay Langly, (MD) November 14, 1834, (JP)
   B. Ramsey.
James M. Hook and Betty Jane Herring, (MD)February 20, 1861.
Joseph A. Wilson and Margaret J. Hamilton, (MD) December 13,
   1860, Groom is from Augusta County.
Moses Bennett and Lousinda McKamey, (MD) November 22, 1834,
   (MG) R. S. McAfee.
Solomon Craghead and Elizabeth Dunlap, (MD) November 13,
   1828, (UK) David Kirkpatrick.
Edward Hickman and Emma J. Miller, (MD) March 25, 1869,
   Groom and Bride are both from Montgomery County.
G. J. Triplett and Lucy E. Smith, (MD) April 6, 1857.
George Bentley and Polly Swearinger, (MD) April 1, 1866.
James S. Tuttle and Martha L. Boone, (MD) May 21, 1846, (MG)
   Noah Flood.
Jas. Wm. Bradley and Nancy F. Craghead, (MD) June 8, 1847,
   (MG) Wm. W. Redman.
Oliver W. Cruse and Phebe E. Carter, (MD) December 1, 1856.
A. Harrison and A. Craig, (MD) June 28, 1831, (MG) Theo.
   Boulware.
William J. Gray and Lydia E. Bell, (MD) March 15, 1860.
D. Wilkins and Sue Gorham, (MD) May 21, 1857.
David Huff and Sally Swan, (MD) February 21, 1841.
James Boyes and Jemima Freeman, (MD) February 12, 1833, (JP)
   John R. Barry.
Robert Gilman and Mariah Coons, (MD) October 29, 1841, (JP)
   A. Northphen.
George W. Crain and Mary Hays, (MD) December 14, 1854, Groom
   is from Audrain County.
Willis E. Dorton and Harriet Lepard, (MD) April 5, 1848.
R. Hudnel and Amanda A. Scott, (MD) July 4, 1869.
Cyrus R. Scholl and Mary Jane Maughes, (MD) October 3, 1852,
   (UK) Alia B. Suethen (sic).
Henry T. Wright and Elizabeth Jameson, (MD) February 24,
   1848, (ED) M. P. Wills.
Robert H. Tate and Sarah M. Kelsick, (MD) October 24, 1849.
G. W. Sutton and Martha Pettus, (MD)May 15, 1853, (UK) Mich.
   Bright, Groom and Bride are both from Boone County.
Albert G. Humphreys and Mary Jane Long, (MD) April 8, 1857,
   Bride is from St. Charles.
Joseph P. Wiseman and Eliz. Jane Robinson, (MD) February 28,
   1844, (MG) B. R. Johnson.
James Bowen and Polly Mages, (MD) February 1, 1844, (MG)
   Jacob Coons.
Edwin Swon and Sarah Ellis, (MD) December 5, 1861.
Willoughby I. McGary and Susan M. Smart, (MD) May 10, 1869,
   (UK) D. M. Grandfield.

Isaac F. Coons and Amanda Houly, (MD) October 2, 1851, (MG)
T. M. Allen.
John J. Husto and Mollie T. Hutchinson, (MD) April 16, 1868.
John Monteer and Susanna Bryan, (MD) December 21, 1837, (JP)
J. A. Burt.
Andrew Y. Rodgers and Rachael Pierce, (MD) December 12,1861.
William A. B. Craghead and Nancy May, (MD)February 25, 1848,
(MG) Jas. M. Green.
Walter Robertson and Mary Eliz. Martien, (MD) September 9,
1853.
John Robt. Crawford and Mary Jane Hall, (MD) January 12,
1854, (JP) John Winn.
James Moore and Vicy Ann Smith, (MD) May 10, 1827, (MG) Wm.
Coats.
Rawley H. Crow and Lucinda Boyd, (MD) March 27, 1845, (MG)
Jacob Ligler.
Calvin Hoveck and Martha A. Biva, (MD) July 8, 1857.
John Smith and Lucinda Eliz. Garret, (MD) March 24, 1858.
James Robinson and Jane Darby, (MD) April 13, 1848.
Elijah Bennet and Tirah Hisey, (MD) January 11, 1854.
William C. White and Harriet Ann Drinkard, (MD) April 29,
1856.
Charles Utter and Lucy A. Reynolds, (MD) October 21, 1869.
Meady Mills and Mary Jane Jennings, (MD) January 28, 1855,
(JP) Robert Jones.
Robert C. Boyce and Asinah (sic) Ann Murphy, (MD) March 24,
1830, (UK) D. M. Kirkpatrick.
Edward Dewland and Lucinda Miller, (MD) December 10, 1846,
(UK) John Green.
J. G. Morris and Marcy C. McCelland, (MD)September 20, 1859.
Geo. W. Stucker and Mildred McCall, (MD) February 10, 1854.
Marcelas Threlkild and Eliza Smith, (MD) August 16, 1857.
Charles Hobbs and Mary Craig, (MD) August 7, 1845, (MG)Theo.
Boulware.
William Clark and Sarah Wadley, (MD) November 2, 1826, (JP)
Jas. Henderson.
Alfred Moon and Martha Young, (MD) July 8, 1847.
Samuel Berry and Frances H. McCall, (MD) February 8, 1866.
Glover Smart and Elvira Day, (MD) February 5, 1834, (UK)
Geo. Hopkins.
Simeon Crago and Francis A. Kertley, (MD) August 4, 1841,
(MG) Geo. T. Key.
Charles Hill and Sarah Tatrum, (MD) March 14, 1850.
Arbickle Sangstu (sic) and Eliza Jane Hamilton, (MD) June 6,
1839, (MG) J. S. Yantis.
Mastin Vaughn and Caroline WIlburn, (MD) November 26, 1834,
(MG) J. Ham.
David Yount and Caty Waggoner, (MD) December 12, 1833, (UK)
Beverly A. Ramsey.

Azariah F. Cobb and Mrs. Sally Wilson, (MD) August 6, 1858.
John S. Marlow and Eliza Ann Garrett, (MD) May 31, 1855.
Milton V. Davis and Jane C. Dunlap, (MD) January 1, 1840,
     (MG) J. L. Yantis.
James Cobb and Ann Boone, (MD) December 31, 1829.
James Hugh Batt and Nannie G. Duncan, (MD) March 25, 1862.
Elihio (sic) Hardin and Mrs. M. Willcoxen, (MD) November 23,
     1857.
John Coons and Eliz. J. Ridgeway, (MD) January 15, 1859.
James M. Simcoe and Mary E. Humphreys, (MD) February 15,
     1866.
John White and Melinda Gathright, (MD) January 21, 1857.
Robert Craghead and Nancy C. Hall, (MD) October 17, 1861.
Charles E. Winscott and Margaret J. Clingman, (MD) March 27,
     1870.
Samuel Creed and Ellen Tincher, (MD) September 19, 1867.
Samuel Duly and Sarah Emiet, (MD) June 23, 1847, (ED) Jacob
     Coons.
John H. Crow and Mary Jane R. Ferguson, (MD) December 19,
     1844, (MG) Jacob Ligler.
Mason Wise and Hettie B. Fullilove, (MD) October 7, 1868,
     (UK) D. M. Grandfield.
Stephen N. Bell and Amanda M. Blackburn, (MD)August 4, 1842,
     (MG) R. C. Hill.
Ervin VanBibber and Mary Bosher, (MD) May 8, 1853, (JP) J.
     A. Burt.
Jacob Crowson and Martha Miller, (MD) April 27, 1848.
William Major and Martha Sanders, (MD) January 25, 1844,
     (UK) Geo. B. Hopkins.
William J. Denny and Mary Ann Branch, (MD) September 15,
     1853.
J. T. S. Hinton and Sarah F. White, (MD) October 28, 1866.
John Truitt and Eliz. J. Kimbrough, (MD) January 14, 1856.
Jackson Harris and Rachel Harris, (MD) September 26, 1854.
Robert W. Criswell and Martha A. H. Hudson, (MD) October 15,
     1856.
William Craighead and Josephine Dunn, (MD) January 28, 1869.
Francis Doyle and Caroline Cleveland, (MD) February 5, 1857.
Benj. W. S. C. Craghead and Margaret Ann Douglass, (MD) Oct-
     ober 21, 1857.
Philip Gillaspie and Emily Blackwell, (MD) January 28, 1857.
Wyatt Williamson and Frances T. Callaway, (MD) December 20,
     1848.
John Bowen and Eliza J. M. Newsom, (MD) November 11, 1868.
Coswell West and Matilda Bryan, (MD) February 20, 1845,
     (UK) Chas. A. Ming, Groom is from Boone County.
Goodman Cowles and Eliz. A. Davis, (MD) January 13, 1853,
     (MG) Robert A. Younger.
Thomas G. Dulin and Mrs. Maria Sutton, (MD)February 22,1857.

William M. Duly and Amanda Dozier, (MD) December 17, 1856.
William Gillmore and Sarah Quinn, (MD) December 22, 1831,
  (JP) Horace Sheley.
Pino (sic) Glover and Sallie N. Bell, (MD) March 20, 1860.
John F. Heron and Rosa White, (MD) November 9, 1865.
Andrew Herrin and Latina E. Crook, (MD) March 14, 1850,
  (UK) Absalom Rice.
Wm. Henry Woolery and Martha Ann Morris, (MD) March 15,
  1854, (UK) Levi M. Gwin.
Vincent Vandiver and Julia Stephenson, (MD) February 12,
  1857.
Graham Turner and Mrs. Lucinda Baskett, (MD) March 30, 1856.
David Wilcoxen and Martha Blythe, (MD) October 28, 1841,
  (UK) Benj. Wren, Groom is from Boone County.
David Todd and Frances Crowson, (MD) April 11, 1850, (UK)
  Thos. P. Stephens, Groom is from Howard County.
Joseph T. Mosely and Nanny J. Criswell, (MD) September 6,
  1868.
William H. Thomas and Mary Rogers, (MD) February 19, 1861.
Dabney H. Crank and Mary Ann Stanley, (MD) March 18, 1841,
  (MG) Geo. Smith.
Lewis Swearigen and Lucretia Hibbert, (MD)February 21, 1867.
William Tuck and Sarah Armstrong, (MD) May 4, 1840, (JP) R.
  Brandon.
Isuau (sic) Moreor and Ophelia Livingston, (MD) February 4,
  1838, (UK) B. A. Ramsey.
Richard Hayden and Mary Ann Puckett, (MD) March 1, 1866,
  (JP) John Jolly, Groom is from Greene County.
James Sims and Margaret Isham, (MD) May 22, 1834, (MG) Wm.
  Duncan.
J. W. Smart and Martha A. Knight, (MD) December 22, 1867,
  (JP) J. O. Craighead.
James Herron and Sally Jane Nite, (MD) June 17, 1841, (UK)
  Absalom Rice.
George Craig and Hannah Atwater, (MD) March 15, 1838, (UK)
  John F. Young.
Isham McDonold and Clarinda Larue, (MD) May 26, 1853, (MG)
  John P. Jesse.
Gustav Sippett and Henrietta Frank, (MD) November 7, 1857.
Robert T. Hays and Mary E. Fitzgerald, (MD) March 21, 1867,
  (UK) Wm. B. Walthall.
Garland Crews and Lucrecia Baker, (MD) March 27, 1870, (ED)
  W. C. Ridgway.
Thomas Bradley and Cynthia Swan, (MD) December 8, 1853, (MG)
  Jas. E. Hughes.
Joshey (sic) B. Hansard and Mary J. McGee, (MD) June 10,
  1868, (MG) W. H. Sipple.
David C. Givens and Susan P. Fisher, (MD) September 8, 1852.
S. A. Dunlap and Susan E. Mosly, (MD) April 15, 1856.

Wilson B. Crago and Octava Mizzingo, (MD) November 28, 1850.
William Davis and Eliza Baker, (MD) May 30, 1831, (MG) Allen McGuire.
J. W. Dawes and Nannie Boulds, (MD) June 19, 1870.
Joseph Watkins and Martha W. Dyers, (MD) November 22, 1837, (MG) R. L. McAfee.
Jasper I. Bond and Mary L. Smith, (MD) February 24, 1869.
Albert Herring and Nancy Jane Hill, (MD) May 9, 1857.
George W. Criswell and Mary Karney, (MD) February 18, 1852.
James W. Suggett and Mildred A. Gilpin, (MD) March 5, 1868.
Dr. A. N. C. Tate and Mary Eliz. Wilson, (MD) February 23, 1854, (MG) W. W. Robertson.
James P. Day and Sarah J. Mosely, (MD) January 29, 1846.
George Dorris and S. Colton, (MD) May 5, 1864.
Thomas Tucker and Betsy Harper, (MD) May 2, 1823, (JP) Thos. Fisher.
Raleigh H. Crow and Susan W. Gray, (MD September 7, 1854.
Robert M. Hazelet and Louisa C. Houf, (MD) January 2, 1861.
Charles Thimnu (sic) and Frances Kennett, (MD) October 31, 1843, (MG) W. W. Robertson.
Henry Stults and Margaret A. Houf, (MD) July 8, 1852.
William T. Day and --- Paget, (MD) February 27, 1850, (UK) Geo. B. Hopkins.
Benjamin L. Bradley and Margaret E. Dehaven, (MD) April 12, 1859.
John Herring and Amanda Jane Knight, (MD) June 18, 1846.
James M. Turley and Mattie C. Beeding, (MD) June 26, 1854.
Hankerson Ware and Eliza J. Watkins, (MD) July 14, 1840, (UK) J. L. Yantis.
John S. M. Thomas and Mary J. Hall, (MD) January 31, 1856.
Chas. M. Ward and Ema Smith, (MD) July 6, 1862, Groom is from Jefferson City.
William Vanover and Mary Loyd, (MD) November 18, 1850.
James E. Wilks and and Hanna Kelsick, (MD) March 2, 1869, Groom and Bride are from Montgomery County.
James M. Davis and Mary E. Whyte, (MD) April 25, 1861.
Samuel S. Swepster and Martha Suey (sic) Nobles, (MD) January 9, 1861.
Isaac N. Hockaday and Sarah K. Shortridge, (MD) December 23, 1841, (MG) Absalom Rice.
James Dinsmon and Margaret Macannon, (MD) November 25, 1841.
John Davis and Mary Jane Turner, (MD) July 5, 1845, (JP) Chas. A. Ming.
William H. Thomas and Elizabeth Collier, (MD) August 22, 1850, (MG) Absalom Rice.
Richard Turner and Nancy Price, (MD) October 6, 1842.
John T. Deshazo and Cahrlotte Walker, (MD) June 22, 1837, (JP) Jas. Stewart.

S. Creasy and M. F. Craighead, (MD) February 15, 1870.
Addison D. Sowers and Emeline Hinton, (MD) April 14, 1867.
R. Smith and Mrs. Susan Wagner, (MD) December 27, 1864.
Nath. Bradley and Mary Pemberton, (MD) March 13, 1845, (MG)
Jacob Coons.
James M. Turman and Margaret A. Everhart, (MD)June 26, 1854.
Richard Swan and Eliz. Ann Groom, (MD) December 1, 1842,
(MG) Noah Flood.
John Syms and Sarah Jane Moseley, (MD) June 15, 1854.
John L. Taler and Martha Wilkerson, (MD) August 31, 1835,
(MG) Wm. Coats.
Arthur Bradley and Mahaley Tharpall, (MD) May 24, 1855.
O. P. Thomas and S. A. McCartey, (MD) December 25, 1859.
Herod Utt and Rebecka Grig, (MD) September 23, 1863.
Franklin Criswell and Sarah J. Cosby, (MD) March 9, 1859.

B O O N E   C O U N T Y
(Callaway County Connections Only)

Book A, 1820 to 1841

Isaac Vincent of Callaway County and Parthenia Orr, (MD) Au-
gust 18, 1825.
Samuel Jamison of Callaway County and Malinda Harris,
(MD) August 10, 1826.
Granville Jamison of Callaway County and Eliza Neskutt,
(MD) March 1, 1837.
Gibson H. Emmons of Callaway County and Elizabeth Hatton,
(MD) January 13, 1828.
Nathan Barnes of Callaway and Tremanda Garnett, (MD) Septem-
ber 24, 1829.
Rile Langley of Callaway County and Matilda Taylor,
(MD) November 4, 1830.
William Ridgeway of Callaway County and Paulina Renfro,
(MD) April 19, 1831.
Thomas Suggett of Callaway County and Polly Patton, (MD) No-
vember 23, 1830.
Dr. WM. M. Duncan of Callaway County and Susan W. Harris,
(MD) October 6, 1831.
Joshua Selby of Callaway County and Ann Selby, (MD) March 4,
1832.
Louis Sharp and Jane Callaway of Callaway County, (MD) March
6, 1832.
Harrison Lynes and Mary Ann Gray of Callaway County,
(MD) August 28, 1833.

Thomas Ridgeway and Elizabeth Stephens, (MD) June 30, 1832, Groom and Bride are both from Callaway County, Groom's father is Ninian Ridgeway.

Benjamin Cason of Callaway County and Mary Hawkins, (MD) December 12, 1833.

William Stephens of Callaway County and Pamelia Renfro, (MD) March 13, 1834.

John H. Brooks of Callaway County and Harriet Barget, (MD) January 17, 1834.

Robert Nichols of Callaway County and Priscilla Wren, (MD) March 28, 1836.

James Thomas of Callaway County and Hannah Jane Waters, (MD) October 5, 1836.

Edmond Baker of Callaway County and Mary Bailey, (MD) November 9, 1836.

John James of Callaway County and Susan Harris, (MD) February 16, 1837.

Robert Nevins of Callaway County and Mary Ann Ridgeway, (MD) May 25, 1837.

Elkanah Hereford of Callaway County and Lucille Helm, (MD) March 15, 1838.

George Smith of Callaway County and Elizabeth Little, (MD) 9, 1838.

Cephias Selby of Callaway County and Lucinda Pemberton, (MD) October 8, 1840.

Book B, 1841 to 1849

Joseph Brown of Callaway County and S..A. Barnes, (MD) December 3, 1841.

Allen Old of Callaway County and Rebecca Winterbower, (MD) April 28, 1842.

Ruben Dorton of Callaway County and Eliza Ann Wilson, (MD) July 27, 1843, Bride is the daughter of Eli Wilson.

Milton Bennett of Callaway County and Ruth McMickle, (MD) December 12, 1844.

John Blythe of Callaway County and Priscilla Spry, (MD) May 31, 1846.

William F. Vanhorn and Sarah Kimbrough of Callaway County, (MD) December 15, 1846.

Richard Chaney of Callaway County and Elizabeth Pemberton, (MD) December 9, 1846.

Anthony Zumwalt of Callaway County and Martha Peak, (MD) December 1, 1847.

Thomas Nesbitt of Callaway County and Mary Bryan, (MD) December 4, 1847.

Martin Nichols of Callaway County and Caroline Crump, (MD) April 6, 1848.

Elijah Bennett of Callaway County and Casandra Vanlanding-
ham, (MD) October 19, 1848.
Benjamin Elley of Callaway County and Caltha (sic) Pemberton
(MD) March 15, 1849.
Harris M. Tibbets of Callaway County and Lucinda M. G.
Roberts, (MD) April 21, 1849.
George W. Kimbrough of Callaway County and Kitty Miller,
(MD) August 7, 1849.

MISSOURI STATESMAN
COLUMBIA, MO

March 23, 1855.
On March the 13th Betty Ann Baker, the daughter of Joseph
Baker of Callaway County, married Philip Hooper of Chariton
County. The marriage service was performed by Elder T. P.
Stephens.

August 24, 1855.
On August the 14th Russella Gibbs, the daughter of Robert F.
Gibbs of Boone County, married John S. James of Callaway
County.

October 26, 1855.
On October the 4th, Rev. D. Coulter married William N. Moore
to Margaret Ewing. The bride is the daughter of Capt. P.
Ewing of Callaway County.

November 9, 1855.
On November the 1st, Samuel Sapp, of Boone County, married
Mary Jane Watson. John K. Watson, of Callaway County, is the
father of the bride.

August 29, 1856.
On August the 20th, Ed Wigginton married John F. Crews, of
Boone County to Louisa Baker. She is the daughter of Thomas
Baker of Callaway County.

July 17, 1857.
On July the 15th, Rev. Green Carey married James Long, of
Boone County, to Mrs. Susan E. Crews. The father of the
bride is Creed Carter of Callaway County.

December 4, 1857.
Robert Ward, of Callaway County, was married to Emily Jane
Mourning, the daughter of Daniel Mourning. The marriage
services were performed by Elder E. E. Chrisman.

March 5, 1858.
On February 25th William Thomas, of Callaway County, married
Elizabeth Griffin, the daughter of Jesse Griffin of Boone
County. The marriage service was performed by Elder B. Wren.

June 11, 1858.

Peter McCrea, Callaway County, married Mary F. Cruse on June the 6th. She is the daughter of Stanley Cruse of Boone County. The marriage services was performed by Elder T. M. Allen.

November 26, 1858.

Rev. E. M. Martin, of St. Louis, married Dr. M. M. Maughas to E. C. L. Offatt. She is the daughter of Eli Offatt of Callaway County.

February 11, 1859.

Wm. Truitt, of Callaway County, married Ann Eliza Pemberton, the daughter of Harvey Pemberton of Boone County. The service was performed by T. M. Allen.

April 29, 1859.

On April the 21st, William H. Chiles, of Callaway County, married Delila Ann Davis. She is the daughter of James Davis. B. Wren, Elder, performed the marriage service,

March 14, 1862.

On February 16th, James P. Thomas, of Callaway County, married Salie McDaniel, the daughter of Wm. McDaniel of Benton County. The marriage service was performed by Rev. Wm. Gray.

July 14, 1862.

Rev. J. H. Tuttle on June the 4th married A. Leopard to Nancy Clatterbuck. Cagely Clatterbuck, of Callaway County, is the father of the bride.

August 22, 1862.

On August the 14th, William H. Smith married Die Curd, the daughter of Gen. John Curd of Callaway County. The marriage service was performed by Rev. Martin.

November 18, 1864.

In Fulton on September 13th, George W. Beilama married Sallie F. Thomas. She is the daughter of Solomon Thomas. They are all from Callaway County. The marriage services was performed by Rev. Steerbargen.

May 26, 1865.

Dr. Archilles Wilkerson married Lou Baker, the daughter of Martin Baker, on May the 10th. The marriage service was performed by W. W. Robertson.

July 1, 1865.

Elder J. M. Robinson on June 25th married D. W. Barnes of Boone County to Susan Glasgow. Nathan Glasgow, of Millersburg, Callaway County, is the father of the bride.

August 31, 1866.

On August the 16th, George Calvert of Audrain County, married Mary N. Carter. She is the daughter of J.G. Carter, of Callaway County.

March 22, 1867.

On March 20th, Wm. M. Davis married Laura Loyd of Callaway

County. The marriage service was performed by Elder J. M. Robinson.

February 14, 1868.

Rev. Burnham on January the 30th married John R. Carter to Martha Fletcher. The bride is the daughter of John F. Fletcher. They are all of Callaway County.

December 3, 1869.

On November the 25th, William S. Cullberton, of callaway County, married Sarah Frances King, the daughter of George King, of Boone County. The marriage service was performed by Elder T. M. Allen.

R E P U B L I C A N
J E F F E R S O N C I T Y, M O

May 21, 1842.

In Cllaway County, J. M. Duncan of Jefferson City, married Mrs. Mary E. McAfee. The marriage services were performed by Rev. R. I. MaCuff.

P E O P L E S T R I B U N E
J E F F E R S O N C I T Y, M O

October 3, 1866.

On September the 9th, William G. Dixon of Cole County, married Hattie Thornhill, the daughter of Nelson Thornhill of callaway County. The marriage services were performed by W. Penn.

E X P R E S S
L A F A Y E T T E C O U N T Y, M O

April 22, 1845.

On March 26th, John W. Robinson, of Callaway County, married Dorcas Griffith, the daughter of St. Charles. The marriage services were performed by Rev. Geo. Smith.

June 2, 1853.

On May 24th, William B. Maxwell of Cass County married Mary
E. Smith. She is the daughter of Elkanah Smith of Callaway
County. The marriage rites were given by Rev. M. M. Modi-
sett.

March 15, 1856.

On February 19th, Thomas F. Gutherin married Mary Elizabeth
Clatterbuck. She is the daughter of O. Clatterbuck. The
marriage ceremony was performed by Rev. Coulter. They are
all of Callaway County.

February 6, 1858.

John W. Howe married Sarah Walls in Audrain County. She is
the daughter of W. H. Walls of Callaway County.

On January 14th, John Thatcher of Callaway County married
Permelia Smith of Audrain County. She is the daughter of J.
T. Smith of Audrain County.

M E T R O P L I T A N
J E F F E R S O N   C I T Y, M O

September 14, 1847.

On the 29th of August, George Bartley married Margaret Jane
Moore. She is the daughter of Whaton Moore of Callaway
County.

September 28, 1847.

On September 14th, John S. Broadwater of Callaway County
married Margaret Jane Trimble. She is the daughter of Mrs.
Ann Trimble.

BLY, 94
BLYTHE, 29 38 47 56 67 69 77
   113 116
BOARD, 15 38 39 55 73
BOAZ, 60 65 71 109
BODE, 73
BOEJE, 76
BOGGAS, 45
BOGGES, 75
BOGGESS, 32
BOGGS, 39
BOGIE, 89
BOGUE, 49
BOISE, 36
BOLES, 70 91 92
BOLIN, 56
BOLTON, 23 42 93
BONA, 50 54 56 73 109
BONALD, 99
BOND, 71 75 114
BOOKER, 40 71
BOON, 24 56 69 86 90 95
BOONE, 4 9 16 23 33 40 44 74
   81 85 86 97 110 112
BOOTH, 5 25 26 55
BOSHER, 112
BOSWELL, 3 6 15 42 69 75
BOULDS, 114
BOULWARE, 1 2 4-6 8 10 13 15
   17 20-23 25 26 28 29 31-33 36
   41 43-46 48 49 51-54 56-64 66
   68-71 75-78 80-82 84-87 89 91
   92 94 96-99 101 102 104 106
   107 110 111
BOURD, 67
BOURLAND, 106
BOURN, 41 49
BOWAN, 17
BOWDEN, 40
BOWDOIN, 44
BOWEN, 5 16 19 44 65 71 75 107
   110 112
BOWIS, 17
BOWLAN, 9
BOWLES, 54 95 96
BOWLIN, 61
BOWMAN, 13 45 82 107
BOYCE, 98 104 111
BOYD, 1 6 8 9 18 21 25-27 39 41
   44 55 56 66 67 75 111
BOYER, 25

BOYES, 74 101 110
BRACKBILL, 6
BRACKENRIDGE, 14 107
BRADFORD, 43 76 101
BRADLEY, 3 10 13 45 47 67 71
   77 80 92 110 113-115
BRADLY, 17 102
BRADNER, 65
BRADWELL, 69
BRAGG, 42
BRAHAM, 101
BRALEY, 20
BRANCH, 21 26 33 40 56 106 112
BRANDENBURG, 5 36 79 81 84
BRANDON, 11 26 27 34 45 69 73
   88 90 91 103 113
BRANGHTON, 61
BRANHAM, 7 36 42 50 81
BRANHAN, 98
BRANNENBURG, 16
BRANSON, 31 82
BRANUM, 80
BRASHEAR, 4 7 83
BRASHEARS, 95
BRASHER, 44
BRATTON, 8 30 73 83
BRECKBILL, 42
BRECKENRIDGE, 7
BREEDING, 44
BREWER, 84
BRIANT, 22 74
BRIDGES, 1 73
BRIGHT, 5 7 30 42 65 78 99 110
BRINGWATT, 70
BRISTO, 82
BRITE, 11 15 36 39 41
BRITT, 63
BROADWATER, 71 76 79 120
BROCKMAN, 75
BROCON, 29
BROOKMAN, 46
BROOKS, 17 18 47 54 62 72 82 90
   91 93 95 116
BROTHERS, 62
BROUGHTON, 12 91 92 93 109
BROUN, 36
BROWES, 3
BROWN, 3 9 10 12 13 18 20 21 23
   25-27 42 49 50 57 58 60 63 68
   71 72 74 77 79 81 85-87 90 91
   94 102 116

DAWSON (continued)
35 38 57 62 68 71 98 100
DAY, 1 3 4 9 11 23 24 27 28 31-
33 41 48 52 54 55 57 58 62-64
67 68 74 83 85 87 97 100 108
111 114
DEAN, 28 56
DEARING, 26 37 41 47 61 102 103
DEBO, 6 31 78 101
DECKER, 103
DEERING, 88
DEGARNET, 69
DEGROTT, 32
DEHAVEN, 13 104 114
DELVIN, 106
DENIUS, 61
DENNY, 112
DERBY, 22
DERIEUX, 15 16
DERREUX, 49
DERRING, 37
DERRIT, 77
DESHAZO, 114
DETWEILER, 82
DEVORE, 17 41 103
DEWLAND, 111
DICKENSON, 28
DICKERSON, 14 19 52
DICKINSON, 57 61
DICKKOFF, 76
DICKMANN, 44
DICKSON, 1 35 41
DICUS, 27 36
DILL, 36
DILLARD, 1 2 16 23 28 37 40
DILLION, 8 27 46 94
DILLON, 17 40 44
DINKMAN, 74
DINSMON, 114
DINSMOORE, 45
DISHMAN, 27
DIVERS, 15 30 101 108
DIXON, 3 77 19
DOAN, 18 48 56
DODD, 9 44
DODDS, 52 102
DOE, 69
DOERRING, 103
DONALD, 54
DONELL, 106
DOOLEY, 23 41

DORRIS, 114
DORSEY, 46 58 68 81 88
DORTING, 107
DORTON, 56 58 110 116
DOUBLEDAY, 69 100
DOUGHERTY, 8 58 63 84 91 99
103
DOUGLAD, 58
DOUGLAS, 17 38 44 56 76 95 97
DOUGLASS, 10 16 18 28 37 40 42
45 49 50 64 72 80 82 87 88 90
92 96 97 99 101 105 108 112
DOUGLY, 85
DOWNY, 101
DOYAL, 96
DOYALE, 103
DOYEL, 84
DOYLE, 58 69 98 112
DOZIER, 17 27 50 70 80 106 113
DRENNAN, 12 39
DRINKARD, 13 37 102 106 111
DRISCAL, 91
DRISCALL, 74
DRISKALL, 84
DRISKELL, 5 34
DRISKILL, 14
DUANE, 44
DUBY, 41
DUDLEY, 13 17 19 31 46 66 67 71
72 81 82 91 108
DULEY, 53
DULIN, 32 52 112
DULY, 112 113
DUNAVANT, 9 83
DUNCAN, 1 6-8 10 11 17 19 25 27
31 34 35 41 43 45-48 50 54 55
57 62 75 76 81 82 86-90 92 93
95 97 100 103 112 113 115 119
DUNCH, 52
DUNHAM, 5 15 48 65 92 98 106
DUNLAP, 15 20 21 23 62 100 110
112 113
DUNLOP, 62
DUNN, 14 23 32 54 66 70 73 92
112
DUNNAVANT, 38 93
DUNNICA, 86 100
DURBEE, 44
DURFEE, 11
DUVALL, 30 103
DYCEN, 29

HAM (continued)
52 54 62 65-67 69 73 76-79 81
85 90 93 97 99 101-103 107
108 111
HAMBLIN, 20 60 73 78 100
HAMIBLIN, 16
HAMILTON, 3 10 14 20 21 23 25
27 35 40 42 44 50 53 55 56 61
69-71 79 110 111
HAMLEY, 57
HAMM, 24
HAMPTON, 7 40
HAMS, 48
HANA, 102
HANNA, 60 81
HANNAH, 64
HANS, 73 77
HANSARD, 3 12 35 41 113
HANSBERRY, 10
HAPEY, 73
HARD, 1
HARDIN, 21 27 28 33 36 61 100
112
HARDING, 6 36 44
HARKINS, 13 19 28 93
HARLAND, 33 55 63 96
HARMAN, 5
HARMON, 42
HARNDON, 67
HARPER, 11 23 25 34 67 88 101
114
HARRIS, 1 3 9 23 37 45 46 55 56
72 75 78 79 81 83 86 95 99 103
105 106 112 115 116
HARRISON, 1 7 9 13-15 20 23 24
30 39 43 45 50 57 59-61 67 69
70 72 77 81 86 87 102 103 110
HARROW, 6
HARRYFORD, 22
HARRYMAN, 32 65
HART, 11 67 72
HARVER, 20
HARVEY, 20 67 69 71 74 81 106
HARVIE, 83
HASE, 80
HASKINS, 8
HASLER, 30
HATCHER, 33 81
HATTON, 63 70 99 108 115
HAW, 101

HAWKINS, 11 22 35 41 46 52 78
82 87 106 108 116
HAYDEN, 45 113
HAYDON, 61
HAYES, 95
HAYNER, 77
HAYNES, 13 30 59 62 84 101
HAYS, 5 15 20 26 44 51 55 64 66-
68 74 87 89 96 101 107 110 113
HAYTMAN, 55
HAYTON, 100
HAZELET, 114
HAZELRIGG, 17 82
HEAD, 45
HEART, 24 100
HEASICK, 20
HEINNY, 50
HELLER, 14
HELM, 73 116
HENDERSON, 5 6 9 13 18-21 25
27 33 34 36 41 42 45 48 55 64
70 73-75 78 80 83 93 105 111
HENDRICKS, 109
HENDRIX, 27 70 92
HENLEY, 74
HENRDON, 65
HENRECH, 99
HENSHAW, 79
HENSLEY, 71 87 95
HENSLY, 75
HEREFORD, 17 18 79 116
HEREYFORD, 100
HERING, 32 44
HERNDERSON, 37
HERNDON, 14 35 55 89 100
HERON, 47 113
HERRIFORD, 4
HERRIMAN, 98
HERRIN, 113
HERRING, 5 6 12 20 21 33 37 54
63 84 99 103 110 114
HERRON, 25 55 113
HERRYMAN, 27
HERSMAN, 33 50
HESS, 30 79
HEWER, 40
HIBBERT, 113
HIBBERTS, 13 82
HICKENBOTTOM, 27
HICKERSON, 5 53 77 100 106

131

HICKMAN, 110
HIGHFIELD, 29
HILBORN, 70
HILE, 107
HILL, 5 7 16 26 31 32 36 59 75 79
   86 93 105 106 108 111 112 114
HILLER, 24 36 73 81
HILTON, 43
HINKE, 100
HINLEY, 20
HINSKAFER, 79
HINTON, 28 36 50 64 108 112 115
HISEY, 68 87 111
HISS, 107
HITE, 60
HOALMAN, 5 26
HOALT, 76
HOBBS, 25 111
HOBSON, 7 9 30 36 74
HOCKADAY, 3 41 43 68 74 80-82
   88 98 114
HOCKENSMITH, 83
HOCKINS, 94
HODGE, 30 104
HOLDERMAN, 28
HOLEMAN, 54
HOLIDAY, 92
HOLLADAY, 98
HOLLAND, 8 18 19 57 80 81
HOLLIDAY, 50
HOLLIS, 46
HOLLIWAY, 63 77
HOLLOWAY, 29 45
HOLMAN, 63 68 72 94
HOLT, 3 6 11 14 15 17 18 22 27
   36 50 53 57 59 61 64 66 68 69
   75 80 84 88 94 101 103 105
HOMESTEAD, 79
HOMMAN, 10
HOOK, 8 31 35 63 68 75 77 110
HOOPER, 117
HOOVER, 32
HOPE, 5 6 42
HOPKEINS, 64
HOPKINS, 3-5 9 15 27 31 37 40
   43 64 67-69 72 78 84 86 93 94
   98 111 112 114
HOPPER, 2 7 42
HOPSON, 43 57 62
HORAIN, 76

HORD, 13 27 29 44 55 64 71 79
   103
HORDE, 79
HORN, 2 95
HORNBICKLE, 28
HORNBUCKLE, 1 4 11 26 40 66
   67 79 88 104 108
HORNER, 94
HOSMAN, 50
HOT, 55
HOUCHENS, 104
HOUCHINS, 30
HOUF, 2 95 98 114
HOUGH, 52
HOULY, 111
HOUSE, 25
HOUSEMAN, 19
HOUSER, 41
HOUSTON, 12 80
HOVECK, 111
HOW, 23
HOWARD, 1 4 5 15 16 43 67 79
   105 107 109
HOWE, 7 35 58 88 96 106 107 120
HOWISER, 6
HOWISON, 108
HOXEY, 59 85 100
HOXSEN, 86
HUBBARD, 1 45 75
HUBBERD, 17
HUDDLESTON, 11 33 58
HUDNEL, 110
HUDSON, 6 8 43 44 53 54 60 63
   64 84 90 98 102 106 109 112
HUFF, 61 63 90 110
HUFFMASTER, 2 53
HUGH, 107
HUGHART, 18 73
HUGHES, 10 28 30 34 37 43 57 58
   71 93 95 99 101 103 108 113
HUGHS, 16 39 60 105 108
HULL, 93
HULTS, 96
HULTZ, 93 101
HUME, 16 49
HUMES, 47
HUMPHRES, 30
HUMPHREY, 85
HUMPHREYS, 2 28 35 42 52 53
   67 75 110 112

132

MCMAHAN (continued)
55 98 106
MCMICKLE, 116
MCMILLIN, 13
MCMURTY, 20 22 34 44 46 74 82
97 98 101 104
MCNEAR, 66
MCNEILEY, 80 98
MCPHEETERS, 24 45 53 92
MCQUENTIN, 2
MCRINNEY, 77
MCROBERTS, 32 99
MCVEIGH, 63
MEACHAM, 9
MEAD, 45 59 81
MEADOWS, 13 28 53 62
MEDCALFF, 58
MEDDERS, 104
MEDE, 98
MEDOE, 92
MEDOWS, 3
MEELOR, 104
MELOANY, 2
MENG, 63 84 85 104
MENIFEE, 28 92
MEREDITH, 8 32 39 43 76 87
MERIDITH, 83
MERRYMAN, 17
METCALF, 47
METEER, 95 101
MEUR, 73
MEYER, 21
MEYERS, 69
MILES, 27
MILLER, 3 5 6 8 9 11 12 14 17-
20 25 26 28-32 36 40 44 48-51
53-56 58 59 64 65 69 70 72-75
78 79 81 83-85 88 90 91 95 97
99 100 101 105-107 109-112
117
MILLIKEN, 48
MILLS, 8 13 111
MILONE, 30
MING, 5 8 21 32 38 41 60 63 70
75 77 81 82 84 90 106 112 114
MIRES, 78
MITCHELL, 22 38
MIVIS, 105
MIZZINGO, 114
MOAD, 5 80
MODISETT, 120

MODISIT, 83
MOMAN, 11
MONROE, 21 39 96
MONTEER, 111
MONTGOMERY, 103
MONTJOY, 12 45
MOODY, 53
MOON, 6 15 19 20 32 33 49 55 63
76 92 111
MOORE, 6-8 10-13 23 26 28 31
33 35-39 41 43 48 49 52 53 56-
59 67 69 72 73 82 83 91 93 102
103 107-109 111 117 120
MORELAND, 69
MOREOR, 113
MORGAN, 34 47 53 56 70 106 107
MORREE, 4
MORRIS, 14 17 28 34 47 54 56 65
85 96 109 111 113
MORRISON, 8 42 65 87
MORROW, 29 32 53 63
MORTZ, 43
MOSBY, 64 67 74
MOSELEY, 28 34 36 96 115
MOSELY, 6 22 29 33 48 84 113
114
MOSES, 27
MOSLEY, 7 42 73 107
MOSLY, 113
MOSS, 11 12 17 50 74 79
MOURNING, 8 117
MOXLEY, 15 19
MOZUIGO, 66
MUIR, 9 21 38 66 85 91 92 96
MULDOR, 49
MULDROW, 39
MULLENS, 29
MUMFORD, 22
MURDOCK, 37 83
MURPHY, 16 17 20 22 39 47 73
81 111
MURRAY, 2 53 66 84
MURRY, 15 61
MUSGROVE, 2 5 6 15 66 76
MUTCHMORE, 48
MYERS, 3 13 16 19 32 36 39 47
51 68 72 108
NALE, 71
NAMER, 41
NANCE, 3 103
NASH, 7 15 18 28 50 53 94

NASHUM, 40
NEAL, 4 10 24 30-33 38 40 73
NEALE, 63
NEFF, 2 26 53
NEIDACKER, 8
NEIL, 55 70 105
NEILL, 7 19 21 22 25 30 32 56
    59 65 71 73 81 96 100 105
NEILLE, 9
NELSON, 17 85
NESBIT, 51 63 76 97
NESBITT, 43 45 116
NESKUTT, 115
NETHERTON, 22
NEUKOMN, 86
NEVINS, 3 4 6 8 17 18 21 24 26
    35 41-43 50 52 55 57 60 61 65
    66 74 75 79 81 87 88 93 103
    116
NEWBOLT, 95
NEWLAND, 54 62 75 87
NEWLON, 34
NEWMAN, 1 23 31 44 53 59 97
NEWSOM, 12 16 18 20 31 48 56
    65 83 99 107 112
NEWTON, 2 4 11 41 84 93
NICCLE, 89
NICHOLS, 3 5 11 12 15 22 24 30-
    33 35 36 39 41 45 51 53 54 59
    62 66 68-71 73 75-77 84 85 87
    94 95 97 98 107 110 116
NICHOLSON, 34 49 56 78 88
NICKELL, 52 99
NICKELS, 28
NICKEN, 83
NIGHT, 53
NITE, 113
NOBLE, 58
NOBLES, 114
NOFLET, 70
NOLAND, 21 29 93 106
NORFLEET, 9 10
NORFLET, 62 69 85 107 109
NORFLETT, 72
NORRIS, 56
NORTHCUTT, 16
NORTHPEN, 15 33 34 42 63 68 77
    99 110
NORTHWAY, 26
NOWELL, 32
NUM, 85

NUNLEY, 88
NUNN, 62
NUNNELLY, 70
O'DANIEL, 83
OBERN, 23
OFFATT, 118
OFFETT, 94 109
OFFUTT, 7 31 61 66 108 109
OGAN, 43
OLA, 62 63
OLD, 75 90 116
OLDE, 52 63 81
OLDHAM, 4 15 41
OLHAM, 97
OLIVER, 4 7 8 12 24 32 34 38 44
    46 61 69 70 73 83 103
ORDWAY, 78
OREAR, 98
ORGAN, 51
ORME, 5
ORR, 115
ORSBORN, 108
OSCLEY, 101
OSLIN, 48
OSTEN, 84
OSTES, 103
OVERALL, 47
OVERFELT, 5 40 74 109
OVERSTREET, 109
OVERTON, 12 14 41 52 62 64 68
    69 73 79 82 88 96 99 102
OWEN, 4 14 15 18 31 41 68 81 97
    107 108
OWENS, 2 43 107 109
OXENDINE, 48
OXLEY, 28
PACE, 4 18 31 34 41 49 51 53 77
    106
PADGET, 37
PADGETT, 47 52
PAGE, 94
PAGET, 114
PAIN, 100 104
PAINTER, 18
PALMER, 14 18 60 64 80 96 100
PANNEL, 97
PANNELL, 96
PARIS, 64
PARKER, 9 22 32 51 74 91
PARKS, 69
PARMER, 73 97 106

140